THE BRAHUI LANGUAGE

THE BRAHUI LANGUAGE

PART I
INTRODUCTION AND GRAMMAR

BY

DENYS DE S. BRAY, I.C.S.

GYAN

Published by

GYAN

Gyan Publishing House
5, Ansari Road
Daryaganj, New Delhi-110002
Phone: 011-47034999, 9811692060
E-mail: books@gyanbooks.com

Distribution Network
gyanbooks.com
India, USA, Canada, UK, Australia, France

ISBN : 978-81-212-4251-6 (PB)
First Published, 1909

2nd Impression 2020

Printed at: Gyan Press, Delhi.

The Brahui Language
Author: Denys De S. Bray

THE
BRAHUI LANGUAGE

PART I

INTRODUCTION AND GRAMMAR

BY

DENYS DE S. BRAY, I.C.S.

CALCUTTA
SUPERINTENDENT GOVERNMENT PRINTING, INDIA
1909

PREFACE.

THE language spoken in and round Kalat, the capital of the Khanate and the meeting-place of Sarawan and Jhalawan, is regarded by most Brahuis as preserving the purest form of their speech, and it is this language which is analysed in the following pages. While passing reference is made to the more important divergencies between the Sarawan and Jhalawan branches of the language, I have not allowed myself to be tempted aside into the interesting bypaths of dialectical variants. I have been content to state what I regard as the standard usage, undeterred by the consciousness that, however clearly defined the rule, exceptions might possibly be culled from some dialect or other to confound it.

Four years' residence in Baluchistan has left me free to pursue the study of Brahui independently of the work of my predecessors, and of the authorities quoted at the end of this volume the only one from which I have wittingly derived assistance is Bishop Caldwell's 'Comparative Grammar of the Dravidian or South-Indian Family of Languages.' Here, however, my debt has been great. Although Bishop Caldwell, working on material necessarily very imperfect and often incorrect, accorded Brahui but a cursory examination in his masterly treatise, his lucid analysis of the grammatical system of the Dravidian languages yields an insight into the structure of Brahui which would otherwise be hardly possible.

To Mr. T. O. Hughes of the Political Department I owe my first introduction to this strangely neglected field of linguistic research, and throughout my labours he has generously allowed me to draw on his intimate knowledge of the Brahuis and their language. It has been my singularly good fortune that my manuscript passed through the expert hands of Dr. Sten Konow, the editor of the Dravidian section of the Linguistic Survey of India, and much of my material has been recast in the light of his valuable suggestions.

But it is, after all, to the Brahuis themsêlves that I have been most indebted, and to none more than to Mirza Sher Muhammad, son of Ghaus Muhammad, Zahri, to whose patient and critical mind much of the accuracy and fulness of this analysis of his mother-tongue is indirectly due.

D. DE S. B.

Quetta, January 1908.

CONTENTS.

INTRODUCTION

INTRODUCTION.

The Brahuis.

Who the Brahuis[1] are, and whence they have found their way into Baluchistan, are questions that still await answer. Even the origin of their name is obscure. The fanciful derivation from *ba-roh-ī*, 'hill-man,' may be dismissed at once, despite the fact that the people about the Helmand are sometimes called, by distinction it might seem, *nā-rohī* or men of the plain; the explanation that they are the old inhabitants of *Biroea* is only valuable as embodying their own cherished tradition that they came from Aleppo, while the more plausible suggestion that they are the descendants of an eponymous hero *Brāho* or Ibrahim, though ingenious, is not wholly convincing.

Although the Khanate of Kalat may nowadays be regarded as the home of the Brahuis, they are found in varying numbers in most parts of Baluchistan; northwards they reach into the Afghan district of Shorawak; to the west they stretch along the Nushki trade-route through the sparsely populated Chaghai tract as far as Seistan, where a small colony has set its abode. Numerically they are the strongest tribe in Baluchistan, numbering roughly 300,000 souls, or more than thrice the strength of the Baluch actually resident in the country to which he has given his name.[2] But their numerical strength is deceptive, for the Brahuis at the

---

[1] The name of both people and language is *Brāhūī*; a common corruption of it is *Brohī*.

[2] *Vide* the Baluchistan Census Report of 1901. The statistics do not of course cover Persian Mekran, to which the term Persian Baluchistan is sometimes applied. It is particularly unfortunate that no linguistic census was taken in Baluchistan.

present day are not a separate race but an amalgamation of independent units, bound together by the bond of common good and ill. The gathering of these units round a Brahui nucleus into a semi-military organisation, subdivided into two main groups, the Sarawans and the Jhalawans, the uplanders and the lowlanders, with the Khan of Kalat at their head, forms the history of the rise of the Brahui Confederacy.

The Brahuis themselves have no false idea of the purity of their race. The popular opinion on the subject is summed up very fairly in the analysis of the Brahui tribe furnished by the ex-Khan of Kalat for the last Census. According to him, the true Brahuis who came from Aleppo are only represented by the Ahmadzai (the ruling family of Kalat), the Iltazai, Mirwari, Gurgnari, Sumalari and Kalandrari; the Bangalzai, Langav and Lahri are Baluch; the Raisani, Sarparra and Shahwani are Afghans; the Kurd and Mamasani (or Muhammad Hasni) came from Persia; the Mengal, Bizanjav, Sajdi and Zahri are Jadgal or Jats; while the Muhammad Shahi and Nichari are the oldest inhabitants of the country. Into the accuracy of this analysis it is not necessary to enter here. Though it cannot be accepted in its entirety, and leaves out of account the heterogeneous composition of many of the sub-sections themselves, it at any rate bears eloquent witness to the conglomerate nature of the Confederacy.

But despite the mixed character of the race it is as a rule not difficult to recognise the typical Brahui. Somewhat below the medium height, with oval face, round eyes, and high, slender nose, he is framed in a less imposing mould than the Pathan or Baluch proper.

The Brahuis are essentially a pastoral people, breeders of sheep and goats; in the more favoured parts of the country they rear horses and cattle. Lazy and unenterprising, they make poor agriculturists. The extremes of heat and cold and the general poverty of the country necessitate periodical migrations, and in the winter there is an exodus of the Jhalawans through the Mula pass into Sind, and of the Sarawans down the Bolan to the Kachhi plain. But though nomads in this restricted sense, they cling with a strange tenacity to their somewhat inhospitable country, in marked contrast to the world-travelled Pathan. They are law-abiding and amenable to the influence of their particular Sardar, yet have no liking for the trammels of regular discipline. Their distaste for discipline and their home-keeping instinct are among the chief reasons why the race with its warlike traditions is almost unrepresented in our army.

Though not so laughter-loving as the Pathan, the Brahui is not without a quiet sense of humour. He is childishly fond of show; he is at the same time remarkably uncleanly in his person. He is no fanatic: his normal attitude towards matters religious is one of philosophic calm. His faith is by no means fashioned according to the strict letter of Muhammadan orthodoxy. Any attempt on the part of the mullah to encroach on mundane affairs is jealously resented, and even within the sphere of religion his influence is curiously limited. Signs are indeed not lacking that it is only in relatively modern times that Islam has gained a firm footing among the people. To this day belief in evil spirits, who may be warded off by charms and exorcised by sacrifices of blood and the frenzy of the devil-dancer, is all but universal.

The Brahui regards his duty towards his neighbour as one of his first duties towards his God, and more careful housewives than one have been divorced by their indignant husbands for neglecting to show due hospitality when left in charge of the home. Extravagantly hospitable himself, he makes inordinate demands on the hospitality of others. As Nasir Khan the Great used to say, the Brahuis have only to see a bone in your hand, and they will run up like dogs from all sides for a bite.

He has little of the Pathan's pride of race and language. On the contrary, though he may naturally be chary of putting the admission into words, he usually accepts as a matter of course the claims of both Pathan and Baluch to be his superior in race, and certainly displays a distinct alacrity to trace a non-Brahui descent whenever he can do so with decency. It is significant that no Baluch with proper pride would stoop to give his daughter in marriage to a Brahui; the Brahui, needless to say, marries his daughter into a Baluch family without a scruple.

This lack of proper racial pride is probably intimately related to the diffidence of the Brahui as to his language. There is a very general feeling among his neighbours that Brahui is a strange language, a jargon too uncouth for 'gentility,' and the feeling is shared in some measure by the Brahuis themselves, who do not hesitate to employ Baluchi or Pashtu on the slightest excuse. It must be remembered that, thanks to intermarriage in the individual family and the mixed character of the race, nearly every Brahui is at least bilingual. The present Khan of Kalat, for instance, used to talk Brahui to his mother and Baluchi to his father and brothers. Some of the Brahui tribes hardly speak Brahui at all; thus the Mirwaris, true Brahuis though they are reputed to be, speak Baluchi almost to a man.

The Brahui Language.

The heterogeneous character of the Brahui tribe is reflected in his language. Not only Baluchi and Persian but Sindhi and Panjabi have been laid under tribute to swell his vocabulary. In view of the large Baluch admixture in the race it is not surprising to find considerable traces of Baluchi in the language; the influence of Pashtu on the other hand has been curiously small. But the predominant element is Persian—including of course Arabic—which has made its way into the language, largely no doubt through Baluchi but probably to an equal extent directly. Geographical contiguity is chiefly responsible for the extensive contributions of Sindhi, and for the less important borrowings from Panjabi and other languages. The extent to which these additions have been made varies naturally in the different tribes according to their geographical position; thus the speech of the Jhalawans, and notably of the Zahris, contains a large Sindhi leaven, while Baluchi has made marked encroachments on the Sarawan dialects. The standard language, which is analysed in this work, is the Middle Brahui spoken in and near Kalat, where Jhalawan and Sarawan meet.

That the Brahui vocabulary has been susceptible to outside influence is not surprising. It is rather a matter for surprise that the language has been able to maintain a vigorous individuality, instead of succumbing, as many isolated families and one of the purest sections, the Mirwari, have succumbed, to the Aryan languages which hem it in around. Nor must the other side of the question be overlooked: it would not be hard to point to many traces of Brahui influence in the Baluchi vocabulary, and even Sindhi, at any rate the Sindhi of the frontier, could probably be shown to be a debtor as well as a creditor, though of course to a much lesser degree.

But however greatly the Brahui is indebted to alien races for the peopling of his tribe and for the vocabulary of his language, the nucleus of both tribe and language seems to be essentially his own. Eliminate all foreign elements from his tribe, and we are left with a people whose kinship with the races to which it has opened its ranks, or by which it is geographically surrounded, has, to say the least, yet to be proved. And if we lop off the foreign overgrowth which has twined itself so luxuriantly round his speech, there is laid bare the trunk of a language, helplessly crippled it is true, but preserving from the wreckage its internal structure practically unscathed. And it is to the internal structure or grammatical system of a language that we must look, and not to the accretions, suggestive witnesses though these are to the subsequent chapters in its life's history, to discover the source from which it has sprung. An analysis of Brahui discloses no kinship to the Aryan languages which have contributed so richly to its vocabulary, but reveals a clear and unmistakable resemblance to the Dravidian languages of Southern India, only to be explained on the assumption that it is descended from the same stock.

The Relationship of Brahui to Dravidian.

The Brahui language is agglutinative, and in this aspect it belongs, speaking in the broadest sense, to the same stage of development as the Dravidian language-group. This, indeed, proves little or nothing; but the argument of kinship rests on a surer foundation than a casual analogy of structure. The grammatical relations of the noun in Brahui are shown, as in Dravidian, by means of suffixes, and most, if not all, of the suffixes, whether expressive of case-relations or of plural number, are traceable to the same source as Dravidian. Even more direct is the evidence of the pronoun, that faithful repository of the secret of a language's origin. Of the personal pronouns, the pronoun of the second person in both numbers is in essentials the same as in Dravidian, and a Dravidian relationship is discernible in the pronoun of the first person, despite the ravages wrought by phonetic decay. The reflexive in Brahui and Dravidian has preserved one uniform type with singular consistency, while the Brahui demonstratives are only explicable in the light of their Dravidian counterparts. The family likeness is but thinly disguised in the interrogatives, and several of the indefinite pronouns are stamped with the same birthmark. The Dravidian relationship of the first three numerals, often, though perhaps erroneously, regarded as only less significant witnesses to the origin of a language than the personal pronouns, is hardly open to question, and it is interesting to find that Brahui and Dravidian, in the absence of an ordinal proper formed from the first cardinal, employ the same device and even, it would appear, the same root to express it. The case of the verb is naturally more complex, but the evidence cannot be gainsaid. The most palpable analogies are to be found in the pronominal terminations of the plural, in the formation of the causal, and above all in the organic negative conjugation. These do not, however, exhaust all the relevant points in the evidence; indeed, though the Brahui verb is not devoid of characteristic peculiarities of its own, it may safely be said—and the remark applies with equal force to the language as a whole—that a full understanding of it would be impossible without the help of the Dravidian languages.

This kinship of the language of the Brahuis on the north-west frontier of the Indian Empire with the remote Dravidian languages of the south is of such signal interest that it seems advisable to sketch in lightly this skeleton outline of the evidences on which the kinship is claimed. But room cannot be found in this essay for an exhaustive treatment of the theme: gaps will necessarily be left in the arguments, difficulties will be glossed over, all but the most salient features omitted, and the conclusions stated in an inevitably dogmatic form. A full presentation of the case in all its ramifications must in fact be reserved for a separate volume.

The Brahui noun more especially asserts its claim to kinship with Dravidian in the suffixes it employs to express the plural number and case-relations. The essential mark of the Brahui plural is *-k*. This is identical with one of the suffixes in Gondi, and there is little doubt that these two languages have preserved the initial portion of the characteristic plural suffix *-kaḷ* (*-gaḷ*) of Dravidian, just as nothing but the final portion *-l-u* has survived in Telugu. That *-kaḷ* (*-gaḷ*) seems properly applied in the Dravidian language-group to neuter nouns is no serious objection, even apart from the fact that the Dravidian usage itself is by no means uniform. Though probably a mere coincidence, it is of some interest to find that *-gal* appears in Brahui, but less commonly than in Baluchi, as a suffix with plural significance: *duz-gal*, for instance, means 'thieves,' and the *Mēngal* were originally, apparently, the Mens. The Dravidian rational plural suffix *-ar*, which is by the by undoubtedly enshrined in the Brahui verbal terminations of the second and third persons plural, is often coupled with the irrational plural suffix *-gaḷ*, and this compound rational plural *-argaḷ* seems on all fours with the compound suffix *-s-k* of what may be called the 'personal' plural in Brahui, the *-s-* of which appears to have been derived from an original *-r* according to a common phonetic interchange. A plural suffix *-sk*, it may be remarked, is found both in Kui and Gondi.

There is only one declension of the Brahui noun. As in Dravidian, the suffixes by which case-relations are expressed are the same in the singular and plural, with one exception. There is, however, this difference in the declension of the two numbers: in the singular the suffixes are added directly to the crude base; in the plural (and this applies partially to the reflexive and both numbers of the personal pronouns) they are added to an oblique base. Both systems of declension are found in Dravidian, though not with the same differentiation in the case of the two numbers.

There are two genitive suffixes in Brahui, *-nā* for the noun singular, and *-ā* for the noun plural and the personal and reflexive pronouns. Both suffixes are employed in Gondi. It is interesting to note that there are parallels in Dravidian to this specialisation in the use of the two suffixes. Thus *-a* forms the plural genitive of all nouns in Telugu without exception, while *-ni* is similarly confined to the singular. Again, although *-in* is the genitive suffix most commonly used in Tamil, *-a* is the classical genitive suffix of the personal and reflexive pronouns.

The Brahui dative-accusative suffix *-e* is the same in form as the Malayalam *-e*, which is no doubt related to the Tamil *-ei*. The objection that these suffixes in Dravidian express the accusative only is not serious. Such extensions of meaning crop up everywhere; thus '*him*,' an original dative, and the German '*euch*,' an original accusative, have to serve in the modern languages as dative and accusative alike, while instances occur in plenty in the minor Dravidian dialects. A fact more hard to account for would have been the absence of a Brahui representative of *-k* (with variants), the universal dative suffix in the Dravidian language group. There seems, however, no reason to doubt that the suffix *-ki*, which denotes much the same as a dative of interest, is traceable to this root. Yet another representative is apparently to be found in the latter part of the suffix *-iskā*, 'up to,' which seems to be an example of the compounding of two case-signs by a process familiar both in Indo-European and Dravidian. The initial portion *-is* appears in Brahui as a separate suffix meaning 'at,' and it is clear that the coupling of case-suffixes meaning 'at' and 'to' would result naturally in a compound suffix meaning 'up to.' If the Brahui *-is* is related to the Dravidian locative *-il*—and the phonetic interchange has ample authority—the suffix *-is-kā* would constitute a perfect parallel to the Tamil locative-directive *-il-ku*, compounded as this is with a locative and dative.

The Brahui instrumental *-aṭ* is not infrequently used with a *quasi*-locative force, and it seems probable that it is derived from the same source as the locative *-aṭī*. Obvious analogies are afforded by Telugu and Tulu. In Telugu the classical instrumental *-ṭa* (*-ta*) is identical with the locative, and is derived from the inflexional *-ṭi* (*-ti*), which is itself sometimes used as a locative. Similarly the Tulu instrumental *-ḍ'du* seems closely related to the locative *-du* or *-ḍ'*, *-tu* or *-ṭ'*. The resemblance of the Telugu suffixes to the suffixes in Brahui is particularly strong.

But perhaps the most striking example of the relationship of the Brahui and Dravidian case-suffixes is to be found in the conjunctive. Not only is *-tō*, the abbreviated form of the Telugu conjunctive, identical with the suffix in Brahui, the longer form *-tōḍu* seems to be preserved in the Brahui full-word *tud*, 'accompanying,' 'in company with.' If this is the case, the evidence of Brahui would apparently have a relevant bearing on the vexed question whether the Tamil *-ōḍu* or the Telugu *-tōḍu* represents the truer form of the Dravidian conjunctive suffix.

It is an interesting feature of Brahui that all but the three first numerals have been borrowed from outside, a fact which is expressed in another form by their neighbours in the taunt that they have had to teach the Brahuis to count beyond three. The numeral is in fact an epitome of the whole language: the bulk of the numerals as of the vocabulary of the language generally have been grafted from outside; but this foreign overgrowth is linguistically far less significant than the native roots. Few races which can boast a developed language at all have had to borrow the first three numerals, however much they may have to thank the outside world for the rest of their arithmetical stock-in-trade.

While all but the first three cardinals have been drawn, often in a corrupted form, from Persian, the first three are regarded by the Brahuis themselves as their own exclusive property. A comparison with Dravidian will satisfactorily disprove such an idea. One of the peculiarities of these numerals is that each presents itself in a two-fold shape: *asiṭ*, *iraṭ*, *musiṭ* are nouns of number, while *asi*, *irā*, *musi* are numeral adjectives. The Dravidian numeral is two-fold in precisely the same way. But the family likeness strikes much deeper. The root of the second numeral in Brahui *ir-* is absolutely identical with the root throughout Dravidian. It may seem unjustifiable to relate *as-* to *or-*, the root of the first numeral in Dravidian, but the interchange not only of *r* and *s* but also of *o* and *a* is otherwise established. The connection between *mus-* and *mur-*, the Dravidian root of the third numeral, is more easily detected, for the included vowel has been left unchanged.

As in Dravidian, the ordinals in Brahui are formed from the cardinals by means of suffixes. To this general rule Brahui and Dravidian have one exception in common. In both the first ordinal is founded not on the first cardinal, but on a base meaning 'front,' 'before.' This device is of course familiar enough in the Indo-European language-group, but the relationship of the Brahui base *muh*, *mon*, to the Dravidian *mu*, *mun*, seems unmistakable.

We pass on to the personal pronouns with the feeling that the Dravidian kinship will reveal itself here if anywhere. And the evidence is clear. Especially is this the case with regard to the pronoun of the second person, nominative singular *nī*, plural *num*. *Nī* is indeed the normal form of the second person singular throughout Dravidian; the nominative plural in classical Kanarese is *nīm*, while *num* is one of the oblique bases in Tamil. The fact that the more characteristic form of the Dravidian plural, of which the Tamil *nīr* is a typical representative, reappears, docked of its initial consonant, in the form *īr* (with variants) as a pronominal termination in the Dravidian verb, is not without significance, for this termination with slight modification, and in the negative verb with hardly any modification at all, is consistently used in Brahui.

The ordinary forms of the Dravidian pronoun of the first person are *ān, yān, nān* in the singular, with *ām, yām, nām* in the plural, in which the final *-n* and *-m* are almost certainly mere marks of number; the triple forms are probably variations of the same base. There can be no doubt of the relationship of the Brahui first person plural *nan* to the Dravidian *nām*. Apart from the fact that in the peculiar circumstances of the case there is no need for a pluralising particle in Brahui, the change from *-m* to *-n*, which is in itself not uncommon and which occurs indeed in the Dravidian pronouns, would be induced naturally by the attraction of the initial *n*.

There remains the first person singular *ī* with its oblique base *kan-*. Though Caldwell, while regarding *nī, num, nan* as Dravidian, was unable to recognise any Dravidian relationship here, it would be strange if the pronoun of the first person were derived in the singular from a source other than that of its plural and the pronoun of the second person in both numbers, and it is doubtless a right instinct to endeavour to trace its origin to the same stock before adopting Caldwell's forlorn comparison with the Babylonian *ānaka*. And we may do so, I think, without misgiving. If the final *-n* of the Dravidian pronouns is merely a mark of singular number, it would be no matter for surprise to find that it is liable to be dropped. It is in fact discarded regularly in the second person singular, *nī* being rarely ousted by the full form *nīn*; Tulu goes a step further and discards both initial and final *n*, leaving the vowel *ī* as the sole representative of the second person singular. The same has been the case with regard to *ē*, the pronoun of the first person singular in

Telugu, and with this Telugu *ē* we may fairly compare the Brahui nominative singular *ī*. It is indeed not impossible that these two dialects have preserved the purest form of the pronoun. The explanation of the appearance of an initial *k-* in the inflexional base involves too elaborate a chain of phonetic interchanges to find a convenient place here.

The relationship of the Brahui reflexive *tēn* to *tān*, which persists throughout the Dravidian language-group, is happily self-evident. The only points of difference lie in the fact that the pronoun in Brahui is common to both numbers, and in slight variations in the idiom. As the final *-n* seems to be simply the sign of the singular number as in the personal pronouns, it is possible that the curious enclitic pronoun of the third person *-ta* (it occasionally appears by the by in the form *-tan*) is derived from the same base, though its use as an enclitic points clearly to foreign influence.

The case of the demonstrative is of peculiar interest. From an internal point of view the Brahui demonstrative is remarkably irregular and manifold in form. The ordinary forms of the nominative singular are *dā* (*hic*), *ē* (*ille*), *o* (*is*), but the oblique cases in the singular, with possibly a few exceptions, are based on *dād*, *ēd*, *od*, forms which may be, and sometimes must be, used in the nominative singular. The presence of this *-d*, which is changed in the oblique cases to *-ṛ-*, cannot be explained from Brahui itself, any more than the strange insertion of *-f-* in the commonest form of the plural, *dāfk*, *ēfk*, *ofk*. It is no mean corroboration of our argument that we have to go to Dravidian for the explanation of both. Dravidian like Brahui has a three-fold demonstrative, the remote, the proximate, and the mediate. They are formed from three demonstrative bases *a*, *i*, *u*, by suffixing the signs of gender and number. In Tamil, to take a typical case, these gender-number suffixes, with the exception of the neuter-singular sign *-d*, begin with a vowel, and require in consequence a euphonic *-v-* to prevent hiatus. Thus the neuter gender demonstratives are *a-du*, *i-du*, *u-du* in the singular, and *a-v-ei*, *i-v-ei*, *u-v-ei* in the plural. It may be safely asserted that herein lies the explanation not only of the Brahui demonstratives singular *dād*, *ēd*, *od*, but also of the plural *dāfk*, *ēfk*, *ofk*, notwithstanding certain difficulties which cannot now be discussed. The *-d* in the singular is in fact a survival of the neuter-singular sign, though it loses all force of gender in Brahui, while the *-f-* is an even more meaningless survival of the euphonic *-v-*. In both cases the *raison d'être* of the consonant has gone, but the sounds themselves have been preserved in much the same purposeless way as the euphonic addition has usurped the initial position in the Telugu masculine singular demonstratives *vāḍu*, *vīḍu*.

It may seem a far cry from the Dravidian *yā-v-ar*, who? (masculine and feminine plural) to the Brahui *dēr*, who? (masculine and feminine in both numbers). But the chain of relationship is complete. *Yāvar* is used in colloquial Tamil as a singular also, and as such is abbreviated to *yār*; *yār*, moreover, in Tulu becomes *yēr*, and finally in both Tulu and Kanarese there is that unexpected change from *y* to *d* which constitutes the last link between the Tamil *yāvar* and the Brahui *dēr*. Nor is this all. *Yā*, the Dravidian interrogative base, is used in High Tamil by itself as a pronoun, and thus the alternative form *dē* of the Brahui nominative and, possibly, the apparently irregular but invariable form *dinnā* of the genitive singular are explained. The shortening of the included vowel in the genitive is characteristically Dravidian.

The interrogative base in Dravidian appears also as *e-*, probably an older and purer form of the base than *yā*, and this in the form *a-* has several representatives in Brahui.

Notable among these are *ant*, what? (*cf.* Malayalam *endu*), *ama*, how? (*cf.* Telugu *ēmi*, why?), *aṭ*, how many? (*cf.* Tamil *ettanai*), and *a-khadar*, how much?—which is especially interesting as being a compound of the Brahui interrogative base *a-* and a corruption of the loan-word *qadr*, quantity.

It is unnecessary in this rapid survey to trace the evidences of a Dravidian relationship through all the intricacies of the Brahui verb; it will suffice to indicate a few of the more palpable features of analogy. As regards the pronominal terminations we are on safe ground in comparing the plural terminations *-n*, *-re*, *-r* with the Dravidian *-m*, *-r*, *-r* (with vowel additions). The peculiar difficulties which beset the terminations in the singular appear to resolve themselves on a closer examination into fresh proof of a Dravidian relationship. Thus the obvious conclusion that the two-fold termination of the first person singular in the affirmative, which appears as *-v* in present-future time and as *-ṭ* in the past and all other tenses which are compounded with the substantive verb, is not in origin pronominal at all, but the distinctive mark of time, is significantly corroborated by the fact that *v* (with phonetic variants *p*, *b*) and *t* are the characteristic marks of present-future and past time respectively in Dravidian.

An apposite confirmation of this explanation is to be found in the organic negative conjugation, one of the most interesting characteristics which Brahui has in common with Dravidian. At first sight it might seem that Brahui employs two negative infixes, *-pa-* (occasionally modified to *-fa-*) in the present-future, and *-ta-* in the past, thus possessing a more complicated system than Dravidian. But viewed in the light of the foregoing explanation, the complexity disappears, and the negative formative, docked of *p* (*f*) and *t*, the signs of time, issues as *-a-*, the fundamental negative formative in Dravidian.

Turning to the causal verb, we find the Brahui causal formative *-if* palpably related to *-vi*, the causal formative in Tamil. It is a curious double coincidence, and probably more than a coincidence, that the sign of present-future time should be practically identical with the causal formative in both languages.

I pass by the case of indefinite pronouns or pronominal adjectives, like *pēn*, other; of demonstrative adverbs, like *dāngī*, *ēngī*, in this and that direction; of postpositional nouns, like *mon*, *muh*, before, *kēragh*, below; and of isolated words of every-day use, like *khaf*, ear, *khan*, eye, *bā*, mouth, *hal*, mouse, *murū*, hare, *khal*, stone, *pī*, excreta, *taḍ*, resistance, *choṭ*, crooked, *chaṭ*, destroyed, *chunak*, small, *hanēn*, sweet, *pūskun*, new, *mutkun*, old, *kuning*, to eat, *hīning*, to lamb, etc., *banning*, to come (roots *ba-*, *bar-*), *bining*, to hear, *allau*, it was not—all of which with numerous others are related to corresponding words in Dravidian according to certain phonetic laws, which are for the most part fairly easily defined. Such words hardly belong to the internal structure of the language, and their evidence, though interesting and important, is subsidiary to the main argument. But I cannot refrain from singling out the obvious relationship of the Brahui words *pālh*, milk, *tēlh*, scorpion, to the Dravidian equivalents *pāl*, *tēḷ*, the special significance of which lies in the fact that the former contain the indescribable aspirated cerebral *lh*, the shibboleth of the Brahui language.

There can be but one verdict on this evidence. This verdict is not that of Caldwell, who summed up his final position in the words "The Brahui language, considered as a whole, seems to be derived from the same source as the Panjâbi and Sindhi, but it evidently contains a Dravidian element," but the converse, first suggested by Lassen in the early days of the study of the language and reasserted by

Trumpp a quarter of a century ago. The Brahui language is sprung from the same source as the Dravidian language group; it has freely absorbed the alien vocabulary of Persian, Baluchi, Sindhi and other neighbouring languages, but in spite of their inroads its grammatical system has preserved a sturdy existence.

One word in conclusion. We can no longer argue with the childlike faith of our forefathers from philology to ethnology, and assume without further ado that this race of Baluchistan, whose speech is akin to the languages of the Dravidian peoples of Southern India, is itself Dravidian; that it is in fact the rearguard or the vanguard—according to the particular theory we may affect—of a Dravidian migration from North to South or from South to North. Such short cuts in ethnology are no longer open to us. The questions with which this essay opened, return to us at its close, but they return with deeper import. Who are these Brahuis, whose habitation is in Baluchistan, and whose language has to stretch beyond their utmost ken over so vast a tract of country and over so many alien languages before it can reach its own kin in the languages spoken by the strange peoples in the far-off South?

GRAMMAR

GRAMMAR.

SOUNDS.

§1. Brahui is not only devoid of literature, it is never reduced to writing except as an artificial feat of skill. The great mass of the people who speak Brahui are in fact illiterate, and the few who can read and write have acquired these accomplishments through the medium of a foreign language, and have as yet made no real attempt to apply them to their mother tongue.

§2. There has accordingly been little hesitation in the selection of the Roman character for the recording of Brahui in this work. On general grounds its advantages are felt to outweigh any that might be offered by the only alternative, a modified Arabic character. The adoption of the latter leads almost inevitably to niceties of fancied orthography to which the Brahui has no counterpart in his speech; it is, for instance, not easy to discard completely the distinction in obvious loan-words between س, ث and ص; ت and ط; ذ, ز, ض and ظ; ک and ق; ا and ع—distinctions which are meaningless to the Brahui, who contents himself in each case with one uniform sound, *s*, *t*, *z*, *k*, *a*. Moreover, apart from questions of artificiality, the Arabic character, overburdened though it may be with an elaborate system of diacritical signs, is incapable of representing the sounds in Brahui fully and without ambiguity, and proves at times definitely misleading. How real these objections are is writ large in the past history of the study of the language.

§3. The vowels with one exception go in pairs, short and long; as *o* is always long, it has been thought unnecessary to burden it with a diacritical mark:—

a, ā; e, ē; i, ī; o; u, ū.

They are sounded generally after the continental fashion, and the only sounds which have no precise equivalent in English are *ē* and *o*, which are pronounced purer than the nearest we possess to them. Practical examples afford the most convenient illustrations:—thus *nan*, we, is pronounced like the English 'nun'; *bāk*, mouths, like 'bark'; *bīn-e*, hunger (acc.) like 'bean-y'; *nē*, to thee, like the German 'Ne-ger' (not like 'nay'); *pin*, name, like 'pin'; *bīn*, hunger, like 'bean'; *hok*, fingers, and *pok*, lost, like the German 'Hokuspokus' (not like 'hocus-pocus'); *nuk*, the roof of the mouth, like 'nook'; *sū*, flesh, like 'sue.'

It is hardly necessary to point out that the sounds recorded in the isolated words do not always retain their full value in the rapidity of ordinary conversation. Thus when several long vowels occur in succession there is a tendency to clip one or more: *tūfakāte ī-ăn-tă pula*, snatch the guns from them, where *ī-ăn-tă* stands for *ī-ān-tā*. Again, a final short *a* is frequently almost entirely elided before a word beginning with a vowel or even with the aspirate:—*kasas rahāi-t' himpak* (for *rahāi-ta himpak*), no one goes near him. The power of the hardly perceptible sound that is left may be conveniently represented by the apostrophe.

§4. The vowels are occasionally nasalised, but chiefly in loan-words; nasalisation is represented in this work by a circumflex sign over the vowel:—*pā̃zda*, fifteen; *sē̃zda*, sixteen; *sirō̃z*, a lute. The nasalisation of a short vowel is somewhat rare: *dā̃z*, dust. In the imitative word *shĩṛshĩṛing*, to neigh, there can often hardly be said to be a true vowel sound at all.

§5. In addition there are the diphthongs—

ei; *ai*; *āi*; *au*.

The diphthong *ei* occurs in a few words only, but some of these are important, as for instance *antei?* why? It has no precise equivalent in English; thus *beik*, grasses, is pronounced neither 'bake' nor 'bike,' but between the two, somewhat nearer the former. The diphthong *ai*, on the other hand, may be readily paralleled in English; thus *aino*, to-day, is pronounced like 'I know' (with a slight emphasis on 'I'); *maiz-il*, stage, like 'mis-er.' It is not to be confused with the heavier diphthong *āi*, which plays an important part as one of the suffixes of the locative. Thus *puṭāi*, on the hair, is pronounced not like 'put I,' but more like 'put aye,' with the broadest pronunciation of 'aye.' The remaining diphthong *au* is pronounced as in German; it has, for instance, the same sound in *maun*, black, as in the German 'Maul.' At the end of a word it is perhaps hardly a true diphthong; it approximates to *av*, into which it resolves before a suffix with an initial vowel: *e.g.*, *kulau*, message, *kulavāk*, messages.

§6. The consonants may be arranged according to the position they occupy in the mouth, from the lips to the back of the throat; it will be observed that the series overlap:—

Labial.		Dental.		Lingual.		Palatal.		Guttural.	
p		*t*		*ṭ*		*ch*		*k*	
b		*d*		*ḍ*		*j*		*g*	
	f								*kh*
	v								*gh*
			s		*sh*				
			z		*zh*				
m				*n*			*ṇ*		
				l *r*			*lh* *ṛ*	*y*	
									h

The majority of these sounds have their counterparts in English, and these it will suffice to illustrate by a few words in which they occur, their pronunciation being indicated by English words composed of the same sounds in brackets. In the case of sounds foreign to English a more detailed description will be given.

p : *pin* ('pin'), name; *kap* ('cup'), half.

b : *buk* ('book'), a kiss; *bas* ('bus'), enough.

m : *mach* ('much' slightly emphasised), date-palm; *hamp* ('hump'), load; *būm* ('boom'), owl.

v is neither the English bi-labial *w* nor the labio-dental *v*. Of the two it more nearly resembles the latter, but differs from it in that the lower lip is drawn slightly further in on to the upper teeth, and touches them more lightly; there is a little more pressure on the teeth when the consonant is preceded by a short vowel.

f : *fām* ('farm'), understand; *bilīf* ('belief'), pregnant. (The sound is never used initially in indigenous words.)

t is unknown to English, nor is it the true dental of Persia, which is formed by touching the tongue almost on the edge of the teeth. It is formed as in Italian by the contact of the tip of the tongue at the spot where the teeth issue from the gums, so as to touch both.

d is the sonant of *t*, and the remarks above apply equally to both.

s : *sīm* ('seam'), border; *his* ('hiss'), ashes.

z : *zū* ('Zoo'), quickly; *būz* ('boose'), muzzle.

ṭ is the ordinary English *t* (and therefore materially different from the cerebral *ṭ* in Hindustani): *būṭ* ('boot'), boot; *ṭīn* ('teen'), tin—both these words are borrowed from English; *chiṭ* ('chit'), rope.

ḍ is similarly the English *d*:—*ḍak* ('duck'), a cut; *ḍāk* ('dark'), bald; *baḍ* ('bud'), a load.

n: *nan* ('nun'), we; *pin* ('pin'), name.

l is pronounced like initial *l* in English:—*līk* ('leak'), a line. Medially and finally it keeps its sound pure, and undergoes no modification as in English. There is thus a perceptible difference between *bil*, a bow, and 'bill,' between *sil-e*, to the skin, and 'silly,' and between *halk*, he seized, and 'hulk.'

r is produced by the vibrations of the tip of the tongue at the front of the hard palate, and the standard English pronunciation therefore supplies no exact parallel:—*ri<u>kh</u>-ēb* (German 'rich-tig'), stirrup; *mār* (German 'Marmor,' Hindustani 'mār'), son.

sh: *shā* ('Shah'), pour; *mash* ('mush'), hill.

zh is pronounced as *<u>zh</u>e* in Persian, and the *z(u)* in the English word 'azure.'

ch: *chank* ('chunk'), a double handful; *pichche* ('pitchy'), to the eye-gum.

j: *jin* ('gin'), a Jinn; *baj* ('budge'), back.

<u>lh</u>: is exceedingly hard to pronounce; it is a harsh aspirated cerebral formed by rolling back the tip of the tongue against the edge of the roof of the palate, letting the back of the tongue rest against the wall of the roots of the teeth, and emitting the sound with some force at both corners of the mouth; the force is occasionally, but not usually, greater at one corner than at the other. The common corruption of the sound among Indian foreigners, *lṭ* (using the Hindustani cerebral *ṭ*), is hopelessly wide of the mark. Though *ḷ* offers itself readily as a symbol for the sound, it has been considered advisable to adopt ***<u>lh</u>***, cumbrous though it is, to mark the harsh aspiration and the exceptional length of the sound.

ṇ is the obscure cerebral nasal of Sindhi and Pashtu (sometimes transliterated *nr*). It occurs chiefly in words borrowed from one or other of these languages, and its use generally points to Sindhi influence, under which it frequently displaces *ṛ* especially when preceded by a nasalised vowel.

ṛ is even more difficult for an Englishman to acquire than *lh*; indeed among some Brahuis themselves a certain difficulty is experienced (§18). It is formed by the contact of the tip of the tongue far back on the palate, so as just to touch the soft palate. The Hindustani *ṛ*, in which the contact is at a point considerably more forward, is a very imperfect approximation.

y **:** *yā* ('Ya-hoo,' German 'Ja,' Persian, Hindustani 'yā'), or.

k **:** *kuk* ('cook'), flocks; *chik* ('chick'), a pinch of something.

g is the same as the English hard *g*:—*guḍ* ('good'), after; *bag* ('bug'), a herd of camels.

kh is pronounced like the Arabic-Persian *khe*, *i.e.*, like *ch* in German and in the Scotch word 'loch':—thus *kharāb*, bad, *bēkh*, root, are pronounced just as in Hindustani.

gh is somewhat less guttural than the Arabic *ghain*, and initially and medially is pronounced as in Hindustani:—thus *gharīb*, poor, and *lāghar*, lean, are pronounced like the same words in Hindustani. At the end of a word, as *e.g.*, in *shāgh*, pour, it is less heavy.

h **:** though the aspirate at the beginning of a word which is sounded with emphasis is distinctly felt deep down in the throat, in ordinary conversation it is often hardly perceptible, and even dropped altogether :—*e.g.*, *hata, ata*, bring; *hēs, ēs*, he brought. The usage in fact is so uncertain that it is not always possible to determine whether the more correct form of a particular word contains an aspirate or not.

§7. The consonant series might be made more complete by the inclusion of the aspirated sounds *ph, bh, ṭh, ḍh*, etc., which are pronounced, due allowance being made for difference of pronunciation in the simple consonants, after the manner familiar from Hindustani. But though Brahui wavers for instance between *phok* and *pok*, lost, gone, and between *bhāz* and *bāz*, many, the simple forms in most cases are regarded as the more pure, and a frequent use of aspiration indicates contact with Sindhi and Eastern Baluchi.

§8. Similarly each series might have been given its proper nasal, each with an appropriate diacritical mark, but the result would have been a needless embarrassment to the practical student. Apart from the nasalised vowels (§4) the only nasals which have a separate individuality are the labial *m*, the lingual *n* and the borrowed cerebral *ṇ*. The modifications which the nasal undergoes in combination with a following dental, palatal or guttural are natural and familiar, and can be at once deduced without the use of distinctive symbols. Thus, *zank*, lambing-season, rhymes with 'bunk'; *bing*, he heard, with 'fing-(g)er' (not of course with 'king'); *lānch*, gird up thyself, with 'lanch' (*i.e.*, *lāntch*, not with 'launch,' *i.e.*, *lānsh*); *hanj*, duck, with 'lunge.' It is true English has no equivalents to *-nt* and *-nd*, which occur for instance in *ant?* what? *band*, joint, but this is simply because it does not happen to possess a semi-dental like Brahui.

§9. Again, a place might perhaps have been found among the labials for *w*, but the sound only occurs in combination;

e.g., *dwāzda* (*cf.* 'dw-ell'), twelve, *swār* (*cf.* 'sw-ard'), rider, *gwan* (*cf.* 'Gu-elf'), the pistachio *khanjak*. It is, in fact, merely a convenient method of writing *u*, and though the vowel sound is generally clipped as in English, it is not infrequently sounded in full :—*e.g.*, *duāzda*, *suār*, *guan*.

§10. The Brahui has a marked fondness for doubled consonants preceded by a short vowel. Among the consonants most frequently doubled are *ch*, *kh*, *t* and *l*, while the doubling of *n* and *s* is an important feature in the infinitive and past tenses respectively of a certain class of verbs. At the end of a word the doubling of a consonant is in most cases barely perceptible, though the sound may be slightly heavier than that of a single consonant. Hence with certain important exceptions, chiefly among the verbs and adjectives, it is unnecessary to mark a final consonant as doubled, whereas care must be taken to reproduce an unmistakable doubling in the body of a word :—*e.g.*, *kutte kulle huchchanā randaṭ mon tiss*, he sent off all the flocks to follow the camel. In this connection it may be noted that the Brahui has no particular dislike for concurrent consonants, at any rate in certain combinations :—*e.g.*, *guzhgh*, lucerne roots, *drassam*, goats' hair, *arisk*, persons, *laṛza*, trembling, *mūshkp*, he may not rub.

§11. The main accent, which is for the most part not particularly decisive—only a short included vowel in a suffix being entirely unaccented—falls ordinarily on the root of the word, though it is apt to be attracted to a syllable containing a long vowel or ending in a doubled consonant. In emphatic conversation, of course, the accent becomes definitely marked.

§12. Though hiatus is little felt except in certain combinations in which the copula is concerned, the declension of the noun affords an interesting example of the insertion of a euphonic *ghain* to prevent hiatus between *a*, short or long, and *ā* or *āi* (§§26, 36 *d*). Though this insertion is conveniently termed euphonic, it will of course be remembered that it is dictated not by the ear but by the vocal organs. But the practice is strangely lacking in uniformity: thus in the case of a monosyllabic noun ending in -*ā* the insertion of *ghain* before the case suffixes -*ān* and -*āi* is not permissible, though it is otherwise optional in the declension of nouns ending in -*a* or -*ā* (§36 *d*). A euphonic *ghain* crops up again in the adjective (§84). Before the copula there are in certain cases special devices to bridge the hiatus (§42).

§13. There is a distinct tendency in Brahui towards 'harmonic sequence of vowels;' that is to say, the vowels of a polysyllable are liable to become attracted into harmony with the last vowel. Thus *khi'lat*, robe of honour, appears as *khalat*, *Muhammad* as *Mahmad*, *manzil*, stage, as *mizil* (or as *maizil*, which has been affected by the same tendency). But it is in the conjugation of the verb that this principle is most noticeable: thus *kungusuṭ*, *kungususuṭ*, I had eaten, are the common forms of the pluperfect as opposed to *kungasuṭ*, *kungasasuṭ*, which are the forms obviously indicated by the formation of the tense, and which are also in use (§§221, 222). In the third person singular, *kungasas*, no change is called for as the last vowel is the same as the vowel preceding it, and none is permissible. The secondary form of the past conditional (§209) offers another illustration of the same kind.

§14. Another phonetic principle, which operates however chiefly in loan-words, is metathesis, according to which the consonants in a word are apt to change places. The simplest examples are to be found in words borrowed from Persian: *niām* (for *miyān*), middle; *dalvat* (for *daulat*), riches; *ruskhat* (for *rukhṣat*), dismissal; *bashkh* (for *bakhsh*), portion; *kulf* (for *qufl*), key; *kilba* (for *qibla*), west.

§15. A full consideration of the interchanges among the consonants lies outside the scope of this volume, but a few general remarks will perhaps be of interest. The interchanges fall naturally into three main groups: (1) interchanges which occur within the standard language itself, (2) interchanges in loan-words, and (3) dialectical interchanges.

§16. One of the most remarkable consonantal interchanges in Brahui itself is that between *k* and *t*, which plays for instance a very important part in the declension of the plural noun (§33). An interchange between *d* and *ṛ* is illustrated by the declension of the demonstratives (§127), while the conjugation of the verb points to interchanges between *n*, *r*, *s*, between *lh*, *l*, *s*, and—in the negative—between *p*, *f*, *v*. A consonant sometimes undergoes change owing to its juxtaposition with another consonant. Thus, *m* changes to *n* before *d*: *handā* (for *ham-dā*), this very; while *n* changes to *m* before *b* or *p*: *kumbo*, do you eat, *kumpa*, eat not, from *kun-ing*. Before a sibilant or a dental *r* may be optionally changed to *ṛ*: *harsing* or *haṛsing*, to turn, *larzing* or *laṛzing*, to tremble, *hartomā* or *haṛtomā*, both, *hardē* or *haṛdē*, every day. The occasional dropping of the aspirate has already been noticed (§6). It seems as if it were occasionally employed to mark a distinction of number. Thus one Brahui will say: *hor*, finger, *ok*, fingers; while a second will say the reverse: *or*, finger, *hok*, fingers. If both singular and plural occur in the same sentence, it is certainly idiomatic to distinguish them in this manner: *chākhū nā asi ore taṛēne, yā kulle hole nā?* has the knife cut one of your fingers, or all of them? *Ust*, heart, plural *hustāk*, and vice versâ constitute another example of the kind. In the case of *r* and *g* there is a similar tendency to be dropped. The pluralisation of nouns ending in final *-r* (§29) and the conjugation of the so-called verbs in *-n* (§186) afford striking illustrations of this tendency in the former. In some instances it is indeed difficult to determine from internal evidence whether a final *-r* is radical or not, *e.g.*, *ama?* *amar?* how? The dropping of *g* is exemplified in the imperative plural and the prohibitive of the passive (§275) and in isolated words like *giṛ* or *iṛ*, all, *giṛā* or *iṛā*, some, *hichgiṛā* or *hichiṛā*, nothing.

§17. It will be convenient to confine a brief review of consonantal interchanges in loan-words to the case of words borrowed from or through Persian. The more important variations include changes from *q* to *kh*: *rakht* (from *vaqt*), time, *akhadar?* how much? the last element being derived from *qadr*, quantity (§150); from final *b* to *f*: *shaf* (from *shab*), evening, *sof* (from *sēb*), apple; from initial *b* to *gw*: *gwāzī* (from *bāzī*), play, *gwar* (from *bar*), breast; from *r* to *l*: *shakal* (from *shakar*), sugar. The frequent nasalisation of long *ā* is not without interest: *bā̃z* (from *bāz*), hawk; *bā̃zil* (from *bāzū*), upper arm; *chā̃* (from *chā*), tea.

§18. As regards the numerous dialectical variations it is interesting to note that the Zagr Mengal finds the same difficulty in the pronunciation of the cerebral *ṛ* as the Brahui child learning to talk, and like him gets over the difficulty by using *r* instead: *dārē* for *dāṛē*, here, *dārān* for *dāṛān*, from this man. The Brahui child similarly does not readily master the difference between *s* and *sh*, and we find the same confusion in the Zahri variant *ishto* for *isto*, last night. The Langavs regularly corrupt *gh* into *kh*: *e.g.*, *khalla* for *ghalla*, grain. Again, the people of Zahri cannot pronounce an initial dental followed by *r*, and either drop it altogether or substitute the corresponding lingual: *e.g.*, *rakh* or *ḍrakht* for *drakht*, tree, *rogh* or *ḍrogh* for *drogh*, lie, *rakhkhing* or *ṭrakhkhing* for *trakhkhing*, to burst. A dialectical change from *t* to *ch*, which is analogous to the interchange of *t* and *k* in the standard language (§16) occurs in the important Jhalawan variant *choṭ*, I will give, for the ordinary *ētoṭ* or *tiroṭ*, and in the corresponding formations of the same verb. The converse is found in the Zagr Mengal *tāva* (*tiāva*) I understand, for *chāva*. But regard being had to the negative of *chā-ing*, it seems not impossible that the older form of the root has been preserved in the dialect (§261).

THE SUBSTANTIVE.

Gender.

§19. Gender in Brahui is not expressed by grammatical forms. Most cases in which a valid distinction of sex exists in the mind of the ordinary Brahui, are provided with different words for the masculine and feminine :—

pīra	grandfather,	*balla*	grandmother.
bāva	father,	*lumma*	mother.
mār	son,	*masiṛ*	daughter.
īlum	brother,	*īṛ*	sister.
mālum	father-in-law,	*balghuṛ*	mother-in-law.
sālum	son-in-law,	*malkhuṛ*	daughter-in-law.
khāspar	brother-in-law,	*duskhīch*	sister-in-law.
mē	slave-boy,	*chokarī*	slave-girl.
kharās	bull,	*ḍaggī*	cow.
mat	he-goat,	*hēṭ*	she-goat.
lok	he-camel,	*ḍāchī*	she-camel.

In cases of obvious necessity there are also separate words for the neuter gender.

§20. The Persian device of prefixing *nar*, male, and *māda*, female, is practically confined to cases in which a distinction of sex has little or no value in the workaday life of the Brahui. Thus the Brahui has evolved no separate words for the masculine and feminine of *khazm*, deer, and on the few occasions when a distinction is called for he is content to employ the foreign compounds *nar-āsk*, buck, *māda-āsk*, doe. Though the feminine of *lāgh*, donkey, is expressed by the Persian *māda-khar* (sometimes corrupted to *mācha-khar*), the device is naturally seldom made use of in the case of domestic animals.

§21. Apart from collective nouns like *bāhir*, herd of donkeys, *gala*, herd of horses, *bag*, herd of camels, *gārum*, herd of cattle, *kur*, flock of sheep and goats, there are often separate words for the common gender :– *bandagh*, human being, including *narīna*, man, *zāīfa*, woman; *hullī*, horse, including *nariān*, stallion, *mādiān*, mare; *mēlh*, sheep, including *khar*, ram, *mir*, ewe; *kuchak*, dog, including *narāz*, he-dog, *mind*, bitch.

Number.

§22. There are two numbers, the singular and the plural; there is no trace of a dual. The nominative singular is the simple base; it may end in a consonant or consonants, in short *a*, a long vowel, or the diphthong *ei*. Though several bases end in *-au*, a final *au* is hardly a true diphthong (§5) and is treated for inflexional purposes as *-av*, to which it approximates in sound in this position.

§23. The nominative plural is formed from the base by suffixing *-k*, which is euphonically strengthened in many instances to *-āk*, and—if the noun ends in a short *a*—to *-ghāk*, a *ghain* being usually inserted to bridge the hiatus.

§24. The formation of the plural is most conveniently discussed according to the ending of the base. In the case of nouns ending in a vowel the rules are simple and happily free from exceptions. The rules in the case of nouns ending in a consonant are more complicated and, apart from the inevitable exceptions, secondary forms are not uncommon.

§25. (i) Nouns ending in a long vowel or in the diphthong *ei* form the plural by suffixing *-k* :—

bā	mouth	*bāk*.
urā	house	*urāk*.
dē	day	*dēk*.
bē	salt	*bēk*,

duī	tongue	*duīk.*
hullī	horse	*hullīk.*
kho	pot	*khok.*
taho	wind	*tahok.*
dū	hand	*dūk.*
pū	worm	*pūk.*
bei	grass	*beik*

§26. (ii) Nouns ending in *-a* (no other short vowel is found at the end of a base) form the plural by suffixing *-āk*, usually with a *ghain* to prevent the hiatus :—

lumma	mother	*lummaghāk.*
bāva	father	*bāvaghāk.*
parra	wing	*parraghāk.*
hūrra	thunder	*hūrraghāk.*

The *ghain* is occasionally omitted, and the final *a* is then all but elided before the plural suffix *-āk.* The barely perceptible sound may be conveniently represented by an apostrophe : *lumm'āk, bāv'āk, parr'āk, hūrr'āk.*

§27. (iii) Nouns ending in a lingual (but not *r*, *cf.* §29), a nasal, a sibilant, *-lh* or *-r*, form the plural by suffixing *-k* :—

pāṭ	wood	*pāṭk.*
hēṭ	she-goat	*hēṭk.*
bhāḍ	cavern	*bhāḍk.*
khal	stone	*khalk.*
bil	bow	*bilk.*
sil	skin	*silk.*
khan	eye	*khank.*
pin	name	*pink.*
zān	knee	*zānk.*
sum	arrow	*sumk.*
kāṭum	head	*kāṭumk.*
kholum	wheat	*kholumk.*

bāmus	nose	*bāmusk.*
his	ashes	*hisk.*
rēz	hair-rope	*rēzk.*
mish	earth	*mishk.*
mash	hill	*mashk.*
pīsh	dwarf-palm	*pīshk.*
būzh	tangled hair	*būzhk.*
mazh	a kind of grass	*mazhk.*
tē<u>lh</u>	scorpion	*tē<u>lh</u>k.*
mē<u>lh</u>	sheep	*mē<u>lh</u>k.*
pā<u>lh</u>	milk	*pā<u>lh</u>k.*
īṛ	sister	*īṛk.*
roṛ	calf	*roṛk.*

NOTE (*a*).—The ordinary plural of *masiṛ*, daughter, is *masink;* the form *masiṛk* is rarely heard. The regular plural *īṛk* from *īṛ*, sister, is very occasionally displaced by *ink.* The plural of *duzz*, thief, is always *duzzāk*, the apparent irregularity being no doubt due to the double consonant.

NOTE (*b*).—Secondary forms are not uncommon, especially in the case of bases ending in *-ḍ* :—*kārēz*, subterranean channel, *kārēzk* or *kārēzāk ; kutām*, nest, *kutāmk* or *kutāmāk ; sāl*, year, *sālk* or *sālāk ; boḍ, boṛ*, louse, *boḍk* or *boḍāk, boṛk* or *boṛāk ; bhāḍ*, cavern, *bhāḍk* or *bhāḍāk.* Indeed, apart from the special cases immediately following, the plural of many nouns in *-ḍ* is preferably formed with *-āk : e.g., koḍ*, cave, *koḍāk* (*koḍk*) *; pāḍ*, blunt sword, *pāḍāk* (*pāḍk*).

NOTE (*c*).—Nouns ending in *-ṭ* or *-ḍ*, preceded by a short vowel, form the plural by suffixing *-āk :—*

puṭ	hair	*puṭāk.*
chavaṭ	sandal	*chavaṭṭāk.*
guṭ	throat	*guṭṭāk.*
kaḍ	pit	*kaḍḍāk.*
piḍ	stomach	*piḍḍāk.*

In the last four examples the doubling of the final consonant of the base in the plural is to be noticed. The doubling is similarly effected in the singular before the copula or on the addition of a suffix beginning with a vowel or diphthong.

§28. (iv) Nouns ending in a dental, palatal, guttural or labial (including the semi-diphthong *-au*, but excluding the nasal *m*, *cf.* §27) form the plural by suffixing *-āk* :—

lot	bag	*lotāk.*
nut	flour	*nutāk.*
pit	thorn	*pitāk.*
ust (*hust*)	heart	*hustāk* (*ustāk* *cf.* §16).
gud	clothes	*gudāk.*
lad	grove	*ladāk.*
rand	track	*randāk.*
mach	date-palm	*machchāk.*
huch	camel	*huchchāk.*
hanj	duck	*hanjāk.*
baj	back	*bajāk.*
kuchak	dog	*kuchakāk.*
ḍhok	clod	*ḍhokāk.*
lok	he-camel	*lokāk.*
pug	bhusa	*pugāk.*
ṭung	hole	*ṭungāk.*
sāng	betrothal	*sāngāk.*
lichchakh	mud	*lichchakhāk.*
malakh	locust	*malakhāk.*
tugh	sleep	*tughāk.*
iragh	bread	*iraghāk.*
lap	handful	*lappāk.*
kap	half	*kappāk.*
trump	drop of water	*trumpāk.*
sharāb	wine	*sharābāk.*

kumb	pool	*kumbāk.*
pif	lung	*piffāk.*
harraf	markhor	*harrafāk.*
kulau	message	*kulavāk.*
pishkau	lock of hair	*pishkarāk.*

NOTE (*a*) —The doubling of the final *ch*, *p*, *f* of the base in some of the plurals will be noticed. The same remarks apply as in the case of a final *ṭ* [§27, Note (*c*) *fin.*].

NOTE (*b*).—Variants are not uncommon:—*e.g.*, *mukh*, waist, *mukhk* (*mukhāk*); *likh*, neck, *likhk* (*likhāk*); *tugh*, sleep, *tughk* (*tughāk*); *baj*, back, *bajk* (*bajāk*); *muj*, mist, *mujk* (*mujāk*); *pif*, lung, *piffāk* (*pifk*); *sof*, apple, *sofāk* (*sofk*). The plural of *khaf*, ear, is an invariable exception, *khafk*.

NOTE (*c*).—Especially to be noted are the plurals of *nat*, foot, *khad*, teat, which are formed by assimilating the final consonant with the plural particle *-k*: *nak*, feet, *khak*, teats. Before the copula or a suffix beginning with a vowel (*cf.* §48, foot-note) the *k* is doubled.

§29. (v) Nouns ending in *-r* form the plural by dropping *-r* and suffixing *-k*; the quantity of the preceding vowel in the singular is preserved unchanged in the plural, but if it is short the *-k* is doubled before the copula or a vowel:—

mār	son	*māk.*
ḍaghār	land	*ḍaghāk.*
bēr	plum	*bēk.*
panēr	cheese	*panēk.*
dīr	water	*dīk.*
amīr	chieftain	*amīk.*
or (*hor*)	finger	*hok* (*ok*, *cf.* §16).
laghor	coward	*laghok.*
shūr	clay	*shūk.*
angūr	grape	*angūk.*

shahr	town	*shahk.*
ditar	blood	*ditak.*
khākhar	fire	*khākhak.*
mīr	ewe	*mīk.*
kur	flock	*kuk.*

A long form in *-āk* with the retention of *-r-* is not uncommon in the case of a loan-word: *e.g.*, *amīrāk* for *amīk*, *sardārāk*, chiefs, for *sardāk*. An indigenous noun is occasionally pluralised in this manner, but in the oblique cases rather than in the nominative: *e.g.*, *kasar*, road, *kasarāk*, but better *kasak*; *jammar*, cloud, *jammarāk*, but better *jammak*. A monosyllabic indigenous noun is rarely so pluralised, if indeed, in pure Brahui, ever.

§30. The plural of *arē*, person, *arisk*, might seem at first sight to stand alone. It is, however, clearly related to the curious plural formation in *-āsk* (if necessary, *-ghāsk*) in the case of a proper name, which denotes, not a number of persons of that name, but the family or party of that person, including properly the person himself. Thus, *Bāz Khānāsk* means Baz Khan and his family, *Mīr Hamzaghāsk*, Mir Hamza and his party. The same formation is even found in cases like *filānaghāsk* (§165), so-and-so and his lot, *lummaghāsk*, the mother and her people, *bāvaghāsk*, relations on the father's side, *plēṭcalāsk*, the Political officer and his following. This formation may be termed the 'personal plural.'

§31. It is worth noting that the Brahui has appropriated the Pashtu patronymic ending *-zai* in the form *-zei*, using it with the same meaning as *-āsk*: *Ghulām Mahmadzei*, Ghulam Muhammad and his family. Unlike *-āsk*, however, this ending is treated grammatically as a singular suffix (§37). It is also commonly used as an ordinary tribal suffix.

§32. The suffix *-gal*, which is frequently used in Baluchi to form the plural of animate objects, is sometimes employed in Brahui, especially in the *āvāl* (Arabic *aḥwāl*) or conventional interchange of news after the salutations are over, in which the words are more carefully chosen and the language generally more formal than in ordinary conversation. Common examples of this formation are *duzgal*, thieves, *buzgal*, flock of goats, *zahgal*, flock of kids. Similarly the Rinds are called *Rindgal*, and the *Mēngal* tribe is apparently the tribe of the Mens, though the suffix is now inextricably incorporated with the name itself. Like *-zei*, the suffix is treated as an ordinary singular (§37).

The Declension.

§33. The grammatical relations of the noun are shown agglutinatively by the suffixing of endings. These suffixes are the same for both numbers except in the case of the genitive. But whereas they are added in the singular to the nominative or crude form of the noun, they are added in the plural not to the nominative but to an oblique base: the plural ending *-k* is changed to *-t-*, and except in the genitive and dative-accusative an inflexional increment *-e-* is also attached.

§34. In the following summary of the suffixes of the cases ordinarily recognised, the suffixes in the plural are conveniently shown in combination with the formative; the necessary modifications in the case of nouns whose plural ending is *-āk* or *-ghāk* are obvious:—

	Singular.	Plural.
Genitive	*-nā*, of	*-t-ā*.
Dative } Accusative }	*-e*, to	*-t-e*.
Ablative	*-ān*, from	*-te-ān*.
Instrumental	*-aṭ*, by	*-te-aṭ*.

	Singular.	Plural.
Conjunctive	*-to*, with	*-te-to*.
Locative	*-aṭī*, in	*-tēṭī*.
	-āi, on, towards	*-te-āi*.

§35. Certain variations presently to be discussed notwithstanding, there is properly speaking but one declension. Example :—

	Singular.	Plural.
Nom.	*kharās*, the bull.	*kharāsk*, the bulls.
Gen.	*kharāsnā*, of the bull,	*kharāstā*, of the bulls.
Dat.	*kharāse* to the bull,	*kharāste* to the bulls.
Acc.	*kharāse* the bull,	*kharāste* the bulls.
Abl.	*kharāsān*, from the bull,	*kharāsteān*, from the bulls.
Inst.	*kharāsaṭ*, by the bull,	*kharāsteaṭ*, by the bulls.
Conj.	*kharāsto*, with the bull,	*kharāsteto*, with the bulls.
Loc.	*kharāsaṭī*, in the bull,	*kharāstēṭī*, in the bulls.
	kharāsāi, on the bull, towards the bull.	*kharāsteāi*, on the bulls, towards the bulls.

§36. In the singular declension certain phonetic modifications take place according to the length or ending of the noun :—

(*a*) In the case of a monosyllabic noun, whether ending in a vowel or a consonant, the genitive and conjunctive endings are not attached immediately, but are linked to the crude noun by means of an incremental *-a-* : *māranā*, of the son; *māruto*, with the son; *bā-anā*, of the mouth; *bā-ato*, with the mouth.

(*b*) A somewhat similar modification may naturally take place when an awkward sequence of consonants would result from an exact adherence to the general rule: *gidispanā*, of the span; *kapotato*, with the pigeon; the regular forms *gidispnā*, *kapotto*, are, however, also in use.

(c) In the case of nouns ending in a long vowel the initial vowel of the locative ending *-aṭī* is elided :— *urāṭī*, in the house ; *tūbēṭi*, in the moon ; *hullīṭī*, in the horse ; *khākhoṭī*, in the crow ; *murūṭī*, in the hare. If the noun is monosyllabic, the ending wavers between *-ṭī* and *-aṭī*, the preference being generally given to the former :— *bāṭi* (*bā-aṭī*), in the mouth ; *dēṭī* (*dēaṭī*), in the day ; *dūṭī* (*dūaṭī*), in the hand. That the ending is, as a matter of fact, not *-ṭī* but *-aṭī*, is abundantly proved not only by the case of nouns ending in a consonant, but by the lengthening of the formative increment *-e-* in the locative plural.

(d) In the case of nouns, other than monosyllables, ending in *-a* or *-ā*, a *ghain* may be optionally inserted before the ablative suffix and the locative suffix *-āi* : *lummaghān*, *lumma-ān*, from the mother ; *lummaghāi*, *lumma-āi*, on the mother ; *urāghān*, *urā-ān*, from the house ; *urāghāi*, *urā-āi*, on the house Curiously enough the hiatus is never bridged in the standard language in the case of monosyllables : *bā-ān*, from the mouth ; *bā-āi*, on the mouth. Nor is it felt in the case of any other vowel than *a*, short or long.

(e) As already noted under the plural [§27, Note (c), etc.], certain consonants, notably *ṭ*, *ḍ*, *ch* and *p*, preceded by a short vowel, are usually doubled when followed by a suffix with an initial vowel or diphthong : *laṭ*, stick, *laṭṭe*, *laṭṭato* ; *puch*, clothes, *puchchān*, *puchchaṭī*.

§37. As regards the declension in the plural, little need be said. Due allowance being made for the different forms of the nominative plural, it is of one uniform type. Thus *bāk*, mouths, *bātā*, *bāte*, *bāteān*, etc. ; *lummaghāk* (*lumm'āk*), mothers, *lummaghātā* (*lumm'ātā*); *pāṭk*, wood, *pāṭṭā*; *masink*, daughters, *masintā*; *lotāk*, bags, *lotātā*; *māk*, sons, *mātā*. If in adding the plural suffix *-k* a final *d*, *t* or *r*, preceded by a short vowel, is dropped, the *-t-* is doubled throughout the oblique cases: *khak*, teats, *khattā*, *khatte*, etc.; *nak*, feet, *nattā*; *kuk*, flocks, *kuttā*; *khākhak*, fires, *khākhattā*. The oblique cases of the 'personal plural' are regular: *arisk*, persons, *aristā*; *Bāz Khānāsk*, Baz Khan and his family, *Bāz Khānāstā*. The ending *-zei* on the other hand is treated like a singular: *Ghulām Mahmadzei*, Ghulam Muhammad and his party, *Ghulām Mahmadzeinā*. And the same is the case with the suffix *-gal*: *duzgal*, thieves, *duzgalnā*.

§38. There are a few dialectical variants common enough to deserve note though not imitation. The locative suffix *-āi* sometimesa ppears in Jhalawan as *-ā*: *kharāsā*, on the bull, for *kharāsāi*. Another Jhalawan tendency is to drop the incremental *-e-* in the plural: *kharāstān*, from the bulls, for *kharāsteān*; *kharāstāi*, on the bulls, for *kharāsteāi*. In Sarawan the dative-accusative suffix is sometimes added in the plural directly to the nominative plural: *kharāske*, to the bulls, for *kharāste*, while an even more abnormal form *kharāsko* may occasionally be heard.

Supplementary Cases.

§39. The declension has to be further supplemented by the suffixes *-ki* (*-aki*), for, for the sake of; *-is*, *-isk*, *-ik*, at the place of, in the vicinity of, in the possession of; *-iskā*, *-ikā*, up to. For these, like the suffixes of the traditional cases, are added to the nominative in the singular, and to the oblique base in the plural.

§40. With *-ki* (*-aki*) is formed a case partaking of the nature of a dative. The choice between the two forms in the singular depends on the same principle as operates in the case of the genitive and conjunctive suffixes (§36, *a*). That is to say, unless the noun is monosyllabic, the short form is used: ***kharāski***, for (the sake of) the bull; ***urāki***, for the house; ***māraki***, for the son; ***bā-aki***, for the mouth. In the plural, however, the long form is invariably employed, the inflexional increment being lengthened to *-ē-*: ***kharāstēki***, for the bulls; ***urātēki***, for the houses; ***mātēki***, for the boys; ***bātēki***, for the mouths.

§41. The remaining suffixes are primarily locative in character. The forms *-ik*, *-ikā*, are not used in the noun singular except in combination with the indefinite article; in the plural, however, they are quite common. Both with the indefinite article and in the plural phonetic considerations have given these forms the preference over the ordinary *-isk*, *-iskā*: in the former there has been an unconscious desire to avoid a repetition of the sibilant, in the latter a natural tendency towards brevity; in both cases the suffix is fused with the preceding vowel and appears as *-ēk*, *-ēkā*. Examples: ***sardāris***, ***sardārisk***, at the house of the chief, in the chief's possession; ***jāga-asēk***, at a certain place; ***masinte-is***, ***masinte-isk***, ***masintēk***, with the daughters, etc.; ***drakhtiskā***, up to the tree; ***drakhtasēkā***, up to a certain tree; ***īlumtēskā***, ***īlumtēkā***, up to the brothers. The Persian preposition *tā* frequently precedes a noun with the suffix *-iskā*; in the case of the suffix *-ikā*, its use is somewhat less common: ***tā dēṭikkiskā***, up to daybreak; ***tā mashtēkā***, up to the hills.

§42. Certain of the case-suffixes take on a final consonant for phonetic reasons when they are immediately followed by the present affirmative of the substantive verb. The suffixes so affected are *-to*, *-ki*, *-iskā*, *-ikā*, which take on *-n*, and *-āi*, which takes on *-ṭ*: ***hullī dāsā kanā māraton e***, the horse is now with my son; ***giṛā-as ki nī much karēnus, kul nā̜***

ilumkin e, all that you have collected is for the sake of your brother; *mullānā zor masītiskān e*, the power of the mullah reaches as far as the mosque (and should reach no further—a common saying); *kanā daghārnā had ē mashtēkān e*, the boundary of my land goes up to those hills; *ghallanā mon nuskhalāiṭ e*, the face of the corn is turned to the mill (a proverb somewhat similar to 'like turns to like'). The suffix *-isk*, apparently by analogy, is sometimes strengthened to *-iskin*: *kanā kaṭ kul kanā māriskin e*, all my winnings are with my son.

§43. With the exception of *-isk*, which ending as it does in a consonant stands clearly on a different footing, all these suffixes are necessarily modified in this manner when they immediately precede the present affirmative of the auxiliary verb. Before other parts of the substantive verb the modification is optional: *kanton* (*kanto*) *aff*, it's not with me. If the following word begins in a vowel, the modified form is not uncommon: *kanā banningiskān aḍ ka*, wait for my coming. Otherwise the modification rarely takes place: *kanā māraton tūlh*, sit with my son; and in the case of *-āi* perhaps never.

The Use of the Plural.

§44. After all the rules for the formation of the plural (§23 *seq.*), it is somewhat disconcerting to find that the Brahui often dispenses with the noun plural, and leaves his plural meaning to be gathered from the context. He shows, in fact, a distinct tendency to avoid the plural if the singular will answer his purpose.

§45. The noun qualified by a cardinal number affords an excellent illustration of these remarks. As the number is already defined by the cardinal, the noun is left in the singular: *asi, irā, musi bandagh*, one, two, three men (§97). To pluralise the noun in such cases is not simply considered superfluous; it would be absolutely incorrect. As regards the number of the verb governed by a noun thus qualified by a cardinal, the practice is not uniform; the verb is, however, generally pluralised unless the subject is regarded not as a collection of individuals but as a whole: ***dah bandagh dāsā sāṛī o,*** ten men are now present; ***kanā irā mār bassuno,*** my two sons have come; ***kane dahas huch bakār e,*** I want a string of ten camels or so; ***naneān bīst bandagh aino bass, yāzda pagga barēra,*** a party of twenty of us came to-day, eleven others will come to-morrow.

§46. The same remarks apply generally to nouns qualified by indefinite pronouns like ***aṭ?*** how many? (§152), ***mana,*** some (§153), ***bāz,*** many (§162), which indicate the number sufficiently to allow the noun to be left unpluralised. The governed verb, on the other hand, is regularly placed in the plural: ***aṭ bandagh bassuno?*** how many men have come? ***bāz huch kaskuno,*** many camels have died; ***mana swār mon tiss,*** he sent off some riders.

§47. Even though the noun is not qualified in this manner, it is frequently left in the singular if the expression is indefinite and there is no room for misapprehension: ***num jwāno varnā ure,*** you are excellent young fellows; ***kanā shahraṭī bandagh bāz e,*** inhabitants in my village there are plenty; ***dā rāsto hīt affas,*** these are not true words. The last example also affords an illustration of the not uncommon use of a singular demonstrative with plural meaning as the subject of the sentence (§130).

§48. To avoid the plural some use is made of a jingling repetition of the singular noun: ***hullī mullī,*** horses, ***bīsh mīsh,*** donkeys, ***urā murā,*** houses. This device denotes a plural of a somewhat vague character, which may often be rendered by phrases like 'horses of sorts,' 'donkeys, etc.,' 'house and home': ***tēnā zāīfa māīfae urāghān kashshibo***

ki mēmānk-a[1] *barēra*, turn your womenfolk out of the house as the guests are coming; *nanā kur mure muchchāi mashān miṛāno*, they have driven our flocks and all right off the hill; *tēnā puch muchche much ka darak*, gather up your clothes and the rest of your belongings and take them away. Used as the subject of the sentence such phrases, though singular in form, govern a plural verb: *bīsh mīsh kul gum massur*, all the donkeys and the rest of them went astray. In the cases of *mār*, boy, *mē*, slave, this type of phrase takes the peculiar forms *mār-mator*, *mē-o-mad*: *mār-mator much massur, mulke bēlār*, the lads and youths banded together and ravaged the fields; *mē-o-made pā ki hullītā gēṛe karrir*, tell the slaves and all to clean out the horse-stalls.

§49. These remarks must not be taken to imply that the use of the plural is at all uncommon. On the contrary the plural is always employed if there would otherwise be any chance of ambiguity. Thus, if there is no indefiniteness in the expression, a noun used with plural meaning is necessarily placed in the plural, unless it is qualified by some word indicating plural number such as those illustrated above. Indeed, even a noun qualified by a numeral is invariably pluralised when the numeral is in the definite or absolute form (§98): *hamē bīstangā bandaghāk bassuno*, all those twenty men have come; *handā iraṭṭangā māk pēsh tammār*, both these two lads came forth. In such cases the noun apparently owes its plural suffix to the fact that the qualifying numeral is regarded by virtue of its attributive ending not as a numeral but as an adjective.

§50. Some nouns, indeed, denoting liquids and the like, are frequently used in the plural when the singular is

[1] To avoid misapprehension in this and many examples to follow reference may be made to §333. Words immediately preceding a verb in the present-future or imperfect usually take on a final *-a*. One result of the addition of this suffix may be the doubling of a final consonant [*cf.* 27 Note (*c*), etc.]

required by the logic of English grammar: *ditak*, blood (not necessarily drops of blood), *dīk*, water, *pāḻhk*, milk, *mishk*, earth, *kholumk*, wheat, and so forth:—*dā khavānā dīk chuṭṭāno hināno*, the water of this mashak has all leaked away; *zaghmanā laggingto ditak-ta chaṭ halkur*, as the sword struck him his blood spurtled out. Speaking generally, the singular is confined to the abstract or indefinite use of such words: *baghaire dīrān bandagh zinda mafak*, man can't live without water; *dā hēṭ bāz pāḻh-a ētik?* does this goat give much milk? *kholumnā iragh sā-anāṛān hunēn e*, wheaten bread is sweeter than barley-bread.

The Use of the Cases.

§51. With regard to the cases in general, it is to be noted that if two or more nouns are coupled together in the same grammatical relation, the case-ending need only be affixed to the last noun, the preceding noun or nouns being left in the crude nominative form: *ī sardār o nāibān harrifēṭ, o javāb titavas*, I enquired of the chief and the deputy, but they vouchsafed me no answer; *chār ḍik dānkū hilārnā hēsura onā nihārīki*, they were bringing four balls of parched grain and dates for his breakfast; *ī Shēr Mahmad, Bāz Khān, Ghulām Rasūl, Fakīr Mahmad, kulle baṭingāṭ*, I summoned Sher Muhammad, etc., all of them.

§52. **The Nominative** requires no special note. Passing reference may be made to the occasional use of the simple base absolutely: *naṭ shapād bass*, he came barefooted; *kāṭum pāsh dēāi chirrēngāka*, he was wandering about, head bare to the sun; *tūfak dūṭī salok ass*, he stood gun in hand; *zaghm baḍḍāi dudēngāka*, he was running sword on shoulder.

§53. **The Vocative** is the same as the nominative: *mardaka muskotā hītāte gīrām kappa*, fellow, forget not the words of the men of old. It is commonly prefixed by *ē* or *o*: *ē niāṛī numā khalk arāṛēk e?* lady, where is your village?

o khudānā bandagh nē ant massune? poor creature, what has happened to you? In prayers and invocations the prefix used is *yā*: *yā khudā kane maizilāi rasēf*, bring me, oh God, to my journey's end; *yā paighumbar khudānā kanā dūe halēs*, oh prophet of God, take me by the hand; *yā pīr kane dā balāghān rakkis*, deliver me, oh saint, from this calamity. In a few cases a special word is employed in the vocative: *bābū arāng kāsa?* father, where are you going? *urē dāngī barak*, friend, come here. The word *urē* (*arē*) is also used as a vocative prefix: *urē mār, bash ma*, my lad, get up. It is worth mentioning that a son is ordinarily addressed by his parents as *bāva*, father, and a daughter as *lumma* or *āī*, mother, or even as *balla*, grandmother. The wife if she has children is addressed by her husband as the mother of the eldest child, otherwise by her name. The wife never addresses her husband by name; he is called the father of so-and-so, if there's a child, otherwise *khwāja*, master.

§54. **The Genitive.**—The most interesting idiom connected with the genitive is its use as an independent declinable substantive. The possessive pronoun is treated in exactly the same way (§146), and the usage points unmistakably to an intimate relationship between the genitive and the adjective in its definite form (*cf.* §89). The declension presents certain peculiar features, on which some light is thrown by the declension of the demonstrative pronoun (§127). The following is the declension of a typical example, *īlumnā*, lit. of the brother, the brother's, that which belongs to, or is connected with the brother:—

	Singular.	Plural.
Nom.	*īlumnā*	*īlumnāk.*
Gen.	*īlumnānā*	*īlumnātā.*
Dat. } Acc. }	*īlumnāe*	*īlumnāte.*
Abl.	*īlumnāṛān* (*īlumnā-ān*)	*īlumnāteān.*

	Singular.	Plural.
Inst.	*īlumnāṛaṭ* (*īlumnā-aṭ*)	*īlumnāteaṭ*
Conj.	*īlumnāto* (*īlumnāṛto*)	*īlumnāteto.*
Loc.	*īlumnāṭī*	*īlumnātēṭī.*
	īlumnāṛāi (*īlumnā-āi*)	*īlum.*

The remaining suffixes are similarly attached:—*īlumnāki* (*īlumnāṛki*), for the brother's; *īlumnāṛis*, at the brother's. The plural may be optionally formed after the model of the demonstratives: *-fk*, *-ftā*, *-fte*, *-fteān*, etc. A possessive or genitive noun may be similarly formed from a genitive plural, *e.g.*, *īlumtā*, the brothers'; the declension is on the same lines, except that there are no optional forms in the plural, which is regular throughout: *īlumtāk*, *īlumtātā*, *īlumtāte*, *īlumtāteān*, etc.

§55. The use of the genitive noun is not unlike the English idiom: *kanā hullī batane, kanā īlumnā bassune*, my horse hasn't come but my brother's has; *dā zaghmanā bā kunṭ e, kanā māranānā tēz e*, the edge of this sword is blunt, but that of my son's is sharp; *nanā ispust salīsune, sardārnāṛān bāz duzzāno*, our lucerne has been left standing, but they've stolen a good deal from the chief's; *dā lashshīto rūtipa, Bāz Khānnāṛto rūta*, don't reap with this sickle, reap with Baz Khan's; *kanā urāṭī aff, tēnā īlumnāṭī maroe*, as he's not in my house, he's probably in his brother's; *nanā hullīteāi swār mabo, ē bandaghātāteāi swār mafabo*, ride on our horses instead of riding on the ones belonging to those fellows; *dā huch lāghar e, kanā bāvanāfk pazzor o*, this camel is skinny, but my father's are fat; *Zahrītā māle khalpa, Sumālāṛītāe arāṛē ki khanis chās ki nā e*, don't lift cattle belonging to the Zahris, wherever you see cattle belonging to the Sumalaris, treat it as your own; *tēnā hullīte darak, kanā īlumtāte illē*, take your own horses and leave those belonging to my brothers.

§56. In the foregoing examples the declinable genitive noun is definitely possessive, and instances in which this is not the case are very rare: ***kh**allingnāe kappa, pēn ama ki nī-a pāsa, nan-a kēna,* leave thrashing out of the question, and we'll do anything else as you suggest. In the examples that follow the genitive stands on a different footing; it is used elliptically, or it would perhaps be more correct to say it is governed by the verb and denotes the object in a somewhat vague manner: *tēnā īlumnā bingunuṭ ki daun **kh**afa uṭ,* it's because I've heard of my brother that I'm so grieved; *sardārnā bing, **kh**ushāmadīki-ta pēsh tammā,* he heard of the chief and went out to pay his respects to him; *nanā narringnā kase pāpēs,* don't breathe a word of our flight to any one; *ī bassunuṭ ki tēnā bāvanā nājoṛīnā nēāṇ harrifiv,* I've come to ask you about my father's illness.

§57. **The Dative** combined with the auxiliary is one means of supplying the place of the missing verb 'to have': *kane irā **kh**arās arē,* I've a couple of bullocks. It is used of the agent with the verbal noun of obligation (*cf.* §324): *sarkāre sardāteaṭ rājāk much karifoī o,* the tribesmen are to be collected by Government through the chiefs. It appears to have a terminative force when used with certain verbs which can hardly be regarded as transitive: *ī **kh**āne rasēngāṭ,* I came up to the Khan; *shahre **kh**uṛk karē narrā,* when he got near to the town he ran off.

§58. **The Dative of Interest,** as the case formed with the suffix *-ki* (*-aki*) may conveniently be called, denotes primarily the person or object for the sake of which something is done: *ī tēnā bāvaki dā ḍa**gh**āre dasēṭ,* I sowed this land for my father; ***kh**udānā pinaki nane illē,* for God's name's sake let us go. It may thus be used to denote purpose: *shahranā pulingki hināne,* he's gone to sack the village. Other extensions in its use follow naturally: *e.g., sē**lh**aki Kachchīāi-a kāna,* we go to Kachhi for the winter.

§59. **The Accusative.**—As in Baluchi, Persian and other languages, the direct object is not necessarily put in the accusative. It may either be represented by the crude base, which is the same as the nominative, or be put in the case which the accusative shares in common with the dative. The general rules which govern the choice between the two are much the same as in other languages.

§60. If the object is unemphasised and there is no room for ambiguity, it remains uninflected: *dīr hata*, bring water; and the same is the case if it is qualified by the indefinite article or a numeral: *asi bandaghas kasfēn*, we killed a man; *irā bandagh rāhī kēk*, he sends off two men; *musi hullī saudā karēṭ*, I sold three horses.

§61. On the other hand, the object is naturally put into the accusative, if there is any danger of object being mistaken for subject, as in the proverb *khoe khākhar, bandaghe hīt*, as fire boils a pot, so words stir up a man. More especially is this the case when reference is made to rational objects: *shwān duzze halk*, the shepherd caught the thief; *duzz shwāne halk*, the thief caught the shepherd. Again, if the object is defined, as for instance by an adjective in the definite form (§84), by a determinate numeral (§98) or by a demonstrative or possessive pronoun, the accusative is necessarily used: *chunakkā māre mon ēte*, send out the young lad; *dā shahre illā*, he left this village; *tēnā musi huchche saudā karēṭ*, I sold my three camels; *musiṭṭangā drakhlāte guḍḍā*, he felled all the three trees.

§62. **The Ablative** denotes primarily motion from: *tēnā uraghān pēsh tammā*, he came forth from his house; *tughān bash massuṭ*, I awoke from sleep. Various uses are derived from this fundamental meaning. It is used in a *quasi*-instrumental sense: *huch iraghān hampok ass*, the camel was loaded with food. It is even used of the agent with verbs of passive significance: *nī dā dāvae khalās*

karak, sarkārān mafak, do you decide this case, it can't be decided by Government. As in many other languages, it ekes out the comparison of adjectives (§§92, 93) : ***piḍ bā-ān shēf e,*** the belly is lower than the mouth (a wise saw directed against over-eating). Analogous is its use in cases like the following : ***narringān jang-a karēsa, jwān ass,*** 'twere better you had fought instead of running away. With certain verbs the object is put naturally in the ablative : ***hanjātā vallarān tūfakas khalkus, rad mass yā bēṭ?*** you fired a shot at the flock of ducks, did your shot miss or hit? ***tēnā lummaghān harrifē,*** she asked her mother. The ablative is sometimes used adverbially of time : ***dēān hinār,*** they went by day. Its use with postpositions and prepositions (§352) will be illustrated separately.

§**63.** **The Instrumental** denotes primarily the instrument with which an act is done : ***laṭṭaṭ khalkus-ta?*** did you beat him with the stick? ***dā chukke dūaṭ halkuṭ,*** I caught this bird with my hand. Hence follows its use to express the agent : ***kanā īlumaṭ toning-a mafak,*** he can't be stopped by my brother. It often expresses the manner in which something is done, thus taking the place of an adverb : ***ba khairaṭ,*** come in peace, welcome (the usual salutation); ***kanā kulavāte ode jwānīaṭ pās,*** please give him my messages properly ; ***handā ḍaulaṭ ki nī kārēm-a kēsa pēn kas kanning-a kappak,*** no one can do work in this way you do. By a natural transition it may denote the way by which one goes : ***handā jangalaṭ pāṭ karisa hināka,*** he was going by this wood picking up sticks ; ***lashkar dā kasaraṭ-a barēk,*** the army will come by this road ; ***dākān hinān kūchaghāteaṭ mashteaṭ jalteaṭ,*** from here we went by valleys, bills and torrents ; ***chukkanā vallaras nanā kāṭumaṭ gidārēngā,*** a flock of birds passed over our head

§**64.** **The Conjunctive** expresses primarily companionship : ***ī nā mārato Mastungāi-a kāva,*** I'll go with your son to Mastung. From this primary meaning arise three main secondary uses. The case may denote that something is in the possession of somebody: *kanā tūfak nā īlumton e*, my gun is with your brother; that an act is performed by means of something: *laṭṭato khalkuṭ-ta, zaghmato khaltavaṭ-ta*, I struck him with the stick, not with the sword; or that one act accompanies another: *onā tavārto nan rasēngān*, as he shouted we arrived; *kanā banningto urāe illā, pēsh tammā*, at my coming he left the house and ran out. A particular case of the last use is the use of the suffix with reference to time: *sobato bash mass*, he got up at dawn; *shāmato barēva*, I'll come in the evening. To be noted is the idiom in a case like *sardār nēton e*, the chief's speaking to you.

§65. **The locative in** *-āṭī* denotes primarily rest in, or motion into a place: *kanā shahraṭī tūlik*, he lives in my village; *urāṭī pēhāṭ*, I went into the house. The locative of the infinitive noun affords two important special cases of this use; coupled with the auxiliary it forms the so-called tenses of actuality (§188): *vakhtas ki ī hīt kanningaṭī uṭ, nī niām tammipa*, don't interrupt when I'm speaking; coupled with the finite tenses of *tamming*, to fall, it forms inceptive compound verbs (§299): *hoghingaṭī tammā*, lit. she fell into weeping, she fell a-weeping, she began to weep. The suffix may also have a terminative force: *kanā tūfak kāṭumaṭī-ta laggā*, my shot hit him on the head; *onā likhaṭī chiṛīngas tafok ass*, there was a bell tied to its neck.

§66. **The locative in** *-āī* denotes primarily motion to, or towards: *ī dāsā Kalātāi-a kāva*, I'll now go to Kalat; *kanā urāghāi ba*, come towards my house. Its secondary meaning is motion on to, or rest on: *ode ḍaghārāi biṭēṭ*, I flung him on the ground; *kaṭṭāi-a khāchik*, he lies on the bedstead. The special case of the infinitive noun is interesting:

ī ode narringāi khanāṭ, I saw him on the point of running off. There are several natural extensions of use which require no particular comment.

§**67. The locatives in** ***-is, -isk, -ik*** denote primarily rest in, or in the vicinity of: ***shwān hamo mashis maroe***, the shepherd will probably be about that hill; ***kure handā dūnisk khanos***, you'll probably find the flock at this well; ***murū hamē drakhtātēk gum mass***, the hare disappeared in the neighbourhood of those trees. They have not infrequently a terminative force: ***nē sardārisk zarūr-a dēva***, I'll certainly take you to the chief (or to the chief's place); ***asi jangalasēk bass***, he came upon a jungle. Closely allied is their use to denote in possession of: ***Bāz Khānis ēnakho kholum aff***, there's no wheat in Baz Khan's possession this year; ***naneān asi bandaghasēk tūfak arē***, a certain one amongst us has the gun with him; ***dā khalkanā bandaghātēk bīsh kharās bāz e***, there are plenty of donkeys and oxen in the possession of the men of this village.

§**68. The locatives in** ***-iskā, -ikā***, both of which may be preceded by ***tā***, denote motion up to, as far as: ***dākā Mastungiskā shāzda koh e***, from here to Mastung is sixteen kos; ***nā pin o marrām murriskā hināne***, your name and fame have travelled to distant lands; ***nēān tā bāmusiskā rasēngānuṭ***, I'm sick of the sight of you (a common expression, meaning literally I have arrived from you to my nose, you've become an offence to my nostrils); ***dā hirre huchchātēkā rasēf***, take this camel-colt up to the camels; ***tā ē mashtēkā hin, zū harsēng***, go as far as those hills and return quickly. The use of these suffixes is extended naturally to time: ***tā irā sāliskā o jahān suritau***, for two years he never moved from the spot.

THE ARTICLE.

§69. In most languages the article is one of the last parts of speech to be evolved, and it is not surprising that the definiteness or indefiniteness of the Brahui noun has often to be gathered from the context. Definite article there is none; but the existence of an indefinite article, and the possibility of expressing definiteness and indefiniteness in the attributive adjective (§80) go far to hide the deficiency. If the absence of a definite article would otherwise make itself seriously felt, recourse is naturally had to the demonstratives (§125). Of these *dā* (*handā*), this, and *ē* (*hamē*), that, are never wholly divested of their demonstrative meaning, and the colourless *o* (*hamo*) is generally pressed into service.

§70. The indefinite article *-as* is derived of course from the first numeral (§95). Like the Persian indefinite article *-ī*, which has a similar derivation, it is attached to the end of the noun. More often perhaps than not the noun is at the same time preceded by the numeral adjective *asi*. A difference in meaning between these two forms of the indefinite article is hardly perceptible. Although the Brahui, with his choice for instance of *bandag͟has* and *asi bandag͟has*, is seemingly able to convey the nicer shades of meaning lying between 'one man' and 'a man' which other languages express by means of intonation, such a distinction, if any there be, is too elusive to be reduced to rule.

§71. The noun with both forms of the indefinite article is declinable throughout the singular:—

Nom.	(*asi*)	*bandaghas*, a man.
Gen.	(*asi*)	*bandaghasēnā.*
Dat. / Acc.	(*asi*)	*bandaghase.*
Abl.	(*asi*)	*bandaghaseān.*
Inst.	(*asi*)	*bandaghaseaṭ.*
Conj.	(*asi*)	*bandaghasēto.*
Loc.	(*asi*)	*bandaghasēṭī.*
	(*asi*)	*bandaghaseāi.*

There are the usual supplementary cases: *bandaghasēki; bandaghase-is, bandaghasēsk, bandaghasēk; bandaghasēkā, bandaghasēskā.* The declension has apparently been subject to two opposing influences. On the one hand it seems clearly based not on *as* but on *ase*, which was probably the original form, and which even now obtains in the special case noted below. At the same time the lengthening of the included vowel in the genitive and conjunctive, which is obviously due to coalescence with the initial vowel of the endings *-anā, -ato*, appears to indicate that the base is still felt to be monosyllabic (§36 *a*).

§72. If the indefinite article is immediately followed by the first or second person singular of the present tense of the affirmative substantive verb, it invariably takes the form *-ase*: *ī Brāhūīase uṭ*, I am a Brahui; *nī Brāhūīase us*, thou art a Brahui. In the third person the ordinary form is apparently reverted to: *o Brāhūīas e*, he is a Brahui; it may, however, be noted here that though it is convenient to write the copula separately, it is sounded in very close connection with the preceding word (§251). Before other parts of the substantive verb the ordinary form is used: *ī Brāhūīas affaṭ*, I'm no Brahui; *ī Brāhūīas assuṭ, drogh-a pātavāṭa*, I was a Brahui and wouldn't have lied.

§73. The indiscriminate use of the indefinite article whether preceded or not by the numeral adjective may best be illustrated by a few connected sentences: *ī daro asi bandaghasēto Kalātāi hināṭ; ēṛē urā-asēṭī pēhān, tūsun; tūlingto nanki iraghas bisēr, hēsur; iraghe hamēṛē asi kaṭṭascāi tikhār*, yesterday I went to Kalat with a man; there we entered into a house and sat down; as we sat there they baked us a cake and brought it, and placed it on a bedstead.

§74. Besides serving as an indefinite article proper, this enclitic *-as* performs several other functions. It may express indefiniteness in the plural: *mana dēaseān guḍ haṛsēngā*, he returned some few days later. With this meaning it is frequently attached to numerals (§105): *hazhda yā bīstas hullī kane bakār e*, I want eighteen or twenty horses or so; or to a noun qualified by a numeral: *numā chār dēasēnā guzrān marē*, it may afford you a living for about four days. It is attached appropriately enough to several indefinite pronouns (§153, *seq.*), and gives peculiar but explicable point to *dēr?* who? (§137), *ant?* what? (§141). But when *-as* is found serving to particularise the antecedent of a relative sentence (§427), the question suggests itself whether *-as* in this connection is not something essentially different from the indefinite article, yet the restrictions in its use with the antecedent are significant.

§75. If the numeral *asi* qualifies a noun to which the enclitic *-as* is not attached, it has in the ordinary course the definite sense of 'one.' But just as we can still say in English 'it happened one day,' 'I went out one afternoon,' so in Brahui the adjective of the first cardinal is sometimes used with the force of the indefinite article: *ode asi de khanāṭ ki dā kasaraṭ-a hināka*, I saw him one day as he was going along this road.

THE ADJECTIVE.

§76. The adjective in its crude form is as a rule either a monosyllable or a dissyllabic compound of a root and an ending. It will be useful to give typical examples :—

sharr[1]	good.	*jwān*	good.
zabr	good.	*zaft*	good.
zibr	rough.	*zift*	rough.
shūk	smooth.	*trund*	fierce.
birr	wild.	*koṛ*	abundant.
burz (*buṛz*)	high.	*shēf*	low.
gwanḍ	short.	*kub*	humpbacked.
ṭunṭ	without hands.	*manḍ*	without feet, lame.
shal	crippled.	*choṭ*	crooked.
chaṭ	destroyed.	*chaṭṭ*	lazy, good-for-nothing.
ḍaḍ	hard.	*buss*	dusty.
namb	moist.	*ḍamb*	deep (of water).
sut	thin (of liquids).	*maṭṭ*	thick (of liquids).
tar	shut (of eyes or mouth).	*pist*	open (of eyes or mouth).
must	shut.	*buj*	closed (of bottles, etc.).
pok	lost, fruitless.	*gaṭ*	busy, confined.

[1] In Arabic *sharr* means of course 'evil'; hence the Persian taunt: *inchi qaum ist, khair-i-shān sharr ast*, what a race, evil with them is equivalent to good!

§77. The commonest adjectival ending is *-un* or *-kun* (with *-gun* after *n*):

balun	big.	*murghun*	long.
pūskun	new.	*mutkun*	old.
bārun	dry.	*pālun*	wet.
bāsun	hot.	*bissun*	cooked, ripe.
uskkun	slender.	*hūlun*	thick.
khulkun	soft.	*pā̃gun*	dense.
bīngun	hungry.	*musun*	upside down.
pīun	white.	*maun*	black.
khīsun	red.	*kharrun*	green.

pūshkun yellow.

Other important endings are — *-ēn : kubēn*, heavy, *pudēn*, cold, *hanēn*, sweet, *kharēn*, bitter; *-ak : chunak*, small, *tanak*, thin, *subak* (Persian *subuk*), light, *paṭṭak*, short of stature; *-ar : sabbar*, strong, *nibbar*, weak, *mandar*, short of stature; and *-or : pazzor*, fat, *nizzor*, weak, *laghor*, cowardly.

§78. In the predicate the adjective retains its simple form; it is indeclinable and affected neither by the gender nor by the number of the word to which it relates: *dā zāifaghāk ushkun o*, these women are slender; *hamo ḍaggīte birr kappa*, don't make those cows wild.

§79. **The attributive adjective** plays a comparatively small part in the language. The union of noun and adjective into a grammatical whole involves a certain complexity of thought, to which the Brahui is not always equal. Even such a simple idea for instance as 'a poor man said to his old mother' would naturally evolve itself in the Brahui mind step by step: *asi bandaghas nēstgār assaka, lumma-ta pīr assaka, pārē-ta*, a man was poor, his mother was old, he said to her.

§80. The attributive adjective, though unaffected by the case, number or gender of the noun it qualifies, never appears in the crude form in which it is used in the predicate according to the definite or indefinite force of the grammatical whole of which it forms a part, it must take on an ending expressive of definiteness or the reverse.

§**81.** The ending expressive of indefiniteness is *-o: asi chaṭṭo māras*, a lazy lad; *baluno inămas*, a large reward; *chunakko chukkas*, a small bird; *pēn bissuno āvālas*, another certain piece of news. In the case of *balun*, big, *chunak*, small, the adjectival formative ending may be dropped before the attributive ending: *ballo inămas*, a large reward; *chuno chukkas*, a small bird. The compensating doubling of *l* in *ballo* from *bal-un* will be noted.

§**82.** Nouns with plural meaning qualified by adjectives in the indefinite form are left in the singular: *num jwāno varnā ure*, you are good youths; *ē kul mauno hullī o*, those are all black horses. But except in the nominative the use of the indefinite adjective with nouns of plural meaning is avoided, its place being taken by the definite adjective: *gandag͟hā bandag͟hāteto dē gidārēfpa*, don't consort with bad men. This often explains the definite turn which the Brahui seems to give to his proverbs and wise saws: *jwānangā bēdīte gandag͟hā kutag͟hāk sholira*, (the) bad cooking-stones upset (the) good broth, the equivalent of 'evil communications corrupt good manners.' But the Brahui is otherwise fond of pointing his proverbs by definite expressions.

§**83.** The verbal adjectives, to wit, the adjectival participles, active (§212) and passive (§275), and the so-called noun of obligation (§213), are subject to the same rules as the ordinary adjective: *jwāno kārēm karoko bandag͟has*, lit. a good work doing man, a man who does good work; *tafoko darvāza-as*, a door that is shut; *kunoīo giṛā-as*, an edible thing. The ending, moreover, may be attached to indefinite pronouns when used as attributive adjectives (§150, etc.): *ak͟hadaro drak͟htas?* a tree of what size? *asi kullo dēas*, a whole day. Attributive adjectives may be similarly formed from certain adverbs (§182): *dauno luchcho māras*, such a vicious lad; and even from one of the postpositions (§380): *nēām-bāro sardāras*, a chief like you.

§84. Definiteness in the attributive adjective is ordinarily expressed by one or other of the endings *-angā*, *-ā*. The choice between the two merely depends on the length of the simple adjective. If it is monosyllabic, it takes on *-angā*: *sunangā shahr*, the deserted village; *sakhtangā laṭ*, the hard stick; *kubangā pakhīr*, the humpbacked beggar; *kullangā nan*, the livelong night. In other cases the ending is *-ā*: *pīunā hullī*, the white horse; *murghunā kasar*, the long road; *chunakkā* (*chunā*) *mār*, the little boy, as opposed to *balunā* (*ballā*) *mār*, the big boy, the elder son; *khudānā karokā kārēm*, the work done by God; *kunoīā dīr*, the drinking water. If the adjective ends in *-ā* or *-a*, a *ghain* is preferably inserted before the attributive ending (*cf.* §36. *d*): *zēbāghā* (*zēbā-ā*) *masiṛ*, the pretty daughter; *gandaghā* (*ganda-ā*) *mār*, the bad son.

§85. Although this simple rule for the use of *-ā* and *-angā* is firmly established—it is, by the by, on all fours with the rule for the use of the genitive endings *-nā* and *-anā* in the case of the noun (§36. *a*)—it is not rigidly adhered to in practice. The general principle is however clear enough to justify our regarding such expressions as *zorākangā varnā*, the strong youth, *sakhtā laṭ*, the hard stick, as loose deviations from the normal.

§86. In passing may be noticed the curious attributive endings *-kono*, *-konā*, which attached to the crude noun transform it into an adjective of similarity: *halkono sādāras*, an animal like a mouse; *nā īlumkonā bandagh*, the man like your brother. These may be similarly attached to the pronoun, generally to an abbreviated form of the oblique base: *kankono māras*, a lad like me; *nēkonā zāīfa*, the woman like thee; *nankonā sardāk*, the chiefs like us; *numkono duzz*, thieves like you; *okono luchchas*, a blackguard like him. These formations are specially remarkable in that there are no corresponding crude adjectives which might be used in the predicate. The endings evidently bear some relation to the ending *-kānaī*, which attached to substantives turns them into abstract nouns of similarity: *dā sajjie ki nī hisingaṭī us, Mēngalkānaī kappēs-ta*, don't follow the Mengal fashion with this meat you're roasting; *nī tēnā īlumto Bāz Khānkānaī kappēs*, don't employ the Baz Khan method in the treatment of your brother. Substantives of this class may in turn be transformed into attributive adjectives by the addition of the usual endings: *dā duzkānaīo kārēmas e*, this is an action characteristic of a thief; *nī huchkānaīo dushmanīas kanto harfēnus*, you've harboured a camel-like grudge against me.

§87. In the case of certain words indicative for the most part of order or direction there is another definite ending, *-īko*: *avalīko dē*, the first day; *monīko tū*, the next month; *padīko lashkar*, the rear-guard; *niāmīko huch*, the middle camel; *chappīko nat*, the left foot; *rāstīko dū*, the right hand (an expression which may be used metaphorically as in English: *nī kanā rāstīko dū us*, you are my right hand). This ending is sometimes curtailed to *-ko*: *shēfko mulk*, the low country; *burzko* (*burzānko, burzīko*) *mash*, the high hill. Though the definite adjective in these and similar cases regularly ends in *-īko*, the ordinary forms are generally admissible: *rāstangā, chappangā, shēfangā*, etc In some instances the word, stripped of the definite ending *-īko*, is not an adjective but a substantive: *mon*, front, *pad*, back *niām*, middle. The ordinary genitives of such substantives frequently take the place of a definite adjective: *monanā bandagh*, the first man: *padanā ilum*, the next brother; *niāmanā huch*, the middle camel.

§88. The attributive adjective generally precedes the noun it qualifies, as in the foregoing examples. It may, however, follow it for emphasis: *hullīas jwāno ha<u>l</u><u>h</u> o barak*, get a horse, a really good one, and come; *jāga jwānangā hamod ass ki nī halkus-ta*, the best place was the one you occupied. The adjective may even be separated from its noun: *ēlo baz<u>gh</u>ar o zimīdar assur bēgunāo*, the rest were cultivators and landlords, quite innocent.

§**89.** This leads on to the use of the definite adjective in all its forms as an independent substantive. The declension of the adjective in *-ā*, *-angā*, proceeds on exactly the same lines as the declension of the possessive genitive (§54), except that there is only one form of the plural, *-āk*, *-ātā*, *-āte* and so on: *musi īlumān ballā pārē*, of the three brothers the eldest said; *handā sharrangāe pēhifēr masītaṭī*, they made this good man enter the mosque; *ē hullīāi swār mafa, ēlo jwānangāṛāi swār ma*, don't ride on that horse, ride on the other good one; *dā chunakkāte yala karak*, let these little ones go; *kunṭangā lashshīteto rūtipa, tēzangāteto rūta*, don't reap with the blunt sickles, use the sharp ones; *<u>kh</u>udānā karokā kane manzūr e*, I accept the act of God; *tēnā jirga tūlokāte baṭangā*, he called his jirga assessors; *kahokātā rahīāi tūs*, he sat near the dead; *dā dīr kunoī affas, kunoīāte hata*, this water isn't drinkable, bring the drinking water.

§**90.** The declension of the definite adjective in *-īko* is very similar:—

	Singular.	Plural.
Nom.	*avalīko*, the first one.	*avalīkok.*
Gen.	*avalīkonā.*	*avalīkotā.*
Dat. } **Acc.** }	*avalīkoe.*	*avalīkote.*
Abl.	*avalīkoṛān*, (*avalīkoān*).	*avalīkoteān.*
Inst.	*avalīkoraṭ*, (*avalīkoaṭ*).	*avalīkoteaṭ.*
Conj.	*avalīkoto*, (*avalīkoṛto*).	*avalīkoteto.*
Loc.	*avalīkoṭī.*	*avalīkotēṭī.*
	avalīkoṛāi, (*avalīkoāi*).	*avalīkoteāi.*

The other case-suffixes are similarly attached. As in the case of the possessive noun (§54) there is an optional form of the plural in *-fk*, *-ftā*, etc Examples: *rāstīko pāraghān bafēs, chappīkorān barak*, please don't come from the right side, come from the left; *tēnā rāstīko dūaṭ kappa-ta, chappīkoraṭ ka-ta*, don't do it with your right hand but with your left; *chappīko dūanā swāteto khān hīt-a kattavaka. khiāl-ta bāz rāstīkoteāi assaka*, the Khan wasn't talking to the riders on his left hand, he was chiefly engaged with those on his right.

§91. The indefinite adjective may also stand alone, but it is indeclinable, and its substantive has in fact to be understood: *aga ballo khwāhisa, ī huchche hēsunuṭ, aga rīshīo khwāhisa, ī hēṭe hēsunuṭ*, if it's a big one you want, I've brought the camel, and if it's a bearded one you want, I've brought the goat. But the ordinary idiom is the same as in English: if the noun is omitted its place is supplied by the noun *asiṭ*, one: *nanā bādshā laghoro asiṭṭ e*, our king is a cowardly one; *dā hullī asīlo asiṭṭ e*, this horse is a well-bred one; *ballo mēlhas nēki hattanuṭ, chunakko asiṭto bassunuṭ*, I haven't brought you a big sheep, I've come with a small one. Sometimes instead of *asiṭ* being used, the indefinite article is attached as if the indefinite adjective were a substantive: *dā hullī asīloas e*, this horse is a thoroughbred one; *chunakkoasēto bassunuṭ*, I've come with a small one. If an indefinite adjective is used in the predicate and refers back to a plural subject and is immediately followed by the present affirmative of the substantive verb in the plural, an apparently euphonic final *-n* is added to it: *Mūlanā mashk sakhlon o*, the Mula hills are stiff ones; *nā hatrokā giṛāk kul jwānon o*, the things you have brought are all excellent ones; *nan kul balunon un, num chunakkon ure*, we are all big ones, you are all small.

Degrees of Comparison.

§92. The comparative degree of adjectives may be formed by adding the suffix *-tir* to the positive : *e.g.*, *jwāntir*, *shartir*, better; *battir* (for *bad-tir*), worse. The object with which the comparison is made is not necessarily expressed: *ē nājoṛā arē dāsā battir e*, that sick person is now worse; if expressed, it is in the ablative: *avalān machchi shartir e*, he's a little better than formerly; *Chiltannā mash Murdārnāṛān burẓtir e*, Chiltan hill is higher than Murdar; *kanā tūfaknā sum nāṛān murtir hinā*, the bullet of my gun went further than yours. In passing may be noticed the use of *battir*, worse, as an intensive adverb: *dā battir jwān e, ki ī nē Sēbīṭī har dē khaniv*, it's awfully good that I see you every day in Sibi. The comparative may be used attributively with the addition of the ordinary endings: *dā hullī jwān aff*, *asi jwāntiro hullīas hata*, this horse is no good, bring a better one; *hamē burẓtirā mashāi lagga*, climb that higher hill. Superlative there is none.

§93. But the comparative is no doubt a relatively modern adaptation from without; the positive is in itself capable of rendering the degrees of comparison, especially with the aid of the ablative: *pēnanā malhān tēnā masiṛ jwān e*, one's own daughter is better than another man's son (one of the stock Brahui hits at the son-in-law); *gandaghā alvādān nēstī-ta jwān e*, it's better to have no children at all than bad ones: *kanā hullī kullān jwān e*, my horse is the best of the lot. The thing compared is probably omitted more often than not; there is rarely any difficulty in gathering from the context whether *kanā hullī jwān e* means, for instance, my horse is a good one, my horse is better than this or that, or is the best of all.

§94. The adjective may be intensified by its unusual position in the sentence, by the intonation of the voice, or by the prefixing of some word meaning most, very, quite: ***bāz jwān***, very good; ***sakht khwash***, most happy, and so on. Or recourse may be had to the primitive device of reduplication: ***asi jwāno jwāno huchchas kanki hata***, bring a particularly good camel for me.

THE NUMERAL.

§95. The Cardinal Numbers are as follows :—

1. *asiṭ, asi.*
2. *iraṭ, irā.*
3. *musiṭ, musi.*
4. *chār.*
5. *panch.*
6. *shash.*
7. *haft.*
8. *hasht.*
9. *noh.*
10. *dah.*
11. *yā̃zda.*
12. *dwā̃zda.*
13. *sē̃zda.*
14. *chā̃ṛda.*
15. *pā̃zda.*
16. *shā̃zda.*
17. *havda.*
18. *hazhda.*
19. *nozda.*
20. *bīst.*
21. *bīst o yak.*
22. *bīst o do.*
30. *sī.*
40. *chil.*
50. *panjā.*
60. *shast.*
70. *haftād.*
80. *hashtād.*
90. *navad.*
100. *sad.*
101. *sad o yak.*
102. *sad o do.*
103. *sad o sei.*
200. *do sad.*
300. *sei sad.*
1,000. *hazār.*
100,000. *lak.*
10,000,000. *kroṛ.*

All but the first three (and of course the last two) are adapted from Persian, and even these three are ousted in the compounds by the loan-words *yak, do, sei.* There are a few unimportant variants: thus, the nasalisation in the tens is sometimes omitted. Some of the more backward tribes, such as the Sumalari and Mengal, regularly count by scores: *musi bīst o dah*, 70; *chār bīst*, 80; *irā hashtād*, 160. The higher numbers are rarely used.

§96. Each of the three indigenous numbers presents itself in a two-fold shape: *asiṭ, iraṭ, musiṭ* are nouns of number, while *asi, irā, musi* are numeral adjectives. The nouns of number and the other cardinals used as such are declinable in the singular like ordinary substantives: ***musiṭṭān asiṭ hushār e***, of the three one is wise; ***dā iragh numā chārana e, o chorikas nanā e***, this bread belongs to you four, and a quarter is ours. As in English, the numerals appear now and then in the plural: ***dā kasaraṭ sadāk kāra barēra***, hundreds come and go by this road; ***dā bāghaṭī sadātcāī pul arē***, in this garden there are flowers in hundreds.

§97. Used as adjectives the numerals are of course indeclinable; the qualified noun is in the singular (§45): ***kanā irā mār o***, I've two sons; ***bīst bandagh kaskur hinār***, twenty men died outright. In passing it may be noted that the cardinals are often used elliptically of age as in English: ***dā hullī bāṭī chār e***, this horse is four according to his mouth.

§98. The numeral adjective may take on the ordinary definite endings of the attributive adjective (§84). In this form the numeral adjective acquires something like an absolute force: ***hamē pā̃zdaghā (pā̃zdāngā) rupaīk***, those fifteen rupees in full; ***hamē bīstangā bandaghāk ki kasaraṭ khanān-tā, dād o, bassuno***, as for all those twenty men we saw on the road, here they are, they've come. In the case of the first three cardinals the attributive ending is added curiously enough to the nouns of number: ***hamo asiṭṭā mār e***, he's the only son; ***hamē iraṭṭangā shaskhāte hata***, bring both those two persons. The noun qualified by a numeral in this definite form is, with an obvious exception in the case of the first numeral, always in the plural (§49). The numerals, with the exception of the first, are naturally not used in the indefinite form: ***ī asiṭṭo bandaghase uṭ***, I am a man alone in the world.

§99. The numeral adjective in the definite form may be used as a substantive (*cf.* §89): ***dā kulle rājān hamo asiṭṭā salisune***, of all these tribesmen he's the only one who has survived; *hamē bīstangāk ki nī pārēsa, bassuno batano?* have all those twenty of whom you were speaking, come or not? *musiṭṭāte-ta tiss,* he gave her the three, *i.e.*, the three stones of the Muhammadan divorce, in other words, he divorced her.

§100. **The Ordinals** are formed from the cardinals by suffixing *-imīko,* with the exception of the first, which is the loan-word *aval* with the definite suffix *-īko* (§87). In the case of the second and third ordinals the ordinal suffix is added to the nouns of number:—

First,	*avalīko.*
Second,	*iraṭṭimīko.*
Third,	*musiṭṭimīko.*
Fourth,	*chārimīko.*
Fifth,	*panchimīko,* etc.

§101. There are four words used for the first ordinal more commonly than *avalīko: monīko, muhīko, monanā, muhanā.* These are derived from the nouns *mon, muh,* face, front; the two former are compounded with the definite ending *-īko* (§87), while the two latter are ordinary genitives. The place of *iraṭṭimīko,* second, is sometimes taken by *ēlo,* the other (§167).

§102. The ordinals are primarily adjectives. Used as substantives they are declined after the model of the definite adjective in *-īko* (§90): *iraṭ tēn-pa-tēn hīt-a kēra, musiṭṭimīkonā antas?* when two chat together what business is it of the third?—two's company, three's none. The plural no doubt would be regular, but as in English it is rarely heard.

§103. **Collective Numerals** are formed from the cardinals by adding the termination *-ī: nan dahī barēna harin ki numeān aṭ jangaki pēsh tammire,* we'll come in a body of ten to see how many of you will sally forth to show fight; *lashkare khanāṭ, panchī dahī bīstī aff, bāz e,* I saw the army, it's not a band of five or ten or twenty, it's a host; *asiṭṭīaṭ khudā jwān e*, God in his oneness is good; *Mastungnā kasaraṭ duzzāk chārī o panchīāi barning-a lappasa, moga asiṭṭīaṭ hining mushkil e*, on the Mastung road thieves can't attack a party of four or five, but it's not easy to travel by oneself; *chārī o panchīlo chikār-a topasa*, they won't molest a party of four or five.

§**104. Distributives** are expressed by repeating the cardinals: *ī ofte irā irā rupaī tissuṭ*, I paid them two rupees each. As substantives the distributives are generally used adverbially in the locative in *-āi*, the case-ending being suffixed to the latter numeral only (§51): *ī ofte iraṭ iraṭṭāi tankhā tirisa hināṭa*, I went on giving them their pay two at a time; *bīst bīstāi hisāb karak*, calculate by scores; *lashkar dīrāi much mass, chār chārāi dīr kunisa hināra*, the army collected at the water and the men kept on drinking in relays of four.

§**105. Approximate Numbers** are perhaps most commonly expressed by suffixing the indefinite article to the cardinals (§74): *ī ofte dahas rupaī tissuṭ*, I gave them about ten rupees; *dā kasaraṭ bīstas khanāṭ*, I saw twenty or so on this road; *panchas dē-a marēk ki ī bassunuṭ*, it's something like five days since I came. It is occasionally more idiomatic to attach the indefinite article to the substantive: *dah dēaseān guḍ dākā rāhī maroṭ*, I shall probably start from here after ten days or so. Or approximation may be expressed by coupling two numerals together: *dah pāzda banningaṭī o*, some ten or fifteen are actually coming. Sometimes both modes of expressing approximation are combined: *hazhda bīstas hullī sardārnā monāi hēsur*, they brought about eighteen or twenty horses before the chief; *hamo mēlhte ki nī khanāsus, dahas yā pāzda-as marēra*, the sheep you saw are between ten and fifteen in number.

§106. **Multiplicatives** are formed by adding *-tal* (fold) to the cardinals: *yaktal*, single, *dutal*, double, two-fold, *seital*, three-fold, *chārtal*, four-fold, and so on. The comparative recentness of this formation seems to be indicated by the fact that the forms *yaktal, dutal, seital* are much more common than *asital, irātal, musital*. The shortening of the vowel of *do*, two, in *dutal* will be noticed. The multiplicatives are generally used of cloth and other things which can be actually folded or bent: *dā yaktalo gidas e, dutaloas hata*, this is single-fold cloth, bring some double-fold; *ī onā zag͟hme dutal karēṭ*, I bent his sword double.

§107. **The Fractional Numbers**, with one exception, are adapted from Persian: *seiak*, a third, *chārik*, a fourth (in the case of bread, etc., *chorik*, a quarter), *panchik*, a fifth, and so on. The fractional numbers are chiefly used with reference to the division of land-produce: *nanā mulkān nanā sardār hashtik-a halēk*, our chief takes an eighth from our land. The only indigenous fractional number is *kap*, half: *mēmāne aṭ irag͟h tissus, asiṭ o kappas yā iraṭ o kappas?* how much bread did you give the guest, one and a half or two and a half loaves? To be noted is *sad o kappas*, 150. The Persian word *nēm*, however, is also freely used, and combines naturally with the borrowed numerals: *yak o nēm*, one and a half, *do o nēm*, two and a half, *sei o nēm*, three and a half.

§108. **Numeral Adverbs** are of various kinds. Adverbs of time are expressed by *vār* (*jār*), time: *asi vār* (*asi jār*), once, *irā vār*, twice, *musi vār*, thrice, *chār vār*, four times, *sad vār* (*satar*), a hundred times. The place of *irā vār* in the peculiar sense of 'again' is often taken by *lojār* (for *ēlo jār*) or by *pēndwār* (apparently a contraction of *pēn-do-vār*). In the case of the first three numerals the forms compounded with *vār* are generally ousted by *asīka* (*asīska*), *irāska*, *musīka* (*musīska*), that is to say, the locatives in *-iskā, -ikā* (§41); it will be noted that the final vowel of the case-endings is shortened, and that they are attached, not to the nouns of number as might have been expected, but to the numeral adjectives (for the converse *cf.* §98) : *asīka ki hīte bingus pēndwār harrifpa,* when you've heard a thing once don't ask again ; *ī daro irāska bassuṭ, nē khantavaṭ,* I came twice yesterday but didn't see you ; *ī nē irāska musīka pārēnuṭ ki dā kasaraṭ bafa,* I've told you twice and thrice not to come by this road. *Asīka,* properly 'once,' also means 'for a while' : *num asīka himpēre,* don't go for a few minutes. *Asīkato,* which appears to be an example of the combination of two case-suffixes, *-ik* and *-to,* means 'all at once,' 'suddenly' : *ofk hīt-a karēra, ī asīkato pēhāṭ,* they were gossiping together when all at once I entered. *Satar* a hundred times, is commonly used metaphorically : *bāva satar ganda marē, mārān jwān e,* be the father ever so bad, he's a better man than his son ; *nī satar zorāk marēs, ī nā khaloī affaṭ,* you may be as strong as a lion, yet I'm not the man to be beaten by you. Numeral adverbs of quantity are expressed by coupling the cardinals with *handākhadar* (or variants, §150), this much : *musi handākhadar dīr hata,* bring three times as much water as this ; *andākhadar ki arēs, bīst andākhadar marēs, kaneāi banning-a kappēsa,* though you become twenty times the man you are, you won't be able to cope with us.

THE PRONOUN.

The Personal Pronouns.

§109. There are three personal pronouns: *ī* and *nī* for the first and second persons, and the enclitic *-ta* for the oblique cases of the third person. The missing nominatives of the third person are supplied by the demonstratives, which also afford optional and generally emphatic forms of the oblique cases. The terminations of the verb are in themselves sufficient to indicate the person, and the pronouns are not infrequently omitted.

§110. The plural of respect has no place in Brahui; if used at all, it is used by those only who have learnt its force in other languages. A man of rank is often addressed in the third person as *khwāja*, master: thus *khwāja joṛ e, khwājanā māk joṛ o?* is the master well, are the master's sons well? is the proper salutation to a chief instead of the ordinary direct queries *nī joṛ us, nā māk joṛ o?* are you well, are your sons well?

§111.

The First Person.

	Singular.	Plural.
Nom.	*ī*, I.	*nan*, we.
Gen.	*kanā.*	*nanā.*
Dat. Acc.	*kane.*	*nane.*
Abl.	*kaneān.*	*naneān.*
Inst.	*kaneaṭ.*	*naneaṭ.*
Conj.	*kanto.*	*nanto.*
Loc.	*kanēṭī.*	*nanēṭī.*
	kaneāī.	*naneaī.*

The Second Person.

	Singular.	Plural.
Nom.	*nī*, thou.	*num*, you.
Gen.	*nā*.	*numā*.
Dat. / Acc.	*nē*.	*nume*.
Abl.	*nēān*.	*numeān*.
Inst.	*nēaṭ*.	*numeaṭ*.
Conj.	*nēto*.	*numto*.
Loc.	*nēṭī*.	*numēṭī*.
	nēāi.	*numeāi*.

The supplementary cases are *kanki*, for my sake; *kane-is*, *kanēsk* (*kane-isk*), *kanēk*, with me, at my house, in my possession; *kanēskā* (*kane-iskā*), *kanēkā*, up to me; the plural and the second person are declined on the same model.

§112. There are several peculiar features in this declension: the use of *-ā* as the suffix of the genitive singular; the appearance of the inflexional increment *-e-* in the singular as well as in the plural, together with the special case of the second person singular; the omission of the increment in the conjunctive of both numbers and also in the case compounded with the suffix *-ki*; and the fact that the plural is not formed by means of the pluralising particle *-k*.

§113. Examples: *ī numto barēva*, I'll come with you; *sardār nēton e*, the chief is speaking to thee; *numeān dēr dēr hināno?* from among you which ones have gone? *naneaṭ narring-a mafak*, no fleeing can be done by us; *numēṭī dā zore khampara*, I don't see this power in you; *kanēṭī nume kārēm e?* have you any business with me? *har nēki badīas mass*, *nēāiṭ e*, whatever the result, good or ill, the responsibility is on thee; *nā kūs kane-is* (*kane-isk*, *kanēk*) *aff*, thy shirt is not with me; *numā īlum isto nane nanēsk gidārēfē*, your brother spent the night with us last night; *nanēskā* (*nanēkā*) *tēne rasēf*, bring thyself up to us.

The discussion of the enclitic use of the pronouns of the first and second persons may be conveniently postponed (§117) until after the discussion of the third person enclitic pronoun.

§114. The Enclitic Pronoun of the Third Person, singular *-ta*, plural *-tā*, which refers to animate and inanimate objects indifferently, is only used in the oblique cases. The place of the missing nominatives is supplied either by the repetition of the noun itself, or by one of the demonstratives, or if there is no room for ambiguity, noun and pronoun may be omitted altogether. Of the demonstratives the colourless *o* (*hamo*) is generally employed, the definite *dā* (*handā*), this, and *ē* (*hamē*), that, being reserved for cases in which some emphasis is required. When reference is made to one or more objects, all three demonstratives may be brought into play, and by their means the ambiguity which often attaches to the pronoun of the third person in English is generally avoided, notwithstanding the fact that the sex of the demonstrative has to be gathered from the context.

§115. The simple *-ta* (*-tā*) represents the genitive, dative and accusative. The other cases are formed by suffixing the enclitic to the ordinary case-endings, which are in turn suffixed to a base *ī-* :—

	Singular.		Plural.
Nom.	—	he, she, it.	— they.
Gen. } Dat. } Acc. }	*-ta*.		*-tā*.
Abl.	*ī-ān-ta*.		*ī-ān-tā*.
Inst.	*ī-aṭ-ta*.		*ī-aṭ-tā*.
Conj.	*ī-to-ta*.		*ī-to-tā*.
Loc.	*ī-ṭī-ta*.		*ī-ṭī-tā*.
	ī-āī-ta.		*ī-āī-tā*.

To these may be added *ī-ki-ta*, for him, her, it; *ī-is-ta*, *ī-isk-ta*, in his, her, its possession, etc.; *ī-iskā-ta*, up to him, her, it, with analogous formations in the plural. Though unimportant in practice, the occasional variant *-tan* deserves notice as bearing on the probable derivation of *-ta* from the reflexive *tēn*, corresponding to the derivation of the enclitic *-ka* from *kan-* in the case of the first person (§117).

§116. The simple enclitic *-ta* (*-tā*) is properly attached to the end of the word to which it stands in the closest relation: *bāva-ta pārē*, his father said; *bāva pārē-ta*, the father said to him; *zaghm-tan kaneān gum mass*, I lost his sword; *khalkut-ta*, I struck him. It may thus be attached to the case-ending of the noun it defines: *tayārī mass barāmnā-tā*, preparations were made for their marriage. It may refer in the same sentence to different objects: *bāva-ta pārē-ta*, his (or her) father said to her (or him). Similarly the compound forms, related as they generally are to the sentence as a whole, are ordinarily placed last in the sentence: *sardār harrifē īānta*, the chief asked him; *masir hinā ītotā*, the girl went with them; *zāīfae ki khanā, bash mass dudēngā īāita*, when he saw the woman, he arose and ran towards her; *dā puchche mūghā īkitā*, she sewed this cloth for them. But if the compound forms stand in intimate relation to some particular element in the sentence, they naturally take their place after it: *asiṭ īṭītā hushār assaka*, one among them was wise. Their position in the sentence is, however, often arbitrary: *nī ītotan hinak, nē shikārnā jahe nishān-a ētik*, you go with him, he'll point you out the shooting-ground; *hullīe kanā īaṭta hatarifis*, please get my horse brought by him.

§117. The Enclitic Pronouns of the First and Second Persons.—On the analogy of the pronoun of the third person, *-ka* and *-ne* are not infrequently used, especially in Jhalawan, instead of the ordinary genitive, dative, accusative of the first and second persons singular: *malhte-ka hich pāpēs*, please don't say anything to my sons; *dā hīte antei pātavēs-ka?* why didn't you tell me this thing? *khalkus-ka*, you struck me; *māre-ne Shālkoṭān hēsuṭ*, I brought thy son from Quetta;

kunē-ne hamē kuchakas ki drust kē-ne, may that dog bite thee that knows thee (a proverb not unlike the Irish 'better the devil you know than the devil you don't know'). These forms are even used instead of the reflexive (*cf.* §120): *kārēme-ka khalās kattanuṭ, ama nēto barēv?* I haven't finished my work, how can I come with you? *sabakhe-ne yāt kattanus?* haven't you got your lesson by heart? In some dialects the use of an enclitic genitive, dative, accusative is even extended to the plurals of the first and second persons. The Nicharis, for instance, make use of expressions like *khalkus-nan*, you beat us, *pārēn-num*, we said to you, instead of the ordinary *nane khalkus*, *num pārēn*. This usage is, however, inadmissible in the standard language.

§118. In the other oblique cases the genitives of the two pronouns, plural as well as singular, are linked enclitically with the base *ī-* by means of the ordinary case-endings: *ī-ṭi-kanā dā zore khanisa ki nī daun-a pāsa?* do you see this power in me, that you speak thus? *dauno kārēmas ītonā karē ki kasas dushmanto kapp*, he dealt with thee in a way no one would deal with his enemy; *nanā māle īānnanā pulār*, they looted us of our property; *musāfirīān ki bassur, īkinumā ant hēsur?* when they returned from their journey, what did they bring for you? In the case of the singular pronouns the enclitic forms *-ka* and *-ne* often oust the ordinary genitives in this formation: *dā kārēme ki īkika karēs, handun chās ki kane bahā-aṭ halkus*, if you did this work for my sake, please consider me your humble servant (lit. that you purchased me with a price); *ī-is-ka harchi ki khanis nā e*, all you may see in my possession is yours; *hamo dā kārēme īaṭne karifik ki malāmat karife-ne*, he'll make thee do this thing to get thee blamed; *nā ilum ki dākā hinā, bāz pīmāz taṛē īāine, magu hich matau-ne*, when thy brother left here, he told many a lie about thee, but there was no harm done thee (lit. he cut many an onion on thee, or *bajāi-ne*, on thy back).

It may be noted in anticipation that the genitive of the reflexive (but not of the interrogative or demonstrative) is similarly used enclitically in the compound forms (§121).

The Reflexive Pronoun.

§119. It is curious that the nominative of the reflexive pronoun, *tēn*, has only been preserved in the foreign compound *tēn-pa-tēn* (*tēm-pa-tēn*), lit. self by self, amongst ourselves, yourselves, themselves (*cf.* 385). The place of the nominative is taken by the instrumental in much the same way as in English: *dā kārēme tēnaṭ khalās karēr*, they finished this work (by) themselves; *ī tēnaṭ hināṭ*, I went myself. The oblique cases are formed after the model of the personal pronouns; the declension is the same for both numbers:—

Gen.	*tēnā*, of self, of selves.
Dat. / **Acc.**	*tēne.*
Abl.	*tēneān.*
Inst.	*tēnaṭ.*
Conj.	*tēnto.*
Loc.	*tēnēṭī.*
	tēneāī.

The supplementary cases are: *tēnki; tēne-is, tēnēsk* (*tēne-isk*), *tēnēk; tēnēskā* (*tēne-iskā*), *tēnēkā.* The only case which presents a deviation from the model of the personal pronouns is the instrumental, *tēnaṭ*, based as it is not on the oblique base but on the crude form.

§120. The reflexive, which may be used of any person in any number, refers back properly—but not exclusively as will be shown presently—to the subject of the sentence; *ī tēne biṭiva huchchān*, I'll throw myself from the camel; *biṭpa tēne*, don't throw thyself; *nājoṛ karē tēne*, he feigned himself ill; *salā karēn tēn-pa-tēn*, we took counsel one with another; *iragh tēnki dabo*, take food for yourselves;

ofk nē tēnto zarūr-a dēra, they will certainly take you with them; *tēnēṭī dā zore khampara*, I don't see this power in myself; *dā māre tēne-is darak ki dāṛē hoghik*, take this lad away to thy house as he's crying here; *huchchātā much kanningnā kārēmc tēneāi harfēnun*, we've taken on ourselves the task of collecting the camels. The genitive naturally supplies the place of a possessive when referring to the subject of the sentence; as a rule it follows its noun unless some emphasis is required: *bāvac tēnā pārēs*, thou didst say to thy father; *ī tēnā bāvaghān khar karēṭ*, I lost my temper with my own father. The ablative has sometimes the special meaning of 'at one's own cost': *aga kanto naukar-a salīsa iragh tēncān kun, ī nē chaṛa dah rupaī ētiva*, if you'll take service with me, your board must come out of your own pocket, and I'll simply give you ten rupees.

§121. The genitive of the reflexive is used enclitically to form certain oblique cases in the same way as the genitive of the first and second personal pronouns (§118): *ī dā giṛāte muchchāi ī-ki-tēnā halkunuṭ*, I've purchased these things one and all for myself; *nī kanā kulle kharche īāntēnā ētisa*, thou wilt give me all my expenses out of thy own pocket; *o kane ītotēnā sardāris darē*, he took me personally into the chief's presence; *mēmānte kulle isto ī-is-tēnā jah tissun*, we gave all the guests lodging at our house last night.

§122. The reflexive may refer to the logical (not necessarily grammatical) subject of the sentence: *kane tēneāi bāvar aff ki dā hīt kane yāt sale*, I've no faith in myself that this saying will stick in my mind; *ofte tēneāi bāvar aff*, they have no faith in themselves; *nume tēnā kārēm karoī e*, you've your own work to do.

§123. Another use of the reflexive when referring otherwise than to the subject of the sentence is to emphasise a noun or pronoun by standing in apposition to it: *kanā tēnā hullīc hata*, bring my own horse; *dā ḍaghār numā tēnā e?*

is this land your own? *dēre dēre khalk? kane tēne khalk, kanā māte khalk, nā tēnā īlume khalk,* whom exactly did he strike? he struck me myself, and my sons, and even thy brother; *sardār ki nume khalk, nāib hich pātav-ta? nāibe tēne khalk,* when the chief struck you, did his deputy say nothing to him? why, he struck the deputy himself. Except in the genitive and dative-accusative this usage is possibly somewhat rare: *dērto bass? kanto tēnto bass,* with whom did he come? he came with me myself.

§**124.** But in such cases recourse is had perhaps more generally and certainly more logically to a periphrasis in which *jind,* body, person, is combined with the genitive of the noun or pronoun, a device which appears to have been introduced into the language from Baluchi or Sindhi: *ḍaghār nā jindanā e yā nī chaṛa bazghar us?* is the land thy own, or art thou simply the cultivator? *antei kanā māre khalēre? nā mār antas marē? nan nā jinde khalēna,* why do you beat my son? what does thy son matter? we'll beat thee thyself. The periphrasis is often used emphatically as the subject of the sentence: *nā urā māte tēnā kasfēne, jind-ta hināne,* thy wife (lit. house) has killed her sons, and she herself is fled; *sardārnā jind hamoṛē tūs,* the chief himself sat there. Less commonly *jinde* precedes the noun or pronoun and is treated like an adjective: *jinde sardārāi nē-a dēva,* I'll take you to the chief himself; *jinde kane kholum aff,* I've no wheat myself; *ī jinde īlumān dā hīle binguṭ,* I heard this from the brother himself. The final vowel of *jind-e* appears to be a reminiscence of the Persian *iẓāfat* like the final vowel of *kull-e, muchch-e,* and other pronominal adjectives (§156).

The Demonstratives.

§**125.** There are three demonstratives, the near demonstrative *dā,* this, the remote *ē,* that, and *o,* which lies in meaning midway between the two, and is therefore generally employed when a demonstrative is required to take the place of a definite article or of the pronoun of the third person. In addition to these there are *handā*, *hamē*, *hamo*, compounded with the Persian *ham*. Though intensive in form, these, like their Baluchi counterparts, are not always intensive in force.

§126. Used as adjectives the demonstratives precede the noun and are naturally indeclinable: *dā zāīfae hamē bandaghto mon ēte*, send this woman with that man. To be noted are the forms *dārako*, *ērako*, *orako*, in which stress seems to be laid on the element of position: *ērako khaṛ kanā ass*, yon ram used to belong to me.

§127. Used as substantives they are fully declinable:—

Singular.

Nom.	*dā*, *dād*, this.	*ē*, *ēd*, that.	*o*, *od*, this, that.
Gen.	*dānā.*	*ēnā.*	*onā.*
Dat. } **Acc.** }	*dāde.*	*ēde.*	*ode.*
Abl.	*dāṛān.*	*ēṛān.*	*oṛān.*
Inst.	*dāṛaṭ* (*dādaṭ*).	*ēṛaṭ* (*ēdaṭ*).	*oṛaṭ* (*odaṭ*).
Conj.	*dāṛto* (*dāto*).	*ēṛto* (*ēṭo*).	*oṛto* (*oto*).
Loc.	*dāṭī.*	*ēṭī.*	*oṭī.*
	dāṛāi.	*ēṛāi.*	*oṛāi.*

Plural.

Nom.	*dāfk.*	*ēfk.*	*ofk.*
Gen.	*dāftā.*	*ēftā.*	*oftā.*
Dat. } **Acc.** }	*dāfte.*	*ēfte.*	*ofte.*
Abl.	*dāfteān.*	*ēfteān.*	*ofteān.*
Inst.	*dāfteaṭ.*	*ēfteaṭ.*	*ofteaṭ.*
Conj.	*dāfteto.*	*ēfteto.*	*ofteto.*
Loc.	*dāftēṭī.*	*ēftēṭī.*	*oftēṭī.*
	dāfteāi.	*ēfteāi.*	*ofteāi.*

The supplementary cases are: *dāki* or *dāṛki*, for the sake of this one; *dāṛis* (*dādis*), *dāṛisk* (*dādisk*), in the possession of this one, etc.; *dāṛiskā* (*dādiskā*), up to this one, with analogous forms in the case of the other two demonstratives. The forms *dāṛēskā*, *ēṛēskā*, *oṛēskā*, which must not be confused with *dāṛiskā*, *ēṛiskā*, *oṛiskā*, are adverbial demonstratives of place, meaning up to here or there, just as *dāṛē(k)*, *ēṛē(k)*, *oṛē(k)*, mean here or there (§388).

§128. The majority of the cases are clearly to be referred to the nominatives *dād*, *ēd*, *od*, with the change from *d* to *ṛ*. These forms of the demonstratives are purely substantival. The insertion of *f* in the plural is anomalous. Though this form of the plural is universal, the *f* is not infrequently omitted in some Sarawan dialects: *dāk*, *ēk*, *ok*; *dātā*, *ētā*, *otā*; *dāte*, *ēte*, *ote*, etc. Certain Sarawans, notably the Kurds, go a step further and retain the *-k* of the nominative in the dative-accusative, instead of making the usual change to *-t-*: *dāke-tā jitā karak*, place these of them aside (*cf.* §38).

§129. The declension of the intensive forms is on precisely the same lines, *ham-* or *han-*, as the case may be, being simply prefixed. The Haruni Muhammad Hasnis and some other Jhalawans corrupt *handā*, *handād* into *hannā*, *hannād*, which they decline in the ordinary way: *hamo duzz ki nī pārēs hannād e*, this is that thief of whom you spoke; *kaneān khulīpa*, *hannāṛān khula*, don't fear me but this man. Finally the aspirate is occasionally omitted in *handā*, etc., but not, curiously enough, in *hamē*, *hamo*.

§130. The nominative forms *dād*, *ēd*, *od*, are invariably used before the third persons present of the affirmative substantive verb: *kanā matlab dād e*, my meaning is this; *kanā īlum hamēd e*, that is my brother. These forms are obligatory in such cases, but their use is not confined to them: *hamo bandaghāteān ki nan isto Khanān*, *chaṛa handād salīsune*, this is the only one who has survived of those men we saw last night. In the dative-accusative singular the case-ending is occasionally omitted: *kane antei pāsa? od pā ki daun kapp*, why do you tell me? tell him not to do so; *ī ēd sakht khalkuṭ*, I beat that man severely. The nominatives singular are often used as nominatives plural, the number being sufficiently indicated by the verb (§47): *dā khāchār*, these slept; *ḍunganā khulīsān o narrār*, out of fear of the gang they ran away. The other cases require no particular comment: *ī oraṭ tēnā kārēme karifpara*, I won't get my work done by him; *kane dāraṭ khalifpa*, don't get me beaten by this man; *harchi ki pāsa, tēnaṭ pā, ēraṭ pārifpa*, whatever you have to say, say it yourself and don't get that man to say it for you; *nā girāk dāṭī affas*, your things aren't in this; *ērto himpa, kanto ba*, don't go with that man, but come with me; *ofteān gila kappa*, don't grumble at them; *tūfak dāris aff*, the gun is not with this man; *dāki panch mēlh tissuṭ*, I gave five sheep for this; *orki kharāsas hēsunuṭ*, I've brought a bullock for him.

§131. The intensive forms, adjectival and substantival, are especially common as the antecedents of a relative sentence (§425): *hamo bandaghas ki dūṭī-ta zaghm ass, Shā Bāz khān ass*, that man who had the sword in his hand was Shah Baz Khan; *handā ki dārē tūlingaṭī e, onā mār e*, this one who's sitting here is his son.

The Interrogative Pronoun.

§132. The interrogatives are *dēr?* who? *ant?* what? *arā?* which. Of these *dēr* refers properly to persons only, *ant* to inanimate objects, while *arā* may be used of either.

§133. *Dēr?* who? which is only used substantivally, is declinable throughout the singular and is applicable to both numbers:—

Nom.	*dēr, dē*, who?
Gen.	*dinnā.*
Dat. / **Acc.**	*dēre.*

Abl.	*dērān.*
Inst.	*dēraṭ.*
Conj.	*dērto* (*dēto*).
Loc.	*dēṭī.*
	dērāi.

The supplementary cases are: *dēki* (*dērki*), for whose sake? *dēris, dērisk*, in whose possession? etc.; *dēriskā*, up to whom? The declension, it would seem, is based partly on *dēr*, partly on the short form *dē*. The genitive is noteworthy.

§**134.** Examples: *dā bandagh dēr e?* who is this man? *dē bassune?* who has come? *dē bassuno?* who have come? *ē masink dēr o?* who are those girls? *nī dinnā mār us?* whose son are you? *nī dēre khanās?* whom did you see? *dērān halkus-ta?* whom did you buy it from? *dā kharās dēraṭ toring-a marēk?* by whom can this bull be stopped? *dērto tūlik?* whom does he live with? *dā iraṭṭe khanās, ant-a chāsa ki luchchī dēṭī e?* you saw these two, what's your opinion—in whom does the villainy lie? *dērāi hinānus?* whom have you gone to? *dēki dīr-a dēsa?* for whom will you take water? *kanā zaghm dēris e?* who has got my sword? *isto dērisk massunus?* whom have you been staying with last night? *pahranā vār dēriskā rasēngāne?* up to whom has the turn for sentry-go got?

§**135.** *Dēr*, though properly confined to persons, is by a natural extension used idiomatically in such phrases as: *nā pin dēr e?* what is your name? *dā shahranā pin dēr e?* what's the name of this village? *khom-ta dēr e?* what's his tribe?

§**136.** The plural is occasionally employed when reference is made to a number of separate individuals: *ant-a chāsa ki dā shahraṭī dērāk bassuno, dākha duzzī karēno?* what's your opinion as to who the men are who have come to this village and committed all these thefts? *dā khalkanā dērāteāi khonanā gumāne dēsa?* which individuals of this village do you suspect of the murder?

§137. The indefinite article is sometimes attached to *dēr* in questions of surprise or contempt: *o dēras marē ki kanc drogh-taṛ pāe?* who the devil is he to call me a liar? *vakhtas ki o khar-a kēk, dēras onā monāi kāe?* when he is wroth, who in truth may stand before him? *dā dunyāṭī dēras bēgham e?* in this world who after all is free from care?

§138. *Ant?* **what?** is used both substantivally and adjectivally. As an adjective it is of course indeclinable; the qualified noun takes on the indefinite article, unless it is used with plural meaning, but even in that case it remains in the singular: *ī nā ant gunā-as karēnuṭ?* what fault have I committed against you? *ant giṛā-asēto khalkunus-ta ki o kor massune?* what thing have you struck him with, that he has gone blind? *ant ant kulau tiss?* what various messages did he give?

§139. As a substantive *ant* is regularly declined; the singular is applicable to both numbers, being rarely displaced by the plural:—

Nom.	*ant?* what?
Gen.	*antanā.*
Dat. } **Acc.** }	*ante.*
Abl.	*antān.*
Inst.	*antaṭ.*
Conj.	*antato.*
Loc.	*antaṭī.*
	antāī.

Antaki? for the sake of what? is the only supplementary case in ordinary use. It means much the same as the interrogative adverb *antei?* why? which seems to be a corrupted or possibly older form of the dative-accusative.

§**140.** Examples: *nā hukm ant e?* what is your command? *ante torēnus?* what are you holding? *ī pārēṭ ki-nēto antanā āvāle ētiv?—tēnā tūfaknā,* I meant to speak to you about what d'you call it?—about my gun; *nā shara antanā e?* what's your case about? *dā antān joṛ massune?* what's this made of? *nī ode antaṭ khalkus ki daun huson e?* what did you strike him with that he's so hurt? *pālhte antaṭī shāghās?* what did you pour the milk into? *tēnā iraghe antāi bisik, pāṭāi yā liḍḍāi?* what does he cook his food on, fuel or dung? *nī antaki bassunus?* what have you come for? *o nē kanā pinaṭ ant o ant pārē?* what particular things did he tell you in my name? A plural is not often employed: *antāte nā bērān karēnuṭ ki nī khar karēs?* what things of yours have I damaged that you got angry?

§**141.** The indefinite article is frequently attached at will without affecting the meaning: *pālhte antasēṭī shāghās?* what did you pour the milk in? *nī antasēki bassunus?* what have you come for? But with a change in the intonation of the voice it is idiomatically used in interrogations of surprise or contempt, as in the analogous case of *dēr?* (§137): *nā hukm antas marē? ī nā khwājanā hukme mannipara,* what's your order to me, when I don't heed the order of your master? *nī antas marēs? ī nēkonā dahe khalēva,* what on earth are you good for? I'll beat half a score like you; *o gharīb antas marē? nī zorākasēto tēne arēf,* what of that poor devil? hit a man your own size (lit. entangle thyself with a strong one).

§**142.** *Arā?* which? is applicable to both animate and inanimate objects. It is primarily an adjective, and as such is of course indeclinable. It means properly 'which of two or more?' *nā arā salā e?* which is your advice (of the proposals under consideration)? as opposed to *nā salā ant e?*

what is your advice (generally)? *dā arā bandagh e?* which man is this? *dā bandagh dēr e?* who is this man? *arā hullī nē dost e?* which horse do you fancy? It is occasionally aspirated: *harā?*

§143. The particular case of the adjective *arā* qualifying the noun *asiṭ* deserves separate notice. The force of the compound *arā-asiṭ?* (*arāsiṭ?*) which one? is much the same as that of the substantival *arā*: *dā musiṭṭān arā-asiṭ kaṭṭā?* of these three which one won? *handā zāīfa arāsiṭnā marēk?* to which one will this woman belong? *harāsiṭṭāi nā gumān e?* on which one does your suspicion rest?

§144. As a substantive *arā* is declinable in both numbers after the general model of the demonstratives:—

	Singular.	Plural.
Nom.	*arā? arād?* which one?	*arāfk?* which ones?
Gen.	*arānā.*	*arāftā.*
Dat. **Acc.**	*arāde.*	*arāfte.*
Abl.	*arāṛān.*	*arāfteān.*
Inst.	*arāṛaṭ* (*arādaṭ, arā-aṭ*).	*arāfteaṭ.*
Conj.	*arāṛto* (*arāto*).	*arāfteto.*
Loc.	*arāṭī.*	*arāftēṭī.*
	arāṛāi.	*arāfteāi.*

The supplementary cases are: *arāki?* or *arāṛki?* for the sake of which one? *arāṛis? arāṛisk?* in the possession of which one? etc.; *arāṛiskā?* (*arādiskā?*) up to which one? *Arāṛē(k)? arāṛēskā?* are interrogative adverbs (§388) meaning where? up to which place? As in the case of the demonstratives (§128) there is a dialectical form of the plural with the omission of *-f-*: *arāk, arātā,* etc.

§145. Examples: *dā ḍaggī arānā e?* to which one does this cow belong? *arāde halkus?* which one did you take? *arāṛaṭ khalkus-ta?* with which did you strike him? *hamo bandagh ki nī pārēs arād e?* the man you spoke of—which is he? (or: where is he? *arād* also meaning where?); *arāṛto bassune?* with which one has he come? *huchchāte arāṛān hēsus?* which one did you bring the camels from? *dā razānteān dīte arāṭī shāghās?* which of these pots did you pour the water into? *tūfak arāṛis e?* which one's got the gun? *dā mēlhtēṭī arā arā nā o?* among these sheep which ones exactly are yours? *arāfk rasēngāno?* which ones have arrived? *arāfteān us?* from what family are you? *dā kārēme arāftēki karēnus?* for the sake of which of them have you done this thing?

The Possessive Pronoun.

§146. The possessive pronouns are simply the genitives of the various pronouns. They are, however, remarkable in that, like the possessive genitive of the noun (§54), they are treated as independent substantives[1], declinable throughout both numbers. There is no need to give the declension; it is the same as that of the possessive noun; there is an optional form of the plural in *-fk*, save in the case of possessives based on genitives plural of the form *-ftā: dāftāk, ēftāk, oftāk, arāftāk;* the phonetic desirability of avoiding the two *f*'s is obvious.

§147. Examples: *dā kuchak kanā e,* this dog is mine; *nā hullī rēsh e, kanānā rēsh joṛ massune,* your horse is wounded, the wound of mine is healed; *tā ki kanā huchche illētanus, ī nāe illēpara,* until you let my camel go, I won't let yours go; *ī tēnā vanḍe harfēnuṭ, num tēnāfte harfbo, ēftāte illēbo,* I've taken my share, do you take yours and let theirs alone; *ē chākhū kunṭ e, kanāraṭ taṛ-ta,* that knife's blunt, cut it with mine; *kanā dilar nāṛto lahr-a kumpak,* your blood isn't so good as mine (lit. my blood doesn't boil with yours); *nā bil kanā māris aff, nāṛis e,* your

[1] Abstract substantives may be formed from some of the possessive pronouns by suffixing *-ī: tēnāīān ēṛē himpa, o kanā dushman e,* for our friendship's sake, don't go there, he's my enemy.

bow isn't with my son, it's with yours; *tēnā razāne hata, tēnā tēlāte kanāṭi shāghpa*, fetch your own pot and don't pour your oil into mine; *nanā kharāsteto nanā tēnā bazghak hināno, numāteto kasas aff*, our own cultivators have gone with our bullocks, there's no one with yours; *aga dā kārēme kanā māraki kappēs, tēnāki ka-ta*, if you won't do this for my son, do it for yours; *nanā ḍaghāteāi nī khiāl-a kappēsa, tēnāfteāi girā-as ki nēān-a marēk, koshish-a kēsa*, you decline to take any trouble over our lands and yet you labour for all you're worth on your own; *num nanā siālāteān khwash ure, tēnātēān antei khar ure?* you're pleased enough with our relatives, why are you annoyed with your own? *nanā konṭāte ki nī daltanus, pēn dinnāte darēnus?* well, if you haven't taken our blankets, whose have you taken?

§**148.** The idiom is occasionally extended to a double genitive: *nā hullīnā laghām kanānāṛān mutkun e*, your horse's bridle is older than that of mine; *nanā khachatlā liṭṭikāk arēr, numāftāk karghok o*, the tails of our mules aren't clipped yet, those of yours are; *nanā urātā karazātēṭī kaṛī arē, numāftātēṭī chaṛa mēkh o*, in the beams of our houses there are rings, while in those of yours there are only nails; *nanā ḍaggītā ākhuk purr o, oftātāk khālī o*, the mangers of our cows are full, those of theirs are empty. But this highly cumbrous mode of expression is generally avoided.

The Indefinite Pronoun.

§**149.** Under this heading it is convenient to discuss several words which partake more or less of the nature of pronouns. Though it is unnecessary to preserve any particular order, certain of the pronouns which are connected by similarity of meaning or use will be grouped together. The list might have been slightly enlarged, but it seems unnecessary to be exhaustive.

§150. ***Dākhadar, dākhar, dākha, dākhas,*** **this much.**
Okhadar, okhar, okha, okhas, **so much.**
Ēkhadar, ēkhar, ēkha, ēkhas, **that much.**
Akhadar? akhar? akha? akhas? **how much?**

The initial *dā, o, ē* are the ordinary demonstrative adjectives, and the pronouns are accordingly found in the intensive forms *handākhadar, hamokhadar, hamēkhadar,* with corresponding variants; the initial *a-* is clearly the particle of interrogation contained in *ant?* what? *arā?* which? *aṭ?* how many? (§152), and one or two other interrogatives. As the latter portion of the pronouns is unmistakably corrupted from the Arabic-Persian word *qadr*, 'quantity,' they are properly demonstratives and interrogatives of quantity, but they are not infrequently used of number also, the demonstratives more especially. They are both adjectives and substantives.

(1) Adjectival use: as adjectives they are of course indeclinable; the qualified noun is in the singular even though reference is made to plural number (§46): ***dākhadar*** (***dākhar, dākha, dākhas***) ***ghalla harf o hata,*** pick up this much grain and bring it; ***okha okhadar kīmat karēno,*** they've fixed such and such prices; ***ēkhas maiva kungunus ki kasas kump,*** you've eaten more fruit than one should; ***akha mēmān bassuno?*** how many guests have come? But if the pronouns are placed in the predicate and the subject of the sentence is used with plural meaning, the subject like the verb is put in the plural: ***mēmānk dākhadar bassuno,*** in such numbers have the guests come.

Attributive use: as adjectives of size they take on the ordinary attributive endings (§80): ***dākhaso bākhoas kung,*** he ate a mouthful this size; ***ēkharo māras e,*** he's a lad that size; ***akhadaro kharās o?*** what size bullocks are there? ***dākhasā dākhasā hullīte ki nī hēsunus, dēr-a halēk-tā?*** who'll take the horses of the size you've brought? They are as usual used as substantives in the definite form: *ēṛē pāṭk tikhok o, hamofteān dākhangā dākhangāte bin o hata,* the sticks are placed there, pick out of them the ones this size and this, and bring them along; *ofteān dākhasāte jitā ka,* those of them this size place on one side.

(2) Substantival use: they are confined to the singular, the declension of which is regular: *nī pā ki ī tēnā mēlhtēki dākhadar-a halēva,* say you'll take so much for your sheep; *hilār akhasnā halkus?* what price did you give for dates? *akhae yala karēs?* how many did you let go? *huchche kholumto hampēnuṭ—akhato hampēnus-ta?—dākhadarto,* I've loaded the camel with wheat—with how much?—with this much. Some of the cases have acquired a specialised meaning: *handākhasato ki nī bassus, nan rāhī-a marēna,* as soon as you come, we'll start; *nan daro kasarāi salīsasun, hīt-a karēna, annā hīte khalās kattavēsun, handākhasaṭī pir malingā,* yesterday we were standing in the road chatting, we hadn't done chatting when the rain began.

The corrupted forms *dīkhadar, dīkhar, dīkha, dīkhas,* are commonly used in Jhalawan with the meaning 'a little': *ī pārēṭ kane dīr ēte, o dīkhadar hēs ki kanā guṭ pālitau,* I told him to give me water, and the amount he brought wasn't enough to moisten my throat; *dīkha sī dā razānaṭī shāgh,* put a little ghi into this pot; *kane dīkhas pālh ēte,* give me a drop of milk.

§151. The interrogatives of the foregoing group together with the demonstratives in the intensive form are used as correlatives: *akha ki harfing-a kēsa, hamokha hata,* bring as much as you can carry; *beṭteān akha ki danning-a kēsa, hamēkha da,* take away as much of the grass as you can.

§152. ***Aṭ?*** **how many?**

There are no demonstratives corresponding to this interrogative of number, their place being supplied by the demonstratives of quantity, *dākhadar,* etc., *supra.*

(1) Adjectival use: the qualified noun is in the singular (§46): *aṭ mār o?* how many lads are there? *aṭ bandaghnā huchchāte darē?* how many men's camels did he carry off? *aṭ tūiskā pir-a kappak?* for how many months will there be no rain? Of course if *aṭ* is used in the predicate, the subject is put in the plural: *māk aṭṭ o?* the lads are how many in number?

An ordinal adjective, *aṭṭimīko?* 'the how manyth?' is formed by adding the ordinal suffix *-imīko* (§100): *dā aṭṭimīko bandagh e ki ī nā padaṭ mon-a ētiva, nī bafēsa?* how many men does this make that I send after you, and yet you won't come? *nī aṭṭimīko dē-a barēsa?* on what day from now will you come? *dā aṭṭimīko go e ki dudēfingaṭī o?* what number race is this they're running off? The pronominal ordinal may be used substantivally like other ordinals (§102): *dā huchchanā katārān ī hashtimīkoe dēva, nī aṭṭimīkoe daros?* of this string of camels I'll take the eighth in order, which number do you think of taking?

(2) Substantival use: *aṭ* is ordinarily confined to the singular, which is declined regularly: *numeān aṭṭanā mēlhte sarkārki darēno?* the sheep of how many of you have they impressed for Government? *duzzāteān aṭṭe tafēno, aṭṭe yala karēno?* of the thieves how many have they bound, and how many have they let go? *dā khavāteān aṭṭaṭī dīr shāghās o aṭṭe bārun illās?* in how many of these water-skins did you pour water and how many did you leave dry? *dā drakhtāteān aṭṭāi chukkāk kutām tafēno?* on how many of these trees have the birds built nests? *ē shalvāre aṭṭāi halkus?* what did you buy those trowsers at? *numeān aṭṭis tūfak arē?* how many of you have got guns? *irā bandaghaṭ ki dā hullī toning-a mafak, aṭṭaṭ toningik?* if this horse can't be held by two men, how many will it take to hold him? *nī tēne aṭṭiskā kaneān ḍakkos?* how often do you intend to hide yourself from me? Some use is made of a jingling form

(*cf.* §48): *aṭṭ-o-maṭṭiskā duzzanā lumma mēḻẖ-a ṭarik?* how many more times will the thief's mother slaughter sheep? (*i.e.*, feasting will turn to hanging before long).

The plural is occasionally employed; it is more vague in character than the singular: *numeān aṭṭāk Sīstānāi hināno?* what numbers of you have gone to Seistan? It is chiefly used in interrogations or exclamations of surprise: *dā jangaṭī aṭṭāk kasfingāno hināno!* what numbers have been killed in this fight!

§153. *Mana, manaṭ,* some, a few.

Of the two forms *mana* is adjectival, *manaṭ* substantival. Herein the pronoun bears a strong resemblance not only to *machchi, machchiṭ*, a little (*infra*), but also to the first three numerals (§96). The indefinite article attached to the noun or pronoun, as the case may be, has a tendency to emphasise the fewness of the number.

(1) Adjectival: the qualified noun remains in the singular (§46): *mana masiṛ hināno,* some girls have gone; *mana dēān guḍ nājoṛ mass*, some days later he fell ill; *mana dēaseān guḍḍ-a barēna,* we'll come after a few days; *mana pāṭas hata,* bring a few fagots.

(2) Substantival: *manaṭ kẖāchār*, some lay down; *manaṭe kẖanāṭ ki hināra*, I saw some going off; *manaṭas kaskur*, a few died. The plural is occasionally employed: *sipāhīteān manaṭāk hināsur, manaṭāk-tā annā hamoṛē assura,* of the sepoys some had gone, while some of them were still there.

Substantival suffix: *i.e.*, *manaṭ* is tacked on to the noun so as to form a kind of compound noun, the case-endings being attached to *manaṭ* alone: *bandagẖ-manaṭe daro kẖalat tissuṭ*, I gave some men robes of honour yesterday; *dē-manaṭān guḍ pēsh tammā*, he sallied forth some days later; *mēmān-manaṭas dāskā rasēngāno*, only a few guests have arrived as yet; *chuk-manaṭaseān kẖalkuṭ*, I had a shot at a few birds.

§154. ***Machchi, machchiṭ***, a little; some.

(1) Adjectival: *ēnakho machchi ghalla kharrisune*, a little corn has sprouted this year; *kane machchi pālh ēte*, give me a little milk. This pronoun sometimes refers to number: *nan machchi bandaghase un, nanā iraghki khulīpa*, we're only a handful of men, don't be anxious about our food. In the predicate *machchi* is ousted by *machchiṭ* if immediately followed by the copula: *ēnakho Shālkoṭaṭī bandagh machchiṭ e*, the people in Quetta this year are few; but *tēnā kirēng tininge machchi ka*, cut your abusing short.

Attributive use: *kane nēto machchiṭo kārēmas arē*, I've a petty business with you; *machchiṭā giṛāghāi nanā takk-a tammipak*, we don't trouble about a trifle (lit. our care does not fall on the trifling thing). It will be noticed that the attributive endings are attached to the substantival form of the word, as in the case of the first three numerals (§98).

(2) Substantival: *pir malingāne? dāskā machchiṭ malingāne, vakhtas ki bāz malingā, kasar-a mafak*, has rain fallen? only a little as yet, as soon as a lot falls the road'll be impassable; *mēmānteān machchiṭnā dūte sillānun, machchiṭ handun tūlok o*, we've washed the hands of some of the guests, a few are still seated as you see; *bāz huch dū tammitav-ne, navā machchiṭas dū tamme-ne*, if you can't lay hands on a number of camels, perhaps you may secure a few. The plural is not very common: *Khudā machchiṭāte bāz-a kēk, o bāzāte machchiṭ-a kēk*, God makes the few many, and the many He makes few.

Substantival suffix: *ī tēnā hullīe bei-machchiṭ tissuṭ*, I gave my horse a little grass; *bei-machchiṭān hullīnā guzrān-a mafak, hadīm ēte*, the horse can't live on a handful of grass, give him grain; *kane pālh-machchiṭas ēte*, give me a drop of milk.

§155. *Giṛā (iṛā), giṛā-as (iṛā-as),* some; something.

Giṛā (*iṛā*) is in reality an ordinary substantive, meaning 'thing': *irā giṛā halkuṭ*, I purchased two things. As a pronoun it is generally used with the indefinite article, and is both adjective and substantive.

(1) Adjectival: the qualified noun is in the singular; it almost invariably refers to an inanimate or irrational object, or else to a rational object like *bandagh* which is commonly used collectively: *kane giṛā-as mēlh bakār e*, I want some sheep; *sardār giṛā-as bandaghto daro dāṛē bass*, the chief came here yesterday with some men; *huch giṛā-as kholumto hampok ass*, the camel was loaded with some wheat. Though the indefinite article is generally attached, it may be omitted: *huchchāi giṛā kholum hampok ass*, there was some wheat loaded on the camel.

(2) Substantival: *lashkarān giṛā-as bassune*, a party of the army has come; *kane giṛā-as ēte*, give me something; *giṛā-as ki kane karoī ass, giṛe karēṭ, hēmon karēṭ*, whatever I had to do, I did it all and got it off my shoulders. If the pronoun is repeated in a linked sentence, the indefinite article is attached as a rule to the last pronoun only: *sardāteān giṛā hināno, giṛā-as hamēṛēk o*, of the chiefs some have gone, and some are still there; *giṛā-tā nane-is massur, giṛā-as-tā nanā illa-is massur*, some of them lodged with us, some with our uncle; *giṛā ī harfēṭ, giṛā tēnā īlume tissuṭ, giṛā-as hamoṛē salīs*, some I took, some I gave to my brother and some was left there.

In apposition: the case-ending is attached to noun and pronoun alike: *duzzāte giṛā-ase bashkhā*, he pardoned some of the thieves; *kharāstā giṛānā likhāi jugh ass, giṛānāṛāi allau*, there was a yoke on the necks of some of the bullocks and none on the necks of others.

§**156.** ***Kul, much, drust, gir,*** **all; the whole.**

Alike in meaning these indefinite pronouns are alike in use. They are at the same time adjectives and substantives. In the predicate they remain unchanged. Used as adjectives proper they appear in the form *kulle, muchche, druste, gire,* in which the final increment seems to be due to a confused idea of the Persian *iẓāfat* (*cf.* §124). The number of the qualified noun depends on whether the meaning of the pronominal adjective is 'the whole' or 'all.' The simple forms are indeed found preceding the noun, but their force is then adverbial, 'exclusively,' 'only,' 'nothing but.' The substantives are either used as ordinary independent substantives, for the most part in the singular, or they are placed in apposition to another substantive: the pronoun remains in the singular, while the substantive is pluralised if necessary; the case-endings are attached to both.

§**157.** ***Kul,*** **all; the whole.**

(1) Adjectival: *kulle mēmānk bassuno,* all the guests have come; *kulle iraghe kungunus?* have you eaten the whole loaf? *ī kulle siālāteān harrifēṭ,* I asked all the relatives; *o tēnā kulle lashkarto koṭāi julau darē,* he made an attack on the fort with his whole force. With the first example may be contrasted the following, which illustrates the adverbial use of the simple *kul*: *kul mēmānk bassuno,* only the guests have come.

Attributive use: *aino kullo dēas gidārēngāne, nī kanā pāraghāi batanus,* to-day a whole day has passed and you haven't been near me; *dushmannā khulīsān nan kullangā nante khanteāi gidārēfēna,* from fear of the enemy we used to spend the livelong nights on the watch (lit. on the eyes).

(2) Substantival: *kul hināno,* all have gone; *kullanā khaire baṭang,* pray for the welfare of all; *kulle kanā banningnā sahī ka,* inform all of my coming; *dā dē kullāi*

baroī e, this day (of trouble) has to come to all. The plural is only occasionally used: *kullāk-a chāra ki nī duzzī karēnus*, all the world knows that you've committed theft.

In apposition: *huchchāk kul kaskuno*, the camels, all of them, have died; *drakhtātā kullanā ṭolāte guḍḍāṭ*, I lopped the top branches of all the trees; *jirga tūlokāte kulle sahī karēs?* did you inform all the members of the jirga? *tēnā lashkarto kullato narrā*, he took to his heels with his whole army.

§158. ***Much***, all; the whole.

(1) Adjectival: *muchche mik hinguno*, all the ewes have lambed; *ēnakhonā muchche fasle malakh kung*, locusts devoured all this year's crop; *muchche mashteāi barf biṭēne*, snow has fallen on all the hills. Compare: *much mashteāi barf biṭēne*, snow has only fallen on the hills. Its use in the predicate may be seen in the so-called compound verbs: *lashkar much mass*, the army collected together; *ī tēnā sangatāte much karēṭ*, I collected my companions together.

Attributive use: *muchcho dēas gidārēngā, nī tēnā kārēme kattavēs*, a whole day passed and you didn't do your work; *hamo khasme ki ī khalkuṭ, ē muchchangā drakhtātēṭī hinā tammā*, the deer I shot ran into that clump of trees and fell (lit. into those collected trees). Passing mention may be made of the abstract noun *muchchī* formed from the adjective *much*: *bile ki khalkuṭ, sum-ta chukkātā muchchīṭī tammā*. when I drew the bow, the arrow from it fell into the thick of the birds; *ī nē muchchīṭī drust karēṭ*, I recognised you among the crowd.

(2) Substantival: *much nājoṛ o*, they are all unwell; *muchchanā kūṭume taṛē*, he cut off the heads of them all; *muchchān zaghmāte-tā pula*, snatch their swords from every one of them. The plural is somewhat rare: *muchchāk khudāṭī umēd-a dēra*, one and all rest their hope in God.

The use of the locative, *muchchāi*, is idiomatic; its force may be represented in English either by an adjective or an adverbial expression, according to the incidence of the emphasis in the sentence: *nanā drakhtāk muchchāi baram karēno, numāfteān manaṭātēṭī hichch-a khampara*, everyone of our trees has borne fruit, and yet I see nothing on some of yours; *kanā jauzanā drakht muchchāi baram e, khulīva ki pinnip*, my walnut tree is laden with fruit from top to bottom and I'm afraid it may break; *ainonā kasaraṭ muchchāi kanā hullī tuḍḍa kunisa bassune*, my horse has come stumbling along every yard of to-day's road; *dā ḍaghār muchchāi bei e, kholum bēkhī machchiṭ e tahṭī-ta*, this land's nothing but weeds, the wheat on it is scanty in the extreme.

In apposition: *shāhidāk much kaneāi drogh taṛēr*, the witnesses lied against me to a man; *duzzātā muchchanā dūte taf*, bind the hands of every one of the thieves; *dā shahraṭī muchchaṭī dārū aff*, there's no medicine in the whole of this village; *ē kirrītēṭī muchchaṭī shakargaz arē?* is there gum in all those tamarisks?

§159. ***Drust***, all; the whole.

(1) Adjectival: *druste lashkar rasēngāne*, the whole army has arrived; *nī druste dē barēsa khwāst kanningki, ī nē hichch-a tifara*, you come every hour of the day begging, but I won't give you anything; *ī druste kārēme karēnuṭ*, I've done the whole work; *druste muskok-a pārēra ki drogh pāpabo*, all the men of old used to say 'don't lie.'

Attributive use: *drusto iraghas hata*, fetch a whole loaf; *kune dā pinnokā shīshae tifa, drustangāe ēte*, don't give me this glass that's broken, give me the one that isn't.

(2) Substantival: *ī drustato nēkī karēnuṭ*, I've dealt righteously with all; *nī druste khalās karēs?* did you finish the whole? *shahraṭī drustāk-a pārēra ki zamīnjumb Hindustānaṭī ballo nuskhān karēne*, they were all saying in

the village that the earthquake had done a lot of damage in India.

In apposition: *hamē mēlhk drust kaskuno,* all those sheep have died; *dā bāgh nanā drustanā e,* this garden belongs to us all; *tēnā siālāteto drustato nā pāraghāi baroṭ,* I'll probably come to you with all my relations.

Drust combines with *dē,* day, and *nan,* night, to form compound words: *dē-drustaṭī irā vār tēnā ḍaghāre dīr toṛēnuṭ,* twice in the whole day I've given my land water; *nan-drust gorīch kashshāne,* the Nor'west has been blowing the livelong night.

§160. *Giṛ (iṛ, gih),* **all; the whole** (especially used in Jhalawan).

(1) Adjectival: *giṛe Brāhūītā pīshkavāk murghun o,* the locks of all Brahuis are long; *ī giṛe dē kārēm-a kēva,* I work the whole day; *giṛe mashteāi shikār arē,* there's sport on all the hills. The somewhat rare variant *gih* does not take on an incremental *-e: gih makhlūk nā āvālān sahī e,* all the world knows about you.

Attributive use: *dā kappīā iraghe mēmāne tifa, giṛvas ete-ta,* don't give that broken loaf to the guest, give him a whole one; *nī ant-a chāsa, ki dā giṛangā kūcha nā maroe?* what d'you think, that you've perhaps bought up the whole of this valley?

(2) Substantival: *giṛ kasarān rad tammār,* they all lost their way; *giṛ khalās mass,* the whole was finished; *tā ki nēān-a marēk, giṛato nēkī ka,* as far as in you lies, deal kindly with all; *giṛe guḍḍa,* fell them all down; *giṛk-a chāra ki nī kanā maṭṭ affēs,* one and all know you're not my equal.

In apposition: *ofk giṛ khāchāno,* they're all asleep; *ḍaggīte giṛe līṛānus?* have you milked all the cows? *kārēme giṛe khalās karēṭ*, I finished the whole work; *sipāhīte-is giṛis zaghm arē*, all the sepoys have swords.

§161. *Tīva, tīvaī*, all; the whole.

This pronoun is very similar to the four immediately preceding, but is used somewhat more laxly.

(1) Adjectival: *kanā tīva fasle dīr loṛā*, the flood carried off all my crop; *nan tīvaī nikāne kuṭṭifēnun*, we've used up all our rations; *tīva pāṭṭe pū kungune*, the boring insect has eaten up all the wood; *tīvaī mulkaṭī malakh tammā*, the locust fell upon the whole countryside. The *quasi*-adverbial use may be noted: *o giṛā-as ki pāik tīvaī drogh e*, all he says is merely lies; *dā ḍaghār tīva bei e*, this field is all weeds.

Attributive use: *tīvo nanas halma karēṭ, maga maizile rasēngtavaṭ*, I posted a whole night but didn't reach the stage; *tīvaghā dē murūtā randaṭ chirrēngāṭ, shikār dū batau*, though I was the whole day after the hares, I got no sport; *ī tēnā tīvaīā ḍaghāre zurrat dasēnuṭ*, I've sown my whole field with *juwári*. The definite attributive adjective may have a *quasi*-adverbial force like the simple adjective: *nī tīvaghā droghaṭ kaneān sharāe kaṭṭiparos*, you won't win the case against me by simply lying.

(2) Substantival: *mēlhte arāng karēs? tīvae bahā karēṭ*, where did you put your sheep? I sold them all; *dā hēṭk tīvaīe kungur*, these goats ate it all.

In apposition: *ispēdāte tīvae guḍḍingaṭī o*, they are cutting down all the poplars; *dā shahraṭī tīva-aṭī duzzāk tammāno*, the thieves have fallen upon the whole village.

§162. *Bāz*, many.

(1) Adjectival: *ēnakho hullītā sailāi bāz bandagh bassuno*, this year many people have come for the horse-show. Though this is the normal construction—the qualified

noun in the singular (§46), the governed verb in the plural, —the noun is occasionally found in the plural: *bāz bandaghāk hajjāi hināno,* many a man has gone on the pilgrimage. If the plural is employed, stress seems to be laid on the large number of separate individuals.

Attributive use: *daro bāzo dostas nanā bāghaṭī muchch ass,* there was many a friend assembled in our garden yesterday; *aino haṛ-dēān bāzo shikāras karēnuṭ,* I've had more sport to-day than usual; *dā bāzangā lashkar ki dāṛē much manningaṭī e, arāngī mon-a kēk?* in which direction will this large army now collecting here set its face? The definite adjective is used in general phrases and the like when an indefinite adjective might seem more appropriate (*cf.* §82): *bāzangā lashkar arāngī ki mon karē, hamē mulke kāṭumaṭ harfik,* a vast army will devastate whatever country it sets out toward (lit. will lift up by the head); *bāzangā dīr faslaki jwān aff,* too much water is bad for the crop.

The abstract substantive *bāzī* may find a place here: *machchiṭā dushmanto jang kanning aṛzān e, maga bāzīnā mone khudā tore,* to fight with a handful of enemies is a small matter, but God may withstand the onset of a multitude.

(2) Substantival: *kane bāz pāpa, ī nā kārēme tēna jwān-a kēva,* don't waste words on me, I'll do your work all right of my own accord; *bāzanā bashkh bāz e,* the share of many is large; *bandagh bāzato jwān e, khudā asiṭṭiaṭ zēbā e,* company is good for man, God in his oneness is beautiful. The plural is occasionally employed: *bāzāk hullīteto dākā gidārēngār, bāzāk kharāsteto,* several passed by here with horses, several with bullocks; *dā ḍaghār bāzāte kungune o bāzātēki khan torēne,* this earth has devoured many a man and has its eye set on many another.

In apposition: *ī mēmānteto bāzato nā jahāi baroṭ*, I'll probably come to your place with the guests, a whole crowd of them; *ī rupaīteāi bāzāi ode sāng-a titavaṭa*, I wouldn't have betrothed her to him for hundreds of rupees.

§163. ***Mānīd***, **a quantity of, a number of.**

Mānīd is never used independently; it invariably follows the noun it qualifies as a kind of plural suffix. The noun remains in the nominative singular; the case-ending is attached to *mānīd*, which is treated like an ordinary singular. The compound of noun and *mānīd* is always qualified by an adjective or pronoun; when the compound is indefinite, as it commonly is, the indefinite article is attached to *mānīd*.

Examples: *Sēbīnā jalsa-aṭī ēnakho ballo sardār-mānīdas muchch e*, there's a large assemblage of chiefs at the Sibi gathering this year; *dākhadaro mēlh-mānīdas ki Marīnā mashaṭī e, pēntīn aff*, there's nowhere such a number of sheep as on the Marri hills; *Mungacharaṭī ēnakho dauno malakh-mānīdas tammā, mulke chaṭ karē*, this year such a swarm of locusts fell upon Mungachar that they devastated the country; *ballo drakht-mānīdaseān maiva hēsunuṭ*, I've brought fruit off a large number of trees; *dauno hal-mānīdas ki dā ḍaghāraṭī khanāṭ, pēn jāga khantanuṭ*, I've not seen elsewhere such a swarm of mice as I saw in this field; *hamē ballā harraf-mānīde ki nan khanān, dāsā hamē mashaṭī aff*, that great herd of markhor we sighted, is on that hill no longer.

§164. ***Būch***, **any at all.**

Būch by itself means literally 'a straw,' 'rubbish': *kanā urāṭī būchas illētano, kulle darēno*, they've not left a straw (*anglice*, a stick) in my house, but have carried off everything; *o daroān dāngī būchas bāṭī kattane*, since yesterday not a morsel has passed his lips.

It is suffixed to the noun, which remains in the crude form. It is declined regularly in the singular; the indefinite article may be attached at pleasure, but the numeral adjective *asi* is never prefixed to the compound: *ē dēaseān ki naukar massunus, giṛā-būchas much karēnus?* from the day you entered service have you saved anything at all? *kasaraṭ ki bassusa bandagh-būch khanās?* as you were coming along the road did you see a single soul? *kasaraṭ dushman-būchato mukābil matavaṭ*, on the road I met with no enemy whatsoever; *nē mār-būchas hum arē? kane tāiskā mār-būch matane*, have you actually any sons at all? to this day not one has been born me.

§165. ***Filāna (filānī),*** **such and such, so and so.**

(1) Adjectival: *filāna sardār ki darbāraṭī numā rahāi tūs, pin-ta dēr ass?* what was the name of such and such a chief who sat near you in the Durbar? *kane pārēno ki filāna tāsīldār vaḍī halkune*, I've been told that the Tahsildar you wot of has taken bribes.

(2) Substantival: *nē kanā pinaṭ dē pārē ki nē filāna kirēng tissune?* who told you about me that so and so had abused you? *ī chāva ki kanā illanā malh Bāz Khānāstā pinaṭ nē sahī karēne ki filānaghāk gandao bandagh o, oftā urāṭī himpa*, I know that my cousin, hinting definitely at Baz Khan and his folk, has given you to understand that so and so are bad lots, and that you shouldn't visit at their houses; *dā filānaghāsk ki numā rahāi tūsura, arāng hināno?* where have what d'you call him and his people gone, who used to live near you? In the last example the personal plural *filānaghāsk* (§30) will be noticed. The variant *filānī*, plural *filānīk*, is not uncommon: *ī pāpara ki numēṭī filānī duzz e, maga num tēnaṭ pāsh kabo-ta*, I won't say that such a one among you is the thief, do you rather produce him yourselves. Another variant, used by hill Brahuis, is *pilāna*.

Here may be mentioned the compound *filān-bāmān*, in which the latter word is meaningless by itself. It is euphemistically used in cursing in combination with the third person plural, present indefinite or past, of *kanning*, to do: *nā filān-bāmāne karēr ki pēndwār kanā jahāi vā barēs*, by all that's unmentionable you'd better beware of coming to my place a second time; *filān-bāmāne kēr, pānē kāe*, for heaven's sake let him go to the dickens.

§166. *Pēn*, other, another.

(1) Adjectival: *kane pēn urā aff*, I've no other house; *ī oṛān khar uṭ ki kanā āvāle pēn bandaghāteto tissune*, I'm annoyed with him for having told my news to other people; *kane pēn hichasto kārēm aff, baghaire nā jindān*, I've no concern with any one else but you yourself. This adjective finds a place in one or two adverbial compounds: *e.g.*, *pēntīn*, elsewhere (§387), in which the last element has now lost its individual existence.

(2) Substantival: *bei giṛā-as ki ēsunus bass e, pēn bakār aff*, what grass you've brought is sufficient, no more's wanted; *pēnanā malh tēnā-a mafak*, another man's son doesn't become one's own (one of many hits at relations by marriage); *tēnānā nan pēnanā dē barēbar aff*, a night at home is better than a day with strangers; *pēne pēnaki ant-a marēk?* what cares one for (the misfortune) of another? *pēnāi itbār kappa*, don't put your trust in another. The plural is both *pēnk* and *pēnāk*: *nā hullīe ī dattanuṭ, pēnk darēňo-ta*, I haven't taken your horse, others have; *harkas ki tēnāfte illā, pēnāteto tammā, kharāb-a marēk*, every one who leaves his kin and consorts with strangers will come to ruin.

In apposition: *dauno shikāras ki kūcha-aṭī e, mashāt pēnāī aff*, there isn't such sport on the hill as there is in the valley: *drakhtāteān pēnān maiva-būch duzzipēs*, don't steal any fruit from any other trees. The use of *pēn* in the former example recalls a familiar Greek idiom.

§167. ***Ēlo*, the other.**

(1) Adjectival: *ēlo hullī kane bakār e*, I want the other horse; *ēlo mēmānk kul hināno, nī antei salīsunus?* all the other guests have departed, so why have you remained? The initial vowel of the adjectival *ēlo* is frequently dropped in one or two adverbial compounds: *e.g.*, *losāl* (*ēlosāl*), next year, *lojār* (*ēlojār*), again.

(2) Substantival: the declension is on the model of the declension of the definite adjective in *-īko* (§90) and there is thus an optional form of the plural with an inserted *-f-*: *ēlonā mālāi zor-a challipak*, one man has no authority over the property of the other; *dāde halpa, ēloe halh*, don't seize this one, seize the other; *ghallaghāk ē urāṭī affas, ēloṭī o*, the grain isn't in that house but in the other; *nā girāk dā huchchāi affas, ēloṛāiṭ o*, your things aren't on this camel but on the other; *dā drakhtāk baram kattano, ēlok kul karēno*, these trees haven't borne fruit yet, all the others have; *tēnāfteān ēlofk jwān affas*, strangers are not better than one's own blood; *kanā āvāle ēlote tifēs*, please don't confide my news to the others; *kane pāsa, ēlofte pāpēsa ki narribo*, you tell me yet don't tell the others to run away.

In apposition: *kaizīnā ēlonā hīte kappa, tēnāe pā*, don't talk of the other prisoner, let's hear of yours; *oṛān baghair sipāhīteān ēlofteān khula*, beware of all the sepoys but him.

§168. ***Asiṭ*, one, some one, a certain one.**

The substantival form of the first numeral (§96) is used as a substantival indefinite pronoun: *asiṭ kane pārē ki pagga pir-a kēk*, some one told me it would rain to-morrow; *ī kasarāi asiṭṭo mukābil massuṭ, laṭṭas dūṭī-ta ass*, I met a man on the road with a stick in his hand. The indefinite article may be attached: *nanā hullīe asiṭṭas isto malāne darēne,* somebody has untied our horse last night and carried it off.

§169. ***Asiṭ ēlo (asi ēlo),*** **one another, each other.**

This combination constitutes the reciprocal pronouns: *bīshk asiṭ ēloe khārēfira,* the donkeys scratch one another; *dā hullīk asi ēloṛto jang-a kēra,* these horses fight with one another; *o harvakht asiṭ ēlonā urāghāi kāra barēra,* they are always exchanging visits at each other's houses.

§170. ***Tomā, tomakā, tomaghā,*** **both.**

(1) Adjectival: the qualified noun is in the plural: *nā tomā hullīte kasaraṭ khanāṭ ki dudēngāra,* I saw both your horses on the road galloping; *ī tēnā tomakā urāte bērifēnuṭ,* I've thatched both my houses; *tomaghā māk-ta narrāno,* both his sons have run away.

(2) Substantival: the pronouns are always pluralised: *irā chuk khanāṭ, tomāte asi tūfakaṭ khalkuṭ,* I saw two birds and brought down both with one shot; *sarkār tomakāte kaiz karē,* Government imprisoned both.

In apposition: *kanā āvāle tēnā īlumteto tomaghāteto pās,* you may tell my news to both of your brothers.

§171. ***Kas, kasas,*** **some one; (with negative) no one.**

This pronoun is substantival only. A difference in force between the two forms *kas* and *kasas* is hardly perceptible; the latter is perhaps the more common of the two. The declension of *kas* is regular. The declension of *kasas,* which presumably contains the indefinite article, is two-fold: it may be declined either like *kas,* or like the indefinite article (§71). Both *kas* and *kasas* are used in the singular only.

(1) Affirmative use: *kane kas pārē ki num ēnakho Kachchīāi kāre,* some one told me you're going to Kachhi this year; *dāṛē kasas arē?* is there any one here? *kasasto ki sarān jwānī karēnus, hamoṛto ākhiriskā jwānī ka,* a

man you've treated well from the beginning, treat him well to the end.

(2) Negative use: *kas pātau ki o dāṛē bassune*, no one said he had come here; *kanto pēn kasas aff*, there's no one else with me; *harkas tēnā kassato jwān e, khudā bēkass kasase kapp*, everybody is happy with his relatives, may God make no one bereft of relatives (*kass*, relative); *kane kasasto kārēm aff*, I've no concern with any one; *kasasēto chikār topa*, don't meddle with anybody.

§**172.** ***Har***, **every, each.**

Adjectival only: *har māre giṛā-as tiss*, he gave each lad something; *har hullīnā likhaṭī pullas tafē*, on the neck of each horse he tied a flower. When *har* qualifies the antecedent of a relative clause, the indefinite article is attached to the noun as usual (§427): *har bandaghas ki drogh-a pāik, mon-ta maun e*, every liar's face is black; *Bolānaṭ ki kāsa, har sardāras ki khanās, chās ki Sarāvānnā e*, every chief you see as you go along the Bolan, you may put down as belonging to Sarawan; *har hītas ki ī nē-a pāva, khaf to-ta*, give heed to every word I tell you.

This pronoun helps to form several adverbial compounds; before a dental -*r* may turn to -*ṛ* (§16): *harvakht*, always, *hardē, haṛdē*, everyday, *hartū, haṛtū*, every month. It combines freely with other indefinite pronouns, as in the examples that follow.

§**173.** ***Harkas***, **every one, everybody.**

Substantival only: *harkas tēnā jāgaghāi hinā*, every one went to his own place. As the antecedent of a relative clause, it regularly takes on the indefinite article: *harkasas ki duzzī karē, ī kaiz-a kēva-ta*, I'll imprison every man who commits theft; *harkasas ki must bass, panch rupaī inām-a halēk*, every one who comes in first will get five rupees reward.

§174. ***Harasiṭ,*** **every one, everybody.**

Substantival only: *dā mosumaṭī harasiṭ langār-a kēk,* everybody ploughs at this season; *harasiṭnā-tā dūṭī khatanā laṭṭas ass,* there was an olive stick in the hand of each one of them.

This pronoun is not to be confused with *harāsiṭ?* the aspirated form of *arāsiṭ?* which one? (§143): *harasiṭ kaṭṭā,* each one won; *harāsiṭ kaṭṭā?* which one won?

§175. ***Hartomā, hartomakā, hartomaghā,*** **both.**

(1) Adjectival: *hartomā māk hināno,* both the lads have gone; *hartomakā masink hoghār,* the two girls wept; *hartomaghā chukkāte yala karē,* he let both the birds go.

(2) Substantival: *hartomāk babo,* come both of you; *hartomakāte khanāṭ,* I saw both; *hartomaghāteto rāhī mass,* he set out with both of them.

As is usual before a dental the -r- may be displaced by ṛ-: *haṛtomā, haṛtomakā, haṛtomaghā.*

§176. ***Hargiṛā (hariṛā),*** **everything.**

Substantival only: *nā hargiṛā jwān e,* everything of yours is excellent; *hargiṛā khwāhiva, nī kane tining-a kēsa?* I want everything, can you give it me? *hargiṛā-as nē bakār e, kane pā,* tell me everything you want.

§177. ***Harchi,*** **any, whatever; everything.**

Harchi is most commonly used as the antecedent of a relative sentence. As an adjective it refers generally, and as a substantive exclusively, to irrational objects. The substantive is declined regularly throughout the singular. Variants like *harchiato, harchito* in the conjunctive indicate indecision as to whether it should be treated as a word of two syllables or one, *i.e.*, as *harchi* or as *har-chi* (*cf.* §36*a*).

(1) Adjectival: *harchi kārēmasēnā nī pās, ī kēva-ta,* mention any work, I'll do it; *harchi mēlhas ki nī kane ētis, ī*

halēva, I'll take any sheep you give me; *harchi bandagh ki dāṛē assur, kul hināno*, whatever people were here, they've all left.

(2) Substantival: *harchi ki pāsa, pā*, whatever you have to say, say; *kanā mār harchiaṭī ustād e*, my son is splendid at anything; *harchiān ki shakk-a kappēsa, tēnaṭ handun marēsa*, if you don't scrutinise everything, of course you'll get like this; *nī harchito* (*harchiato*) *kārēm-a torisa*, you meddle with everything.

§178. ***Hich*** **(with negative), no (adjective); nothing.**

Hich is properly confined to negative sentences, though when it is used as an attributive adjective or adverbially the negative is occasionally omitted. It is both an adjective and a substantive. As an adjective it is applicable to animate and inanimate objects alike, as a substantive to the latter only, except in the special form *hichas*.

(1) Adjectival: the qualified noun remains in the singular; the addition of the indefinite article to the noun accentuates the singular number: *dāṛē must hich shikār matane*, there's been no sport here before; *dā shahraṭī kane hich dushman aff*, I've no enemy in this village; *hich hullīas daun dudēngparoe, ki kanā hullī dudēngik*, no horse in the world will run as mine does; *kane hich dauno dostas aff ki num ure*, I've not a single friend like you. As will be seen in the following paragraphs the adjectival *hich* combines freely with other indefinite pronouns.

Attributive use: *o hichcho bandaghas e* (*aff*), he's a good for nothing fellow; *o hichchangā ḍaghārān nē khudā ēte*, God give you some other than this worthless land.

(2) Substantival: *kanto hichch aff*, I've nothing with me; *kanēān hichchanā harriftau*, he didn't ask me about anything; *khudāghān baghair ī hichchān khulīpara*, save God I fear nothing. The adverbial force of the ablative coupled

with *-bā* (*-bār*), like (§380), is worth noting: *dā chiṭṭe hichchām-bā kishkāṭ*, I broke this rope in a trice (lit. like nothing); *ī nē hichchām-bār-a khalēva*, I'll thrash you like anything. The indefinite article is occasionally attached: *dāṛē hichchas aff*, there's nothing here.

Hichas, no one, nobody, which is not to be confused with *hichchas*, nothing, illustrated in the last example, is of course a substantive only: *dāṛē hichas batane*, no one has come here; *hichas pātau ki o nājoṛ massune*, nobody said he had fallen ill; *kane hichasnā parvā aff, o hichase kanā parvā aff*, I care for nobody and nobody cares for me. It may be declined like the indefinite article: *ī hichasēnā urāṭī pēhitavaṭ*, I entered no one's house.

§179. *Hichkas, hichkasas* (with negative), no one, nobody.

These are used in exactly the same way as *kas, kasas* in negative sentences (§171): *nanā huchchīāk bassuno, numāteān hichkas batane*, our camel-drivers have come in, but not a single one of yours; *ofteān hichkasas khantavaṭ*, I didn't see one of them. They are slightly more emphatic than the simple forms *kas, kasas*.

§180. *Hichiṛā, hichgiṛā* (with negative), no; nothing.

(1) Adjectival: *ī ēnakho hichiṛā kholum bahā kattanuṭ*, I've sold no wheat this year. The indefinite article may be attached for emphasis: *ī nēān hichiṛā-as māl dattanuṭ*, I've taken no property from you at all.

(2) Substantival: *nī hichiṛā tippēsa*, you understand nothing; *o pēn hichiṛā-as pātane*, he has said not a word else. It may be used in a general way of rational objects as in English: *ēṛē ki hināṭ sardāteān hichiṛā khantavaṭ, kul hināno*, when I got there, I saw nothing of the chiefs, they've all gone.

§181. ***Dirse,*** **any one; (with negative) no one.**

This pronoun is regarded as old-fashioned, and is indeed almost obsolete, its place being taken by *kas, kasas,* which it resembles in meaning and use.

(1) Affirmative use: *dā duzz ki dākā narrā, dirse khanā-ta?* did any one see the thief that ran by here? *dirsenā bāva ki sakhī massune, mār-ta zarūr sakhī-a marēk,* any one who is the son of a generous father is sure to be generous himself.

(2) Negative use: *dirse pāp ki ī onā dushman uṭ,* no one may say I'm his enemy; *dirseāi ki kanā gumān ass, dāṛē aff,* the one on whom my suspicion rested is not here. The indefinite article is occasionally attached: *dauno kārēmas kēv ītonā, ki dirseas pāp ki nī hamē bandagh us,* I'd do such a thing to you that no one'd recognise you as the same man.

§182. ***Dauno, daunangā,*** **such as this;** ***ohuno, ohunā,*** **such;** ***ēhuno, ēhunā,*** **such as that;** ***amaro? amarā?*** **what kind?**

These attributive adjectives formed from demonstrative and interrogative adverbs (§388) seem to deserve a place among the indefinite pronouns. There are several variants: *duno, daunā, ohunangā* and so on. The choice between the definite and indefinite forms depends of course on the definiteness or the reverse of the compound expression of which they form a part, but there is often little practical difference of meaning between the two. It will be remembered that the definite form is always used with a pluralised noun (§82). In the case of the demonstratives the intensive forms *handuno,* etc., are not common.

Examples: *kanto dauno kārēmas karē, ki hūkam prīshto kapp,* he treated me in a way a pig wouldn't treat a millet crop : *dauno hīt kane pāpa*, don't tell me such stuff ; *ohuno hullīas ki nā e, kanā bazghatteto bāz arē*, my labourers have plenty of horses like that crock of yours ; *dā amaro urā-as e ki nī tafēnus-ta ?* what sort of hut is this that you've built ? *nī kane daunā sakhtīnā vakhtāi ki kārēm batavēs, pēn chivakht kane kārēm-a barēsa ?* if you don't come to my aid in such an hour of stress as this, when will you ever help me ? *tēnā dēe ēhunangā kārēmtēṭī gidārēfpa*, don't waste your day over that sort of work ; *ohunangā siālān ki nā e, maf, jwān e*, it's better to have no relations at all than the kind yours are ; *nā guzrān amarangā bandaghāteton e ?* with what sort of men do you consort ? The definite adjective may of course be used substantivally : *amarangāte kirēng-a ētisa ?* what sort of men are you abusing ?

THE VERB.

§183. The root of the simple verb is normally monosyllabic, the few exceptions being supplied for the most part by loan-words. The conjugation is agglutinative in structure and surprisingly uniform, for transitives and intransitives, passives, neuters and causals are conjugated on practically identical lines. There is, moreover, an organic negative conjugation which is one and the same for every class of verb. But apart from the inevitable irregular verbs there is considerable variety within this uniformity, notably in the personal terminations or the terminations used as such, which are not consistently the same throughout, and in the formation of the past stem of the affirmative verb. The various tenses, moreover, show interesting signs of belonging to different stages of development.

The Formation of the Affirmative Verb.

§184. The order selected in the following analysis of the formation of the various parts of the affirmative verb has been dictated by several considerations, arising from a review of the verb as a whole in all its developments. It is hardly logical, but it has its compensating advantages. The infinitive owes its prominent position more to the *usus loquendi* of conventional grammar than to its intrinsic importance; yet it serves at the same time to introduce the two tenses of the substantive verb which figure largely in the formation of the conjugation, while a full treatment of the substantive verb itself is more conveniently deferred. Again, the imperative singular presents on the whole the simple base more adequately than the presents or any other part of the verb, and alone supplies the key to one of the main irregularities in the negative conjugation. The various participles are conveniently, if illogically, wedged in between the past conditional and the past stem, for none of them are based on the latter, while two are closely related to the former.

The Infinitive.

§185. The infinitive is a verbal noun ending in *-ing*, and is declined regularly throughout the singular. In the large majority of cases it is formed by adding the termination directly to the base: *bin-ing*, to hear ; *bin-ing*, to pick out ; *kun-ing*, to eat ; *tikh-ing*, to place ; *narr-ing*, to flee. The final consonant of the base is very occasionally doubled in the infinitive: *hall-ing*, base *hal-*, to seize ; *khall-ing*, base *khal-*, to strike ; *bārr-ing*, base *bār-*, to become dry. In *khuling*, *khulīng*, to fear, *saling*, *salīng*, to stand, the infinitive termination seems to waver between *-ing* and *-īng*, but the bases of these verbs are really two-fold : *khul-*, *khulī-*, *sal-*, *salī-*, as appears elsewhere in the conjugation. In a special class of verbs, called neuter verbs (§276), the infinitive seems sometimes to end in *-ēng : rasēng*, to arrive, *aṛēng*, to be entangled; but such forms are simply abbreviated for *rasēnging*, *aṛēnging*.

§186. There is an important group of verbs whose infinitive docked of the termination *-ing* ends in *-n*, single or double, and in whose conjugation—the passive, *cf.* §273, only excepted—the consonant *n* does not figure again. This group includes some of the commonest and most irregular verbs in the language, *e.g.*, *manning*, to become (§256), *banning*, to come (§257), *kanning*, to do (§258), *danning*, to take away (§259), *pāning*, to say, *toning*, to hold. The true nature of the base in such verbs is best indicated by their imperative singular (§191). The imperative singular is two-fold ; the one form is the same as the base as it appears in the infinitive with the omission of the abnormal nasal, while the second form differs from the first only in that it contains a final *-r : e.g.*, *danning*, imperativo singular *da*, *dar ; manning*, imperative singular *ma*, *mar*. Curiously enough, we are debarred by the rest of the conjugation from regarding either form as the true base to the exclusion of the other. Thus in the case of *danning* the presents are founded on the base *da-*, yet the whole of the negative conjugation is to be referred to the base *dar-*; in *manning* we have the exact converse; the presents are founded on the base *mar-*, while the whole of the negative conjugation is to be referred to the base *ma-*. The explanation of the curious infinitives seems to be that they are formed from the base in *-r*, the change to *-n* being induced by the attraction of the nasal in the infinitive termination. This group of verbs may be styled for brevity's sake, but admittedly loosely, 'the verbs in *-n*'. Other verbs which belong in a greater or lesser degree to the group are *anning*, to be (§248), *tining*, to give (§260), *chāning* (more commonly *chā-ing*), to understand (§261), *hunning* (but also *huring*), to look (§262), *hatining* (*hating*, etc.), to bring (§263). But unless otherwise specified the subsequent remarks on the verbs in *-n* will apply to those enumerated in the earlier part of this paragraph only.

The Present and Past Tenses of the Substantive Verb.

§187. The locative of the infinitive noun coupled with the finite tenses of the substantive verb forms a convenient periphrasis which serves to supply the place of what may be termed the tenses of actuality. The present and past of the substantive verb are as follows:—

Present.

Singular.	Plural.
1. *ī uṭ*, I am.	1. *nan un*, we are.
2. *nī us*.	2. *num ure*.
3. *od e*.	3. *ofk o*, (*ur*).

Past.

Singular.	Plural.
1. *ī assuṭ*, I was.	1. *nan assun*, we were.
2. *nī assus*.	2. *num assure*.
3. *o ass*, (*assas*).	3. *ofk assur*, (*asso*)

It will be noticed that the past is based on the present. The alternative forms in the third persons are important as they reappear in the conjugation of the ordinary verb. An instance of this is to hand in the past of the substantive verb itself: the form *assur* is explained by reference to the secondary form *ur* in the present, which is regularly employed by certain tribes, the Zahris for instance, instead of the ordinary *o*. The form *assas* is properly a pluperfect. These tenses will receive further comment when the substantive verb is dealt with as a whole (§248 *seq.*).

The Tenses of Actuality.

§188. The so-called tenses of actuality are therefore of the form *ī ti<u>kh</u>ingaṭī uṭ*, I am in (the act of) placing, *ī ti<u>kh</u>ingaṭī assuṭ*, I was actually placing. It will be sufficient to include the present only in the paradigm, to which these phrases hardly belong at all. For the tenses in which the substantive verb is defective, recourse is had to the auxiliary *manning*, to become (§256): *ī ti<u>kh</u>ingaṭī maroṭ*, I will probably be placing; *ī ti<u>kh</u>ingaṭī massunuṭ*, I have been placing.

The Imperative Singular.

§189. The various methods of forming the second person singular of the imperative from the base may be reduced to three:—

§190. (1) The commonest form of the imperative singular is identical with the simple base:—

Infinitive.		Imperative singular.
bining,	to hear;	*bin*.
bising,	to bake;	*bis*.
kuning,	to eat;	*kun*.
ti<u>kh</u>ing,	to place;	*ti<u>kh</u>*.
rasēnging,	to arrive;	*rasēng*.

Especially remarkable are the imperatives singular of the verbs *tūling*, to sit, *halling*, to seize, *khalling*, to strike, which are formed by changing the lingual of the base to the aspirated cerebral *lh* : *tūlh*, *halh*, *khalh*. The case of *shāghing*, to pour, which besides the regular imperative *shāgh*, forms another, *shā*, by dropping the *ghain* of the base, is noteworthy; a somewhat less common example of the same kind is *ho*, *hogh* from *hoghing*, to weep.

§191. The imperatives singular of the so-called verbs in *-n* (§186) are formed after this method, but constitute a special subdivision by themselves. Each has two forms, corresponding to the two forms of the base :—

Infinitive.		Imperative singular.
manning,	to become ;	*ma*, *mar*.
banning,	to come ;	*ba*, *bar*.
kanning,	to do ;	*ka*, *kar*.
danning,	to take away ;	*da*, *dar*.
pāning,	to say ;	*pā*, *pār*.
toning,	to hold ;	*to*, *tor*.

§192. The verbs in all the subdivisions of this group form a strengthened imperative singular by suffixing *-ak* : *binak*, *bisak*, *kunak*, *tikhak*, *rasēngak*, *tūlhak*, *halhak*, *khalhak*, *marak*, *barak*, *karak*, *darak*, *pārak*, *torak* ; it will be noticed that in the case of the verbs in *-n* the suffix is added to the secondary imperative. Although the suffix tends to impart emphasis, the choice between the strengthened and unstrengthened forms depends as a rule not so much on emphasis as on euphony.

§193. (2) A large number of verbs, including more especially those whose bases end in a doubled consonant or in concurrent consonants, form their imperative singular by suffixing a final *-a* to the base :—

Infinitive.		Imperative singular.
bărring,	to become dry ;	*băra*.
ḍakking,	to hide ;	*ḍakka*.
narring,	to flee ;	*narra*.
taring,	to spin ;	*tara*.
ṭanging,	to hang ;	*ṭanga*.
illing,	to leave ;	*illa*.

§**194.** (3) The imperative singular of a few verbs is formed by suffixing *-e* to the base :—

Infinitive.		Imperative singular.
khuling,	to fear ;	*khule*.
saling,	to stand ;	*sale*.
silling,	to wash ;	*sille*.
păling,	to become wet ;	*păle*.
(*tining*),	to give ;	*ēte*.
illing,	to leave ;	*ille*.

The infinitive *tining* and the imperative singular *ēte* seem to be derived from different roots; the verb is indeed one of the most irregular in the language (§260). The imperatives *khulī*, *salī*, do not belong to this group; they are derived directly from the bases of *khulī-ng*, *salī-ng* according to the first method, just as the somewhat less common forms *khul*, *sal* are derived directly from *khul-ing*, *sal-ing*. And much the same appears to be the case with *illē*, yet a third form besides *illa*, *ille* of the imperative singular of *illing*, to leave. Though the long vowel does not appear in the infinitive, it is preserved, as in the case of *khulī-*, *salī-*, in the presents, the adverbial participle and throughout the negative conjugation. In other words, the long final vowel in all three appears to be an integral part of a secondary base. On the other hand, though *sillē, pālē* sometimes displace the regular forms *sille, pāle,* the long vowel does not maintain its place elsewhere in the conjugation, not even in the imperative plural, and its occasional appearance in the imperative singular is clearly abnormal.

§195. These three methods of forming the imperative singular are not necessarily mutually exclusive. In a large number of verbs the imperative singular conforms indifferently to either of the first two types: *ḍaling,* to gnaw, imperative singular *ḍal* or *ḍala ; hamping,* to load, *hamp* or *hampa ; khoshking,* to rub, *khoshk* or *khoshka.* Moreover nearly all the verbs which form their imperative singular after the third method have an optional form in *-a : ille, illa ; pāle, pāla.* Indeed, all three methods are combined in the case of *khuling, saling, silling : khul* (*khulī* from *khulīng*), *khula, khule ; sal* (*salī* from *salīng*), *sala, sale ; sil, silla, sille* (*sillē*).

The Imperative Plural.

§196. The second person plural of the imperative is formed by attaching the termination *-bo* to the imperative singular, which may become subject to slight phonetic modification.

§197. If the imperative singular is identical with the base, the termination on being attached gives rise as a rule to no modification : *bis, bisbo ; tikh, tikhbo.* If the base ends in *-n,* there is a natural change of *n* to *m* before the labial of the termination : *bin, bimbo ; kun, kumbo.* In the case of passives and neuters of the type *rasēnging,* the termination may be either added directly : *tikhing,* be thou placed, *tikhingbo ; rasēng, rasēngbo ;* or the *g* of the base may be dropped and the *n* changed in consequence to *m : tikhimbo, rasēmbo.* The three verbs which adopt a cerebral *lh* in the imperative singular, revert to the radical lingual in the imperative plural : *tūlh*, *tūlbo* ; *halh*, *halbo* ; *khalh*, *khalbo*. Corresponding to the alternative forms of the imperatives singular *shāgh*, *shā*, *hogh*, *ho*, there are alternative forms in the plural, *shāghbo*, *shābo*, *hoghbo*, *hobo*.

§198. In the case of the verbs in *-n* the termination is in all cases attached to the short form of the imperative singular : *ma*, *mabo* ; *ba*, *babo* ; *ka*, *kabo* ; *da*, *dabo* ; *pā*, *pābo* ; *to*, *tobo*. The imperatives *hur*, *hubbo* from *hunning*, to look, which appears indeed also as *huring* (§262), are not really analogous. There is no other form of the imperative singular besides *hur* ; the imperative plural *hubbo* is formed from *hur* with the phonetic change of *r-b* to *bb*.

§199. If a final *-a* or *-e* is added to the base in the imperative singular, the vowel changes to *-i-* before the plural termination : *bāra*, *bāribo* ; *ḍakka*, *ḍakkibo* ; *narra*, *narribo* ; *khule*, *khulibo* ; *sale*, *salibo* ; *ēte*, *ētibo*. An *a*-sound is, however, occasionally retained : *bārabo*, *narrabo*, *ḍakkabo*. Though the included vowel does not appear again in the affirmative conjugation, it obtains throughout the negative.

§200. If the base, and consequently the imperative singular, end in *-ē* or *-ī*, the long vowel is of course maintained in the imperative plural : *illē*, *illēbo* ; *khulī*, *khulībo* ; *salī*, *salībo*. It is indeed maintained throughout the conjugation. On the other hand, there are no forms in the imperative plural corresponding to the anomalous imperatives singular *sillē*, *pālē*, and the long final vowel is clearly not radical (*cf.* §194 *fin.*)

§201. It follows that if there are alternative forms of the imperative singular, there may be alternative forms in the plural also : *ḍal*, *ḍala* : *ḍalbo*, *ḍalibo* ; *hamp*, *hampa* : *hampbo*, *hampibo* ; *khoshk*, *khoshka* : *khoshkbo*, *khoshkibo* ; *khul*, *khula*, *khule*, *khulī* : *khulbo*, *khulibo*, *khulībo* ; *sal*, *sala*, *sale*, *sali* : *salbo*, *salibo*, *salībo*.

The Present Indefinite.

§202. The present indefinite is formed from the base by adding the following terminations :—

Singular.	Plural.
1. *-iv.*	1. *-in.*
2. *-is.*	2. *-ire.*
3. *-e.*	3. *-ir.*

Thus : *biniv*, I may hear ; *bisis*, thou mayst bake ; *tikhe*, he may place ; *bārin*, we may become dry ; *ētire*, you may give ; *sillir*, they may wash. A long final *-ē* or *-ī* of the base naturally ousts the short vowel of the termination : *illēv*, I may leave ; *khulīs*, you may fear ; *salī*, he may stand. It follows that there may be alternative forms of the present indefinite corresponding to alternative forms of the base : *illiv, illēv ; khuliv, khulīv ; saliv, salīv.* In *chāv*, the ordinary present indefinite from *chā-ing* (rarely *chāning*), to understand, the vowel of the termination is dropped ; it is, however, sometimes retained, *chā-iv* (*chāiv*).

§203. In a few cases the accent is diverted from the base to the terminations, the vowel of which becomes long in consequence :—

Singular.	Plural.
1. *-ēv.*	1. *-ēn.*
2. *-ēs.*	2. *-ēre.*
3. *-ē.*	3. *-ēr.*

Thus : *kunēv*, I may eat ; *kahēs*, thou mayst die ; *hatē* (*hatarē*), he may bring ; *khalēn*, we may strike ; *halēre*, you may seize.

§204. The verbs in *-n* here fall into two groups. In the one, composed of *danning*, to take away, *kanning*, to do, *pāning*, to say, the present indefinite is formed from the short base : *dēv, kēv, pāv* (contracted from *da-ēv, ka-ēv,* *pā-iv*, the base in the first two being unaccented). The third persons singular are *dē* (for *da-ē*), *kē* (for *ka-ē*) and *pā-e*. Analogous are *tēv*, from *tining*, to give, a dialectical variant used by the more wild Brahuis for the ordinary form *ētiv*, and also *chāv* from *chāning* (but more usually *chā-ing*), which appeared in the last paragraph but one.

In the second group, composed of *banning*, to come, *manning*, to become, *toning*, to hold, the present indefinite is formed from the strengthened base in *-r* : *barēv*, *marēv*, *toriv*, the accent falling on the base in the last, and on the termination in the other two. Somewhat analogous are *huriv*, from *hunning*, to look, which also appears, however, as *huring*, and *hatarēv*, from *hatining* (but also *hataring*), to bring, which was cited in the foregoing paragraph.

§205. In the case of *hining*, to go (§264), the present indefinite is derived from a different root from that of the infinitive or the imperatives *hin*, *himbo* : *kāv*, *kās*, *kā-e*. With the obvious exception of the present-future the remaining parts of the verb are based on the same root as the imperative.

The Present-Future.

§206. The present-future is formed from the present indefinite by suffixing *-a*. This statement requires slight modification. The second person plural is left unaltered—the addition of *-a* would tend to make it clash with the third person plural; the termination of the third person singular is *-k* without the addition of *-a*, while except when the root is unaccented the included vowel has a distinct *i*-sound. The terminations are therefore as follows :—

Singular.	Plural.
1. *-iva.*	1. *-ina.*
2. *-isa.*	2. *-ire.*
3. *-ik.*	3. *-ira.*

Thus: *biniva*, I hear, I will hear; *bisisa*, thou bakest, thou wilt bake; *tikhik*, he places, he will place. The present-future follows exactly the same lines as the present indefinite: *illiva, illēva; khuliva, khulīva; dēva, dēsa, dēk; pāva, pāsa, pā-ik* (*pāik*); *kāva, kāsa, kā-ik* (*kāik*).

The Probable Future.

§**207.** The probable future is formed from the base by suffixing *-o-* and adding the present of the substantive verb (§187), the initial vowel of which is elided except in the third person singular; the third person plural is based on the full form *ur*, not on *o*. The terminations are therefore as follows:—

Singular.		Plural.	
1.	*-oṭ.*	1.	*-on.*
2.	*-os.*	2.	*-ore.*
3.	*-oe.*	3.	*-or.*

This tense is exceptionally regular: *binoṭ*, I will (probably) hear; *bisos*, thou wilt (probably) bake; *tikhoe*, he will (probably) place. The only material irregularity lies in the fact that a final radical *-ē* or *-ī* in the base is elided: *illoṭ, khuloṭ, saloṭ*. In the case of verbs in *-n* the tense is formed from the strengthened base in *-r*: *daroṭ, karoṭ, pāroṭ, baroṭ, maroṭ, toroṭ*; similarly *huroṭ, hataroṭ*, but *chā-ot*. *Tining*, to give, is an interesting member of this group of verbs in *-n*: the imperative *ēte*, the presents *ētiv, ētiva*, and the probable future *ētoṭ*, cannot seemingly be referred to the same root—or at any rate to the same form of the root—as the infinitive *tining*. The base of the infinitive reasserts itself, however, in the somewhat rare dialectical variants of the presents, *tēv, tēva*, and in the most common form of the probable future, *tiroṭ*, as well as in the past stem and throughout the negative conjugation. In Jhalawan, it may be noted, the regular form of the probable future is *choṭ*.

Significant light is thrown on *tining* by the compound verb *hatining*, etc., to bring (§263), in which it is unmistakably contained.

The Past Conditional.

§208. In form this tense, which also serves as a past optative, is the past of the probable future. It is formed from the base by suffixing *-o-* and adding the past of the substantive verb (§187), the initial vowel of which is elided. It should be noted that *assuṭ*, *assus*, etc., when used in the formation of tenses contain only one *s*. The terminations are therefore as follows :—

Singular.		Plural.	
1.	*-osuṭ.*	1.	*-osun.*
2.	*-osus.*	2.	*-osure.*
3.	*-osas.*	3.	*-osur* (*-oso*).

Thus : *binosuṭ*, had I heard, I would have heard, would that I had heard ; *illosuṭ*, had I left ; *khulosuṭ*, had I feared ; *karosuṭ*, had I done ; *ētosuṭ*, *tirosuṭ*, Jhalawan *chosuṭ*, had I given. The third person plural regularly ends in *-osur*, but the form *-oso* is also employed occasionally.

§209. The tense is sometimes compounded with the pluperfect instead of the past of the substantive verb (§252), though in this form it is too cumbrous for general use. The formation is chiefly remarkable as affording an example of the harmonic sequence of vowels (§13) ; thus instead of *binosasuṭ* we have as a rule *binosusuṭ*, by the attraction of the final vowel ; on the other hand the original vowel sound is of course maintained in the third person singular, *binosasas*, as it happens to be the same as that of the final syllable.

The Present Adverbial Participle.

§210. The present adverbial participle (like the present adjectival participle and the noun of obligation, *infra*) is also founded on the simple base. It is formed by suffixing *-isa* : *binisa*, hearing; *bisisa*, baking; *tikhisa*, placing. A final radical *-ē* or *-ī* is maintained, and there may thus be two forms of the participle : *illēsa*, *illisa*, leaving ; *khulīsa*, *khulisa*, fearing ; *salīsa*, *salisa*, standing. The participle in the case of the verbs in *-n* is formed from the strengthened base in *-r* : *karisa*, doing ; *pārisa*, saying ; *barisa*, coming ; similarly *tirisa*, giving ; but *chā-isa*, understanding.

§211. Instead of *-isa* we sometimes find *-isa-aṭ*, which can hardly be anything but an instrumental though the participle being purely adverbial is not otherwise declinable, and also *-isau*, which appears to contain the conjunction *o*, 'and' (§433), in spite of the fact that the use of a conjunction to couple the participle to the finite verb seems illogical. These secondary terminations are attached in exactly the same way as *-isa*, from which they do not differ in force : *binisa-aṭ*, *binisau* ; *illēsa-aṭ*, *illisa-aṭ*, *illēsau*, *illisau* ; *karisa-aṭ*, *karisau*.

The Present Adjectival Participle.

§212. The present adjectival participle, or relative participle as it might be termed, is formed by suffixing *-ok* to the base : *binok*, hearing, one who hears ; *bisok*, one who bakes. As in the similar case of the probable future and the past conditional a radical *-ē* or *-ī* is elided : *illok*, one who leaves ; *khulok*, one who fears ; *salok*, one who stands. In the case of the verbs in *-n* the participle is formed from the base in *-r* : *karok*, one who does ; *pārok*, one who says. From *tining* there are three forms : *tirok*, *ētok*, with *chok* in the Jhalawan dialect, one who gives.

This verbal adjective, which may also have a passive significance (§275), takes on the ordinary definite and indefinite endings (§83 *seq.*) when used attributively.

The Noun of Obligation.[1]

§213. The noun of obligation is formed by suffixing *-oī* to the base: *binoī*, obliged to hear, obligation to hear, intending to hear, intention of hearing: *bisoī*, obliged to bake; *illoī*, obliged to leave; *khuloī*, obliged to fear; *saloī*, obliged to stand. In the case of the verbs in *-n* it is formed from the base in *-r*: *karoī*, obliged to do; *păroī*, obliged to say. There are three forms from *tining*: *tiroī*, the commonest of the three, *ētoī*, with the Jhalawan *choī*, obliged to give.

This formation, which in the case of transitives has also a passive significance (§275), takes on the ordinary definite and indefinite endings (§83 *seq.*) when used as an attributive adjective.

The Past Stem.

§214. The past, the imperfect, the pluperfect and the perfect are based on what may be termed the past stem. The past stem, which happens to be the same in form as the third person singular of the past, must not be regarded as an active past participle, of which the language is devoid. It is formed from the base by the addition of *-ā*, *-ē*, or a consonant.

§215. (1) The past stem of by far the largest number of verbs, including all passives, is formed by suffixing *-ā* to the base. It is noteworthy that this is practically the invariable method of forming the past stem of new

---

[1] The designation 'noun of obligation' is not particularly happy, but it is hard to find one exactly to the point. The term 'gerund,' which naturally suggests itself, is apt to be misleading, and fails to cover sufficient range.

importations into the language, unless the base happens to end in *-f*. Examples :—

Infinitive.		Past stem.
bining,	to pick ;	*binā*.
illing,	to leave ;	*illā*.
makhing,	to laugh ;	*makhā*.
tikhing,	to place ;	*tikhā*.
shāghing,	to pour ;	*shāghā*.
rasēnging,	to arrive ;	*rasēngā*.
tikhinging,	to be placed ;	*tikhingā*.

§216. (2) The second group of verbs, those which form their past stem by suffixing *-ē* to the base, includes the causal and all other verbs whose base ends in *-f* :—

Infinitive.		Past stem.
tūlifing,	to make to sit ;	*tūlifē*.
ḍakkifing,	to cause to be hidden ;	*ḍakkifē*.
tafing,	to bind ;	*tafē*.
harfing,	to lift ;	*harfē*.
harrifing,	to ask ;	*harrifē*.

To this group belong certain of the verbs in *-n*, the past stem being formed by suffixing *-ē* to the base in *-r* : *danning*, to take away, *darē* ; *kanning*, to do, *karē* ; *pāṇing*, to say, *pārē* ; *toning*, to hold, *torē*. Though no longer a past, *arē* from *anning*, to be (§250), is probably an analogous formation. The remaining verbs in *-n* form their past stem after the third method.

The other verbs which form their past stem in *-ē* appear to be too miscellaneous to be reducible to rule, *e.g.*, *bising*, to bake, *bisē* ; *biṭing*, to throw, *biṭē* ; *hamping*, to load, *hampē* ; *taṛing*, to cut, *taṛē*. In some cases there are two forms of the past stem, the form in *-ē* being probably the older : *bīṛing*, to milk, *bīṛē*, *bīṛā* ; *dasing*, to sow, to rain, *dasē*, *dasā*. The same even applies to a few verbs whose base ends in *-f* :

gwafing, to plait, *gwafē*, *gwafā*; *rēfing*, to cheat, *rēfē*, *rēfā*; *rofing*, to sweep up, *rofē*, *rofā*.

§217. (3) It is even more difficult to reduce the verbs in the third class to rule. They fall into two subdivisions according to whether the consonant in which the past stem ends is *k* (changing to *g* after *n*) or *s*:—

	Infinitive.		Past stem.
(i)	*khalling*,	to strike;	*khalk*.
	halling,	to seize;	*halk*.
	bining,	to hear;	*bing*.
	kuning,	to eat;	*kung*.
	hīning,	to lamb, etc.;	*hīng*.
(ii)	*anning*,	to be;	*ass*.
	manning,	to become;	*mass*.
	banning,	to come;	*bass*.
	tining,	to give;	*tiss*.
	bāsing,	to become hot;	*bāsis*.
	bising,	to ripen;	*bisis*.
	bārring,	to become dry;	*bāris*.
	kharring,	to sprout;	*kharris*.
	piring,	to swell;	*piris*.
	pirāi-ing,	to run dry;	*pirāi-is*.
	chā-ing,	to understand;	*chā-is*.
	khwāhing,	to request;	*khwāhis*.
	pāling,	to become wet;	*pālis*.
	khulīng,	to fear;	*khulīs*.
	salīng,	to stand;	*salīs*.

A few of these verbs have a secondary past stem in *-ā*: *hīnā*, *khulā*, *kharrā*, *khwāhā*.

To the first subdivision belongs *kah-ing*, to die, *kas-k*, the past stem being derived from a different form of the base, *kas-*, which also appears in the negative and causal. Similarly the abnormal past stems *tūs* from *tūling*, to sit, and *hēs* (commonly *ēs*) from *hating* (with variants, §263), to bring, belong to the second subdivision.

§218. It is thus clear that the past stems of the verbs cannot be marshalled in order according to mechanical rules.[1] There is nothing on the face of it to show, for instance, why the past stem of *bining*, to pick, should be *binā*, while the past stem of *bining*, to hear, is *bing*. In the absence of a deeper insight into the history of the individual verb, the memory in most cases is the only guide, but it soon becomes a tolerably safe one. The list of verbs in the language is not very formidable, and it is the commonest verbs as usual which appear to be least amenable to rule. But while the formation of the past stem has been developed on different lines, the formation of the tenses derived from it presents little difficulty.

The Past.

§219. The past is formed by suffixing the present of the substantive verb (§187) to the past stem, except in the third person singular which remains the same as the crude past stem. The third person plural is compounded with the full form *ur*, though there is also a secondary form in *-o* if the past stem ends in a consonant. If the past stem ends in

---

[1] The foregoing analysis is purely formal. In a subsequent volume I hope to show that the past stem is probably formed in one of two ways: (1) by suffixing a particle indicative of past time, *-ā*, *-ē*, *-k* (with *g* after *n*); (2) by the reduplication of the final consonant of the base. Under the latter heading would fall the verbs enumerated in (3) (ii) above, the explanation being based to a large extent on the interchange of both *r* and *l* with *s*. On the other hand it is not impossible that *-s* itself is simply a sign of past time, though this explanation fails to account for the included vowel in some of the past stems.

a vowel, the initial vowel of the substantive verb is elided throughout. The terminations are therefore as follows :—

Past stem ending in a consonant.	Past stem ending in a vowel.
Singular.	**Singular.**
1. *-uṭ*.	1. *-ṭ*.
2. *-us*.	2. *-s*.
3. —.	3. —.
Plural.	**Plural.**
1. *-un*.	1. *-n*.
2. *-ure*.	2. *-re*.
3. *-ur* (*-o*).	3. *-r*.

Thus: *k͟halkuṭ*, I struck; *bassuṭ*, I came; *mak͟hāṭ*, I laughed; *tafēṭ*, I bound. If the past stem has two forms, there are of course two forms of the past and the other tenses of past time: *rēfēṭ*, *rēfāṭ*, I cheated; *k͟hulīsuṭ*, *k͟hulāṭ*, I feared.

The Imperfect.

§220. The imperfect is formed from the past, as the present-future is formed from the present indefinite (§206), by suffixing *-a*. As in the present-future, the *-a* is not added in the second person plural. The third person plural is always compounded with the full form *ur*. The third person singular is remarkable. In the present-future it is formed by suffixing *-k* only. In the imperfect it is formed by suffixing not only *-k*, but also a final *-a*; moreover, if the past stem ends in a consonant, *-a-* is inserted before *-ka*. The terminations are therefore as follows :—

Past stem ending in a consonant.	Past stem ending in a vowel.
Singular.	**Singular.**
1. *-uṭa*.	1. *-ṭa*.
2. *-usa*.	2. *-sa*.
3. *-aka*.	3. *-ka*.

Past stem ending in a consonant.	Past stem ending in a vowel.
Plural.	Plural.
1. *-una.*	1. *-na.*
2. *-ure.*	2. *-re.*
3. *-ura.*	3. *-ra.*

Thus: *khalkuṭa*, I was striking, I used to strike, had I struck; *bassuṭa*, I was coming; *makhāṭa*, I was laughing; *tafēṭa*, I was binding.

The Pluperfect.

§**221.** The pluperfect is formed from the past stem by suffixing the past of the substantive verb (§187), of which one *s* is dropped, and—if the past stem ends in a vowel—the initial vowel is elided. The third person singular is compounded with the double form *-asas;* if the past stem ends in a consonant, it may also be compounded with the short form *-as*, and this is the rule if the final consonant is *-s*. In the plural the third person ordinarily ends in *-asur*, but a secondary form in *-aso* is not uncommon. If the past stem ends in a consonant the terminations are as a rule not *-asuṭ*, etc., but *-usuṭ*, etc., according to the law of harmonic attraction (§13); the third person singular is obviously unaffected. The terminations are therefore as follows:—

Past stem ending in a consonant.	Past stem ending in a vowel.
Singular.	Singular.
1. *-usuṭ* (*-asuṭ*).	1. *-suṭ.*
2. *-usus* (*-asus*).	2. *-sus.*
3. *-asas*; *-as.*	3. *-sas.*
Plural.	Plural.
1. *-usun* (*-asun*).	1. *-sun.*
2. *-usure* (*-asure*).	2. *-sure.*
3. *-usur* (*-asur*).	3. *-sur.*
(*-uso*) (*-aso*).	(*-so*).

Thus: *khalkusuṭ* (*khalkasuṭ*), I had struck, *khalkasas*, *khalkas*, he had struck; *bassusuṭ* (*bassasuṭ*), I had come *bassas*, he had come; *ma<u>kh</u>āsuṭ*, I had laughed, *ma<u>kh</u>āsas*, he had laughed; *tafēsuṭ*, I had bound, *tafēsas*, he had bound.

§**222.** There is also a double form of the pluperfect, analogous to the double form of the past conditional (§209); that is to say, instead of the tense being compounded with the past of the substantive verb, it may be compounded with the pluperfect (§252): *tafēsasuṭ*, I had bound; *<u>kh</u>alkasasuṭ*, I had seized. The vowels of the termination may be subject to harmonic attraction: *<u>kh</u>alkususuṭ;* and this is regularly the case if the root contains an *u*-sound: *kungususuṭ*, I had eaten. If the past stem ends in *-s*, this formation, in itself redundant and not particularly common, is naturally avoided.

The Perfect.

§**223.** The perfect is formed from the past stem by infixing a perfect formative *-un-* and adding the present of the substantive verb. The ordinary forms of the substantive verb are attached, including *e* and *o* in the third persons, as if the past stem were converted into an independent participle by the addition of the perfect formative *-un*. If the past stem ends in a vowel, the vowel of the perfect formative is elided. The terminations are therefore as follows:—

Past stem ending in a consonant.	Past stem ending in a vowel.
Singular.	**Singular.**
1. *-unuṭ.*	1. *-nuṭ*
2. *-unus.*	2. *-nus.*
3. *-une.*	3. *-ne.*
Plural.	**Plural.**
1. *-unun.*	1. *-nun.*
2. *-unure.*	2. *-nure.*
3. *-uno.*	3. *-no.*

Thus: *<u>kh</u>alkunuṭ*, I have struck; *bassunuṭ*, I have come; *ma<u>kh</u>ānuṭ*, I have laughed; *tafēnuṭ*, I have bound.

The Conjugation of the Affirmative Verb.

§224.

Infinitive: *tikhing*, to place, the placing.

Present adverbial participle: *tikhisa*, placing.

Present adjectival participle: *tikhok*, placing, (one) who places.

Noun of obligation: *tikhoī*, obliged to place, obligation to place.

Imperative.

Place.

Singular.	Plural.
2. *tikh(ak)*.	2. *tikhbo*.

Present of Actuality.

I am (in the act of) placing.

1. *ī tikhingaṭī uṭ*.	1. *nan tikhingaṭī un*.
2. *nī tikhingaṭī us*.	2. *num tikhingaṭī ure*.
3. *o tikhingaṭī e*.	3. *ofk tikhingaṭī o*.

Present Indefinite.

I may place, etc.

1. *ī tikhiv*.	1. *nan tikhin*.
2. *nī tikhis*.	2. *num tikhire*.
3. *o tikhe*.	3. *ofk tikhir*.

Present-Future.

I place; I will place.

1. *ī tikhiva*.	1. *nan tikhina*.
2. *nī tikhisa*.	2. *num tikhire*.
3. *o tikhik*.	3. *ofk tikhira*.

Probable Future.

I will (probably) place.

Singular.	Plural.
1. *ī tikhoṭ.*	1. *nan tikhon.*
2. *nī tikhos.*	2. *num tikhore.*
3. *o tikhoe.*	3. *ofk tikhor.*

Past Conditional.

Had I placed ; I would have placed, etc.

1. *ī tikhosuṭ.*	1. *nan tikhosun.*
2. *nī tikhosus.*	2. *num tikhosure.*
3. *o tikhosas.*	3. *ofk tikhosur.*

Past.

I placed ; I ate (infin. *kuning*).

Singular.	Singular.
1. *ī tikhāṭ.*	1. *ī kunguṭ.*
2. *nī tikhās.*	2. *nī kungus.*
3. *o tikhā.*	3 *o kung.*
Plural.	**Plural.**
1. *nan tikhān.*	1. *nan kungun.*
2. *num tikhāre.*	2. *num kungure.*
3. *ofk tikhār.*	3. *ofk kungur.*

Imperfect.

I was placing ; I was eating.

Singular.	Singular.
1. *ī tikhāṭa.*	1. *ī kunguṭa.*
2. *nī tikhāsa.*	2. *nī kungusa.*
3. *o tikhāka.*	3. *o kungaka.*
Plural.	**Plural.**
1. *nan tikhāna.*	1. *nan kunguna.*
2. *num tikhāre.*	2. *num kungure.*
3. *ofk tikhāra.*	3. *ofk kungura.*

Pluperfect.

I had placed ; I had eaten.

	Singular.		Singular.
1.	*ī tik͟hāsuṭ.*	1.	*ī kungusuṭ.*
2.	*nī tik͟hāsus.*	2.	*nī kungusus.*
3.	*o tik͟hāsas.*	3.	*o kungasas,* *kungas.*
	Plural.		**Plural.**
1.	*nan tik͟hāsun.*	1.	*nan kungusun.*
2.	*num tik͟hāsure.*	2.	*num kungusure.*
3.	*ofk tik͟hāsur.*	3.	*ofk kungusur.*

Perfect.

I have placed; I have eaten.

	Singular.		Singular.
1.	*ī tik͟hānuṭ.*	1.	*ī kungunuṭ.*
2.	*nī tik͟hānus.*	2.	*nī kungunus.*
3.	*o tik͟hāne.*	3.	*o kungune.*
	Plural.		**Plural.**
1.	*nan tik͟hānun.*	1.	*nan kungunun.*
2.	*num tik͟hānure.*	2.	*num kungunure.*
3.	*ofk tik͟hāno.*	3.	*ofk kunguno.*

The above represents the normal conjugation of the typical verb. Reference must be made for variants, etc., to the foregoing paragraphs: *e.g.*, for variants of the adverbial participle to §211; for other forms of the imperative to §190 *seq.;* for other tenses of actuality to §188; for variants of the presents to §203 *seq.;* for shorter forms of the third person plural in the past conditional, the past and the pluperfect to §§208, 219 and 221; for double forms of the past conditional and pluperfect to §209 and §222; and for an optional form of the simple pluperfect to §221. The data given in the list of verbs at §265, read with the sections on the formation of the parts of the verb, will indicate sufficiently the conjugation of practically every important verb in the language.

The Formation of the Negative Verb.

§225. Every verb, active, passive, neuter or causal, may be conjugated negatively. Negation is expressed agglutinatively by means of the negative particle *-a-*, which is inserted into the verb. In the tenses of present-future time (including the past conditional, which is a future perfect in form) the particle of negation is preceded by *-p-*, the sign of present-future time, and in the past tenses by *-t-*, the sign of past time. These signs of time and negation are suffixed to the base. Although all the finite tenses are represented in the negative conjugation, there is no negative infinitive nor participle, whether adverbial or adjectival, while the noun of obligation is generally avoided.

The Tenses of Actuality.

§226. As there is no negative infinitive, negation in the so-called tenses of actuality has to be expressed in the auxiliary.

§227. **The negative present of the substantive verb** is as follows :—

Singular.	Plural.
1. *ī affaṭ*, I am not.	1. *nan affan.*
2. *nī affēs.*	2. *num affēre.*
3. *od aff, affak.*	3. *ofk affas.*

There are several peculiar features in this formation, which will be more conveniently discussed later (§253). It may be noted here that *affaṭ*, *affēs*, etc., when employed in tense-formation, appear as *-afaṭ*, *-afēs*, etc., or more often as *-avaṭ*, *-avēs*, etc., while *aff* becomes the diphthong *-au*.

§228. The present of actuality in the negative verb is therefore of the form *ī tikhingaṭī affaṭ*, I am not (in the act of) placing. Other tenses of the kind may be formed with the remaining negative tenses of the substantive verb (§254) : *ī tikhingaṭī allavaṭ*, I was not placing, etc., and where it is defective with the negative of *manning*, to become

(§256) : *ī tikhingaṭī mafaroṭ*, I will probably not be placing, and so on. These tenses will be omitted from the conjugation of the negative verb (§247).

The Prohibitive.

§229. The second person singular of the prohibitive is formed from the base by suffixing the present-negative sign *-p-a*. The rules for its formation are very similar to those for the formation of the imperative plural of the affirmative verb (§197 *seq.*).

§230. If the imperative singular is identical with the base, *-pa* is ordinarily attached without modifying the base : *bispa*, do not bake ; *tikhpa*, do not place. If the base ends in *-n*, there is a natural change of *n* to *m* before the labial of the termination : *bimpa*, do not hear ; *kumpa*, do not eat. In the case of passives (§275) and neuters (§278) the suffix may be added directly to the base : *tikhingpa*, be not placed ; *rasēngpa*, do not arrive ; or the *g* of the base may be dropped and the *n* changed in consequence to *m* : *tikhimpa*, *rasēmpa*. The verbs which adopt an abnormal *lh* in the imperative singular revert to the radical lingual in the prohibitive, as in the rest of the conjugation : *tūlpa*, do not sit ; *halpa*, do not seize ; *khalpa*, do not strike. Corresponding to the two forms of the imperatives of *shāghing*, to pour, *hoghing*, to weep, there are two forms of the prohibitive : *shāghpa*, *shāpa*, *hoghpa*, *hopa*. The prohibitive *kaspa*, do not die, and indeed the whole negative conjugation of *kahing*, is founded on that form of the base which is utilised in the past stem of the affirmative verb (§217 *fin.*).

§231. The prohibitives of the verbs in *-n* are particularly interesting. In the case of two of them, to wit, *pāning*, to say, and *toning*, to hold, the prohibitives are formed by suffixing the present-negative sign to the shorter form of the base without modification : *pāpa*, *topa*. The short form of the base is also used in the case of *banning*, to come, *manning*, to become, and *tining*, to give, but the sign of present time undergoes a remarkable change from *p* to *f* : *bafa, mafa, tifa*. The infix appears as *f* throughout the present-future tenses of these verbs ; it appears by the by as doubled *ff* in the present of the substantive verb negative (§253). In the case of *kanning*, to do, and *danning*, to take away, the present-negative sign is clearly suffixed to the strengthened base in *-r* : *kappa, dappa*, *-rp-* changing to *-pp-*. Analogous are *huppa*, from *hunning* (*huring*), to look, and *tippa* from *chāning* (*chā-ing*, dialectical variant *tā-ing*), to understand, for the whole of the negative conjugation is founded on the bases *hur* (§262), *tir-* (§261). The doubled consonant is maintained throughout the tenses of present-future time, and the sign of past time *t* is similarly doubled in the past tenses.

§232. If the imperative singular is formed by adding *-a* or *-e* to the crude base, the vowel sound becomes *-i-* before the present-negative suffix : *bāripa*, do not become dry; *ḍakkipa*, do not hide; *narripa*, do not flee; *k͟hulipa*, do not fear ; *salipa*, do not stand. The included vowel is maintained in such verbs throughout the negative conjugation. As already noted, the prohibitive of *tining*, to give, is *tifa* ; there is no formation to correspond directly to the imperative *ēte, ētibo*.

§233. If the base ends in *-ē* or *-ī*, the long vowel naturally maintains its place unchanged in the negative conjugation: *illēpa*, do not leave; *k͟hulīpa*, do not fear; *salīpa*, do not stand.

§234. It follows therefore that there may be alternative forms of the prohibitive (and hence of the negative conjugation generally) corresponding to alternative forms of the imperative : *ḍalpa, ḍalipa*, do not gnaw; *hamppa, hampipa*, do not load; *k͟hoshkpa, k͟hoshkipa*, do not rub ; *k͟hulpa*, *khulipa, khulīpa,* do not fear; *salpa, salipa, salīpa,* do not stand.

§235. The second person plural of the prohibitive is formed, as in the affirmative, by adding the termination *-bo* to the singular: *bispabo,* do not bake; *tikhpabo,* do not place; *bimpabo,* do not hear; *rasēngpabo, rasēmpabo,* do not arrive; *tūlpabo,* do not sit; *dappabo,* do not take away; *tifabo,* do not give; *bāripabo,* do not become dry; *khulpabo, khulipabo, khulīpabo,* do not fear.

The Present Indefinite.

§236. The present indefinite of the negative is formed from the base by suffixing the following terminations, with the same phonetic modifications as in the case of the prohibitive:—

Singular.	Plural.
1. *-par.*	1. *-pan.*
2. *-pēs.*	2. *-pēre.*
3. *-p.*	3. *-pas.*

It will be noticed that the negative sign *-a-* is changed to *-ē-* in the second persons, and is dropped altogether in the third person singular, which thus remains with only the sign of time to denote negation, person, number and tense. In the third person plural there is a change from the *-r* of the affirmative to *-s,* which has been induced no doubt by the apparently abnormal adoption of *-r* as the termination of the first person singular.

Examples: *bispar,* I may not bake; *tikhpar,* I may not place; *bimpar,* I may not hear; *kumpar,* I may not eat; *tikhingpar, tikhimpar,* I may not be placed; *rasēngpar, rasēmpar,* I may not arrive; *tūlpar,* I may not sit; *shāghpar, shāpar,* I may not pour; *pāpar,* I may not say; *topar,* I may not hold; *kappar,* I may not do; *dappar,* I may not take away; *huppar,* I may not look; *tippar,* I may not understand; *mafar,* I may not become; *bafar,* I may not come; *tifar* (Jhalawan *chofar*), I may not give; *kaspar*, I may not die; *bāripar*, I may not become dry; *illipar*, *illēpar*, I may not leave; *khulpar*, *khulipar*, *khulīpar*, I may not fear. The following third persons will be specially noted, though they follow on the same lines as the first person: *maf*, he, she or it may not become; *baf*, he may not come; *tif*, he may not give.

The Present-Future.

§237. The present-future negative is formed in the ordinary way by suffixing *-a* to the present indefinite. The second person plural, however, is left unaltered as in the affirmative (though without the same cause). The third person singular ends in *-k* as in the affirmative, the negative sign, which was omitted in the present indefinite, reappearing as the included vowel. The terminations are therefore as follows:—

Singular.	Plural.
1. *-para.*	1. *-pana.*
2. *-pēsa.*	2. *-pēre.*
3. *-pak.*	3. *-pasa.*

Thus: *bispara*, I do not bake, I will not bake; *bimpara*, I do not hear; *kappara*, I do not do; *tippara*, I do not understand; *bafara*, I do not come; *tifara* (Jhalawan *chofara*), I do not give; *khulpara*, *khulipara*, *khulīpara*, I do not fear.

The Probable Future.

§238. The probable future negative is formed from the base, with the usual phonetic modifications, by suffixing the present-negative sign *-pa-* and the terminations of the affirmative probable future, with an apparently euphonic *-r-* to bridge the hiatus. The terminations are therefore as follows:—

Singular.	Plural.
1. *-paroṭ.*	1. *-paron.*
2. *-paros.*	2. *-parore.*
3. *-paroe.*	3. *-paror.*

Thus: *bisparoṭ*, I will (probably) not bake; *bimparoṭ*, I will (probably) not hear; *kapparoṭ*, I will (probably) not do; *tipparoṭ*, I will (probably) not understand *bafaroṭ*, I will (probably) not come; *tifaroṭ* (Jhalawan *chofaroṭ*), I will (probably) not give; *k͟hulparoṭ*, *k͟huliparoṭ*, *k͟hulīparoṭ*, I will (probably) not fear.

§239. A peculiar form of this tense is heard in Jhalawan. The formative *-o-* of the affirmative probable future is suffixed to the base, and the present negative of the substantive verb (§227) is then attached, its initial vowel being elided. The terminations are therefore as follows:—

Singular.	Plural.
1. *-ofaṭ.*	1. *-ofan.*
2. *-ofēs.*	2. *-ofēre.*
3. *-of.*	3. *-ofas.*

Thus: *bisofaṭ*, I will (probably) not bake; *binofaṭ*, I will not hear; *k͟hulofaṭ*, I will not fear; *chāofaṭ*, I will not understand; *chofaṭ*, I will not give. In the case of the verbs in *-n* the terminations are attached to the strengthened base in *-r*: *karofaṭ*, I will not do.

The Past Conditional.

§240. As in the affirmative this tense is in form the past of the probable future. It is formed from the base in exactly the same manner as the negative probable future except that the past and not the present of the substantive verb is attached. The terminations are therefore as follows:—

Singular.	Plural.
1. *-parosuṭ.*	1. *-parosun.*
2. *-parosus*	2. *-parosure.*
3. *-parosas.*	3. *-parosur* (*-paroso*).

Thus: *bisparosuṭ*, I would not have baked, had I not baked, would that I had not baked; *bimparosuṭ*, I would not have heard; *kapparosuṭ*, I would not have done; *tifarosu*

(Jhalawan *chofarosuṭ*), I would not have given; *k͟hulparosuṭ*, *k͟huliparosuṭ*, *k͟hulīparosuṭ*, I would not have feared. A double form compounded with the pluperfect of the substantive verb (*cf.* §209) is sometimes heard: *bisparosusuṭ*.

§241. In Jhalawan there is a secondary form of this tense, corresponding to the peculiar Jhalawan form of the probable future negative. It is based on the third person singular of that form of the tense, by attaching the past of the substantive verb affirmative, which generally appears as *-ēsuṭ* (*cf.* §245). The terminations are therefore as follows:—

Singular.	Plural.
1. *-ofēsuṭ*.	1. *-ofēsun*.
2. *-ofēsus*.	2. *-ofēsure*.
3. *-ofēsas*.	3. *-ofēsur* (*-ofēso*).

Thus: *bisofēsuṭ*, I would not have baked; *k͟hulofēsuṭ*, I would not have feared; *chofēsuṭ*, I would not have given. The forms *bisofasuṭ*, *k͟hulofasuṭ*, etc., are less commonly heard.

The Noun of Obligation.

§242. The negative noun of obligation is formed from the base, modified phonetically in the usual manner, by suffixing the present-negative sign *-pa-*, and attaching as in the affirmative the termination *-oī*, with the insertion of *-r-* to bridge the hiatus. Thus: *bisparoī*, not obliged to bake, no obligation to bake; *bimparoī*, not obliged to hear; *kapparoī*, not obliged to do; *bafaroī*, not obliged to come; *tifaroī* (Jhalawan *chofaroī*), not obliged to give; *k͟hulparoī*, *k͟huliparoī*, *k͟hulīparoī*, not obliged to fear. In the case of transitives this formation has a passive signification also (§275).

The Past.

§243. The past negative is formed from the base by infixing the past-negative sign *-t-a-*, and attaching the present of the substantive verb negative (§227). One of the concurrent *a*'s is elided[1]; *ff* is changed to *v*, while *aff* in the third person singular becomes the diphthong *-au*.[2] The terminations are therefore as follows :—

Singular.	Plural.
1. *-tavaṭ*.	1. *-tavan*.
2. *-tavēs*.	2. *-tavēre*.
3. *-tau*.	3. *-tavas*.

The variations in the formation of the past run parallel to the variations in the formation of the prohibitive: *bistavaṭ*, I did not bake; *bintavaṭ*, I did not hear; *tūltavaṭ*, I did not sit; *shāghtavaṭ*, *shātavaṭ*, I did not pour; *pātavaṭ*, I did not speak; *totavaṭ*, I did not hold; *kattavaṭ*, I did not do; *dattavaṭ*, I did not take away; *huttavaṭ*, I did not look; *tittavaṭ*, I did not understand; *titavaṭ*, I did not give; *batavaṭ*, I did not come; *matavaṭ*, I did not become; *kastavaṭ*, I did not die; *bāritavaṭ*, I did not become dry; *narritavaṭ*, I did not flee; *khultavaṭ*, *khulitavaṭ*, *khulītavaṭ*, I did not fear.

The Imperfect.

§244. The imperfect is formed in the negative, as in the affirmative, by suffixing *-a* to the past, with similar modifications: the second person plural remains unchanged, while the third person singular takes on *-aka*, the diphthong being resolved into *-av-*. The terminations are therefore as follows :—

Singular.	Plural.
1. *-tavaṭa*.	1. *-tavana*.
2. *-tavēsa*.	2. *-tavēre*.
3. *-tavaka*.	3. *-tavasa*.

Thus: *bistavaṭa*, I was not baking; *tittavaṭa*, I was not understanding; *titavaṭa*, I was not giving; *narritavaṭa*, I

[1] And hence it might be argued that only the past sign *-t-* and the negative present of the substantive verb are attached to the base. The version given in the text seems, on the whole, preferable.

[2] The diphthong is resolved on the addition of the enclitic pronoun of the third person: *e.g.*, *pātav-ta*, he didn't say to him.

was not fleeing; *khultavaṭa*, *khulitavaṭa*, *khulītavaṭa*, I was not fearing.

The Pluperfect.

§245. On the analogy of the affirmative, the pluperfect negative is formed by adding the past of the affirmative substantive verb to the third person singular of the past negative, the diphthong of which is resolved. The form *-ēsuṭ* is generally used instead of *-asuṭ* to avoid the sequence of unaccented syllables (*cf.* §241). The terminations are therefore as follows:—

Singular.	Plural.
1. *-tavēsuṭ* (*-tavasuṭ*).	1. *-tavēsun* (*-tavasun*).
2. *-tavēsus* (*-tavasus*).	2. *-tavēsure* (*-tavasure*).
3. *-tavēsas* (*-tavasas*).	3. *-tavēsur* (*-tavasur*).
	(*-tavēso*) (*-tavaso*).

Thus: *bistavēsuṭ*, I had not baked; *tittavēsuṭ*, I had not understood; *titavēsuṭ*, I had not given; *khultavēsuṭ*, *khulitavēsuṭ*, *khulītavēsuṭ*, I had not feared. The forms *bistavasuṭ*, *tittavasuṭ*, etc., are much less commonly used.

The Perfect.

§246. The negative perfect is formed from the base, modified in the usual manner, by suffixing the past-negative sign *-ta-*, and attaching the perfect formative *-(u)n-* and the present affirmative of the substantive verb. The terminations are therefore as follows:—

Singular.	Plural.
1. *-tanuṭ*.	1. *-tanun*.
2. *-tanus*.	2. *-tanure*.
3. *-tane*.	3. *-tano*.

Thus: *bistanuṭ*, I have not baked; *tittanuṭ*, I have not understood; *titanuṭ*, I have not given; *khultanuṭ*, *khulitanuṭ*, *khulītanuṭ*, I have not feared.

The Conjugation of the Negative Verb.

§247.

Noun of Obligation : *tikhparoī*, not obliged to place, no obligation to place.

Prohibitive.

Do not place.

Singular.		Plural.	
2.	*tikhpa.*	2.	*tikhpabo.*

Present Indefinite.

I may not place, etc.

1. *ī* *tikhpar.*	1. *nan* *tikhpan.*
2. *nī* *tikhpēs.*	2. *num* *tikhpēre.*
3. *o* *tikhp.*	3. *ofk* *tikhpas.*

Present-Future.

I do not place ; I will not place.

1. *ī* *tikhpara.*	1. *nan* *tikhpana.*
2. *nī* *tikhpēsa.*	2. *num* *tikhpēre.*
3. *o* *tikhpak.*	3. *ofk* *tikhpasa.*

Probable Future.

I will (probably) not place.

1. *ī* *tikhparoṭ.*	1. *nan* *tikhparon.*
2. *nī* *tikhparos.*	2. *num* *tikhparore.*
3. *o* *tikhparoe.*	3. *ofk* *tikhparor.*

Past Conditional.

Had I not placed, etc.

1. *ī* *tikhparosuṭ.*	1. *nan* *tikhparosun.*
2. *nī* *tikhparosus.*	2. *num* *tikhparosure.*
3. *o* *tikhparosas.*	3. *ofk* *tikhparosur.*

Past.

I did not place.

Singular.	Plural.
1. *ī tik̲h̲tavaṭ.*	1. *nan tik̲h̲tavan.*
2. *nī tik̲h̲tavēs.*	2. *num tik̲h̲tavēre.*
3. *o tik̲h̲tau.*	3. *ofk tik̲h̲tavas.*

Imperfect.

I was not placing.

1. *ī tik̲h̲tavaṭa.*	1. *nan tik̲h̲tavana.*
2. *nī tik̲h̲tavēsa.*	2. *num tik̲h̲tavēre.*
3. *o tik̲h̲tavaka.*	3. *ofk tik̲h̲tavasa.*

Pluperfect.

I had not placed.

1. *ī tik̲h̲tavēsuṭ.*	1. *nan tik̲h̲tavēsun.*
2. *nī tik̲h̲tavēsus.*	2. *num tik̲h̲tavēsure.*
3. *o tik̲h̲tavēsas.*	3. *ofk tik̲h̲tavēsur.*

Perfect.

I have not placed.

1. *ī tik̲h̲tanuṭ.*	1. *nan tik̲h̲tanun.*
2. *nī tik̲h̲tanus.*	2. *num tik̲h̲tanure.*
3. *o tik̲h̲tane.*	3. *ofk tik̲h̲tano.*

In the above only the most regular forms have been given; for variants reference will be made to the preceding paragraphs. It will be borne in mind that if there is an included vowel between the crude base and the present-negative sign in the prohibitive, the included vowel is maintained throughout the negative conjugation: *e.g.*, *narripa*, do not flee, *narriparoī*, *narripar*, *narripara*, *narriparoṭ*, *narriparosuṭ*, *narritavaṭ*, *narritavaṭa*, *narritavēsuṭ*, *narritanuṭ*.

Auxiliary and Irregular Verbs.

Anning, to be.

§**248.** The substantive verb is defective, and what tenses there are, are not all derived from the same root. The infinitive *anning* is almost obsolete, and its use is seemingly confined to one or two set phrases: *e.g.*, *anningki pās*, *shikār Sēbīnā ḍoraṭī bāz e, maga nē dū tamme*, as a matter of fact (lit. for existence' sake you may say) there's sport in abundance on the Sibi canal, and possibly you may get some; *anningki dā kasaraṭ dīr arē*, as a matter of fact there is water on this road. Imperative there is none, though a trace of one is perhaps preserved in *bash-a*, arise, seeing that there is no verb *bashing*. Nor are there any participles, noun of obligation or perfect. On the other hand, though both present indefinite and future are missing, there are two forms of the present.

§**249.**

The Present.

Singular.	Plural.
1. *ī ut*, I am.	1. *nan un*.
2. *nī us*.	2. *num ure*.
3. *od e*.	3. *ofk o* (*ur*).

The dialectical variant *ur* in the third person plural evidently preserves the original type (*cf.* §16). There are several peculiar features in this tense. It is the only present affirmative in the language in which, due allowance being made for palpable elisions (§204), the included vowel is not *-i-*(*-ē-*), and in which the first person singular does not end in *-v*(*a*). Indeed, though a present in meaning, there seems reason to regard it as a past in origin, like the emphatic present.

§250.

The Emphatic Present.

Singular.	Plural.
1. *ī arēṭ*, I *am*, I exist.	1. *nan arēn.*
2. *nī arēs.*	2. *num arēre.*
3. *od arē.*	3. *ofk arēr.*

§251. This is in form an ordinary past from *anning*, after the model of *ī karēṭ*, I did, from *kanning* (§216). It is more emphatic than *ī uṭ*, and generally implies actual existence: *khudā jwān e*, God is good; *harkas chāik, khudā arē*, everybody knows that God exists; *ī nājoṛ uṭ*, I'm unwell; *ī nājoṛ arēṭ maga tā shahriskā kāva*, I *am* unwell, but I'll go as far as the village. The relationship of *arēṭ* to *uṭ* is in fact analogous to the relationship of *shta* to *dai* in Pashtu, and of *hastam* to *-am* in Persian. The resemblance of *uṭ* to the Persian *-am* is particularly strong, as it is pronounced, especially in the third person singular, in very close connection with the word preceding it, and it would perhaps be more correct to write it as an enclitic (*cf.* §72).

§252. The remaining three tenses of the affirmative, to wit, the past, imperfect and pluperfect, are based on the past stem *ass-*, which is derived from *anning* on the analogy of *mass-* from *manning*, to become (§217).

The Past.

Singular.	Plural.
1. *ī assuṭ*, I was.	1. *nan assun.*
2. *nī assus.*	2. *num assure.*
3. *od ass.*	3. *ofk assur* (*asso*).

The Imperfect.

Singular.		Plural.	
1. *ī*	*assuṭa*, I was.	1. *nan*	*assuna*.
2. *nī*	*assusa*.	2. *num*	*assure*.
3. *od*	*assaka*.	3. *ofk*	*assura*.

The Pluperfect.

1. *ī*	*assusuṭ*, I had been.	1. *nan*	*assusun*.
2. *nī*	*assusus*.	2. *num*	*assusure*.
3. *od*	*assas*.	3. *ofk*	*assusur* (*assuso*).

It will be seen that these tenses are formed from the base *ass-* in the ordinary way. As a matter of fact, there is little difference of meaning between the three; it will be remembered that the third person singular of the pluperfect is largely employed in the conjugation of the verb instead of the corresponding person of the past. The form *assasuṭ* is sometimes used for the more usual form *assusuṭ*, which has been affected by harmonic attraction (§221).

§253. The negative tenses are as follows:—

The Present.

Singular.		Plural.	
1. *ī*	*affaṭ*, I am not.	1. *nan*	*affan*.
2. *nī*	*affēs*.	2. *num*	*affēre*.
3. *od*	*aff*, *affak*.	3. *ofk*	*affas*.

This tense is remarkable as being the only negative present in which the first person singular does not end in *-r*(*a*). In other respects it is not unlike the presents indefinite *mafar*, *bafar*, *tifar*, derived from *manning*, to become, *banning*, to come, *tining*, to give, except for the doubling of *-f-*, the sign of present time (§231) and the second form of the third person singular, which is in reality a present-future, though in no way differing from *aff* in its ordinary use and meaning.

§254.

The Past.

Singular.		Plural.	
1. *ī*	*allavaṭ*, I was not.	1. *nan*	*allavan.*
2. *nī*	*allavēs.*	2. *num*	*allavēre.*
3. *od*	*allau.*	3. *ofk*	*allavas.*

The Imperfect.

1. *ī*	*allavaṭa*, I was not.	1. *nan*	*allavana.*
2. *nī*	*allavēsa.*	2. *num*	*allavēre.*
3. *od*	*allavaka.*	3. *ofk*	*allavasa.*

The Pluperfect.

1. *ī*	*allavēsuṭ*, I had not been.	1. *nan*	*allavēsun.*
2. *nī*	*allavēsus.*	2. *num*	*allavēsure.*
3. *od*	*allavēsas.*	3. *ofk*	*allavēsur.* (*allavēso*).

These three past tenses of the negative of the substantive verb are derived from a root *all-*, which appears to have no connection with the ordinary verbal root. The past is formed by adding to it the negative present *affaṭ* with the usual modifications (§243); the imperfect is formed from the past in the regular manner (§244), and the imperfect in turn constitutes no less regularly the basis for the formation of the pluperfect (§245). A difference in meaning between the three tenses is not often clearly marked.

§255. The substantive verb is otherwise defective. The missing parts are supplied by *manning*, to become. The abnormal features in the conjugation of *manning* and of the other irregular verbs which are presented below have already been examined in the discussion of the formation of the various parts of the verb.

Manning, to become.

§256. There are two bases, *ma-*, *mar-* (§186). With the exception of the first form of the imperative, the whole of the affirmative is founded on the latter, while the whole of the negative is founded on the former. The remarkable phonetic change in the sign of present time in the negative conjugation has already been referred to (§231).

	Affirmative.	Negative.
Infinitive:	*manning.*	...
Pres. adv. part.:	*marisa.*	...
Pres. adj. part.:	*marok.*	...
Noun of obligation:	*maroī.*	*mafaroī.*
Imperative:	*ma, mar, marak.*	*mafa.*
Present indefinite:	*marēv.*	*mafar.*
Present-future:	*marēva.*	*mafara.*
Probable future:	*maroṭ.*	*mafaroṭ.*
Past conditional:	*marosuṭ.*	*mafarosuṭ.*
Past:	*massuṭ.*	*matavaṭ.*
Imperfect:	*massuṭa.*	*matavaṭa.*
Pluperfect:	*massusuṭ.*	*matavēsuṭ.*
Perfect:	*massunuṭ.*	*matanuṭ.*

Banning, to come.

§257. *Banning* is conjugated in exactly the same way as *manning*.

Kanning, to do.

§258. There are two bases, *ka-*, *kar-*. With the exception of the first form of the imperative and the affirmative presents the conjugation, both affirmative and negative, is founded on the base *kar-*. The curious formation of the affirmative presents has been analysed in §204; for the doubling of the signs of time throughout the negative reference should be made to §231.

	Affirmative.	Negative.
Infinitive:	*kanning.*	...
Pres. adv. part.:	*karisa.*	...
Pres. adj. part.:	*karok.*	...
Noun of obligation:	*karoī.*	*kapparoī.*
Imperative:	*ka, kar, karak.*	*kappa.*
Present indefinite:	*kēv.*	*kappar.*
Present-future:	*kēva.*	*kappara.*
Probable future:	*karoṭ.*	*kapparoṭ.*
Past conditional:	*karosuṭ.*	*kapparosuṭ.*
Past:	*karēṭ.*	*kattavaṭ.*
Imperfect:	*karēṭa.*	*kattavaṭa.*
Pluperfect:	*karēsuṭ.*	*kattavēsuṭ.*
Perfect:	*karēnuṭ.*	*kattanuṭ.*

Danning, to take away.

§259. *Danning* is conjugated in exactly the same way as *kanning*.

Tining, to give.

§260. The imperative and the ordinary forms of the affirmative presents are based on the root *ēt-*. If the dialectical and other variants, which have already been mentioned (*tēv*, §204, *ētoṭ*, *choṭ*, §207, etc.), are left out of account, the rest of the affirmative is founded on the base *tir-* and the negative on the base *ti-* after the analogy of *manning* and *banning*.

	Affirmative.	Negative.
Infinitive:	*tining.*	...
Pres. adv. part.:	*tirisa.*	...
Pres. adj. part.:	*tirok.*	...
Noun of obligation:	*tirōī.*	*tifarōī.*
Imperative:	*ēte.*	*tifa.*
Present indefinite:	*ētiv.*	*tifar.*
Present-future:	*ētiva.*	*tifara.*
Probable future:	*tiroṭ.*	*tifaroṭ.*
Past conditional:	*tirosuṭ.*	*tifarosuṭ.*
Past:	*tissuṭ.*	*titavaṭ.*
Imperfect:	*tissuṭa.*	*titavaṭa.*
Pluperfect:	*tissusuṭ.*	*titavēsuṭ.*
Perfect:	*tissunuṭ.*	*titanuṭ.*

Chā-ing, to understand.

§261. The affirmative is conjugated regularly on the base *chā-*, the only peculiarities lying in the not very common infinitive form *chāning* and in the formation of the past stem *chā-is* (§217 ii). The negative conjugation is founded on a base *tir-* on the analogy of *kanning* and *danning*, and implies an obsolete infinitive *tinning*. The dialectical variant *tā-ing* (imper. *tā*, pres. *tāv*, *tāva*, sometimes also *tiā-ing*, *tiā*, *tiāv*, *tiāva*) heard chiefly in the Nushki district, seems to afford a connecting link between the two bases.

	Affirmative.	Negative.
Infinitive:	*chā-ing* (*chāning*).	...
Pres. adv. part.:	*chā-isa.*	...
Pres. adj. part.:	*chāok.*	...
Noun of obligation:	*chāoī.*	*tipparoī.*
Imperative:	*chā*, *chā-ak.*	*tippa.*
Present indefinite:	*chāv.*	*tippar.*
Present-future:	*chāva.*	*tippara.*
Probable future:	*chāoṭ.*	*tipparoṭ.*
Past conditional:	*chāosuṭ.*	*tipparosuṭ.*
Past:	*chā-isuṭ.*	*tittavaṭ.*
Imperfect:	*chā-isuṭa.*	*tittavaṭa.*
Pluperfect:	*chā-isusuṭ.*	*tittavēsuṭ.*
Perfect:	*chā-isunuṭ.*	*tittanuṭ.*

Huring, hunning, to look.

§262. The affirmative is conjugated in the ordinary way on the base *hur-*, with a slight irregularity in the formation of the imperative plural *hubbo* (§198). The negative is conjugated after the model of *kanning* and *danning*.

	Affirmative.	Negative.
Infinitive:	*huring, hunning.*	...
Pres. adv. part.:	*hurisa.*	...
Pres. adj. part.:	*hurok.*	...
Noun of obligation:	*huroī.*	*hupparoī.*
Imperative:	*hur.*	*huppa.*
Present indefinite:	*huriv.*	*huppar.*
Present-future:	*huriva.*	*huppara.*
Probable future:	*huroṭ.*	*hupparoṭ.*
Past conditional:	*hurosuṭ.*	*hupparosuṭ.*
Past:	*hurāṭ.*	*huttavaṭ.*
Imperfect:	*hurāṭa.*	*huttavaṭa.*
Pluperfect:	*hurāsuṭ.*	*huttavēsuṭ.*
Perfect:	*hurānuṭ.*	*huttanuṭ.*

Hating, hatining, hataring, hatiring, to bring.

§263. This verb is clearly compounded with *tining*, to give, which accounts for several curious forms and variants. The first element *ha-* is probably to be traced to *hal-*, to seize. The aspirate is frequently dropped.

	Affirmative.	Negative.
Infinitive:	*hating.* *hatining.* *hataring.* *hatiring.*	...
Pres. adv. part.:	*hatisa.* *hatarisa.* *hatirisa.*	...
Pres. adj. part.:	*hatok.* *hatarok.* *hatirok.*	...
Noun of obligation:	*hatoī.* *hataroī.* *hatiroī.*	*hatiparoī.*

	Affirmative.	Negative.
Imperative:	*hata.* *hatar.*	*hatipa.*
Present indefinite:	*hatēv.* *hatarēv.*	*hatipar.*
Present-future:	*hatēva.* *hatarēva.*	*hatipara.*
Probable future:	*hatoṭ.* *hataroṭ.* *hatiroṭ.*	*hatiparoṭ.*
Past conditional:	*hatosuṭ.* *hatarosuṭ.* *hatirosuṭ.*	*hatiparosuṭ.*
Past:	*hēsuṭ.*	*hatitavaṭ.* *hattavaṭ.*
Imperfect:	*hēsuṭa.*	*hatitavaṭa.* *hattavaṭa.*
Pluperfect:	*hēsusuṭ.*	*hatitavēsuṭ.* *hattavēsuṭ.*
Perfect:	*hēsunuṭ.*	*hatitanuṭ.* *hattanuṭ.*

***Hining*, to go.**

§264. With the exception of the affirmative presents the conjugation of *hining*, both affirmative and negative, proceeds perfectly regularly from the base ***hin-*: *hinisa*, *hinok*, *hinoī*, *himparoī*, *hin*, *himpa*, *himpar*, *hinoṭ*, *himparoṭ*, *hinoṭ*, *hintavaṭ***, etc. The presents in the affirmative are formed from a different base *kā-*[1] (§205).

Present Indefinite.

Singular.		Plural.	
1. *ī*	*kāv*, I may go.	1. *nan*	*kān.*
2. *nī*	*kās.*	2. *num*	*kāre.*
3. *o*	*kāe.*	3. *ofk*	*kār.*

Present-Future.

1. *ī*	*kāva*, I go; I will go.	1. *nan*	*kāna.*
2. *nī*	*kāsa.*	2. *num*	*kāre.*
3. *o*	*kā-ik* (*kāik*).	3. *ofk*	*kāra.*

[1] There is also the curious form *kāmbo*, let us go, I and you, which appears to be compounded of *kān*, first person plural of the present indefinite, and *-bo*, the ending of the second person plural imperative.

List of Verbs.

§265. The various parts of the more important verbs in the language will be deduced without difficulty from the following skeleton table, read with the sections on the formation. The secondary form of the imperative in *-ak* which obtains in a certain class of verbs (§192) has been omitted for the sake of brevity, and the same applies to the optional form of the prohibitive in the case of neuter verbs like *aṛēnging* (§276). As the negative conjugation is formed as a rule from the base as presented in the imperative according to certain well-defined principles, it is ordinarily unnecessary to display the prohibitive separately. In view, however, of the importance of the few abnormal cases a place has been accorded to it in the table. Only the primary meaning of the verb is given. It will be borne in mind that the third person singular of the past is identical with the past stem (§214).

Infinitive.		Imperative. (2nd p. s.)	Past. (3rd p. s.)	Prohibitive. (2nd p. s.)
anning,[1]	be,	...	*ass.*	...
aṛēnging,	be entangled,	*aṛēng,*	*aṛēngā,*	*aṛēngpa.*
aurazēnging,	get excited,	*aurazēng,*	*aurazēngā,*	*aurazēngpa.*
avalēnging,	get confused,	*avalēng,*	*avalēngā,*	*avalēngpa.*
āvāning,	yawn,	*āvān(a),*	*āvānā,*	*āvāmpa, āvānipa.*
banning,[2]	come,	*ba, bar,*	*bass,*	*bafa.*
bārring,	become dry,	*bāra,*	*bāris,*	*bāripa.*
bāsing,	become hot,	*bāsa,*	*bāsis,*	*bāsipa.*
bashkhing,	present,	*bashkh(a),*	*bashkhā,*	*bashkh(i)pa.*
baṭinging,[3]	summon,	*baṭing,*	*baṭingā,*	*baṭingpa.*

[1] *Cf.* §248 *seq.* [2] *Cf.* §257. [3] Also *baṭanging,* §279.

Infinitive.		Imperative. (2nd p. s.)	Past. (3rd p. s.)	Prohibitive. (2nd p. s.)
bēg̲h̲ing,	knead,	*bēg̲h̲(a)*,	*bēg̲h̲ā*,	*bēg̲h̲(i)pa*.
bēling,	devastate,	*bēla*,	*bēlā*,	*bēlipa*.
bēning,	wear,	*bēn*,	*bēnā*,	*bēmpa*.
bining,	hear,	*bin*,	*bing*,	*bimpa*.
bining,	pick,	*bin*,	*binā*,	*bimpa*.
birring,	distinguish,	*birra*,	*birrā*,	*birripa*.
birvinging,	be sifted,	*birving*,	*birvingā*,	*birvingpa*.
bīṛing,	milk,	*bīṛ(a)*,	*bīṛē*, *bīṛā*,	*bīṛ(i)pa*.
bising,	bake,	*bis*,	*bisē*,	*bispa*.
bising,	ripen,	*bis*,	*bisis*,	*bispa*.
bisinging,		*bising*,	...	*bisingpa*.
biṭing,	throw,	*biṭ*,	*biṭē*,	*biṭpa*.
buḍḍing,	drown,	*buḍḍa*,	*buḍḍā*,	*buḍḍipa*.
būk̲h̲ing,	bellow,	*būk̲h̲a*,	*būk̲h̲ā*,	*būk̲h̲ipa*.
buring,	crumble (intr.),	*bura*,	*burā*,	*buripa*.
chā-ing,[1]	understand,	*chā*,	*chā-is*,	*tippa*.
chakking,	taste,	*chakka*,	*chakkā*,	*chakkipa*.
chaling,	crack (intr.),	*chala*,	*chalā*,	*chalipa*.
challing,	be current,	*challa*,	*challā*,	*challipa*.
chanḍing,	shake,	*chanḍa*,	*chanḍā*,	*chanḍipa*.
chaṭṭing,	lick,	*chaṭṭa*,	*chaṭṭā*,	*chaṭṭipa*.
chikking,	pull,	*chikka*,	*chikkā*,	*chikkipa*.
chirrēnging,	roam,	*chirrēng*,	*chirrēngā*,	*chirrēngpa*.
chiṛēnging,	be annoyed,	*chiṛēng*,	*chiṛēngā*,	*chiṛēngpa*.
chiṛing,		*chiṛa*,	*chiṛā*,	*chiṛipa*.

[1] *Cf.* §261

Infinitive.		Imperative. (2nd p. s.)	Past. (3rd p. s.)	Prohibitive. (2nd p. s.)
chonḍing,	gobble up,	*chonḍa*,	*chonḍā*,	*chonḍipa*.
choshing,	soak,	*chosh(a)*,	*choshā*,	*chosh(i)pa*.
chumming,	kiss,	*chum(ma)*,	*chummā*,	*chum(mi)pa*.
churring,	drip,	*churra*,	*churrā*,	*churripa*.
chūshing,	suck,	*chūsh(a)*,	*chūsā*,	*chūsh(i)pa*.
chuṭṭēnging,	be rid of,	*chuṭṭēng*,	*chuṭṭēngā*,	*chuṭṭēngpa*.
chuṭṭing,	drip,	*chuṭṭa*,	*chuṭṭā*,	*chuṭṭipa*.
dāghing,	measure (grain, etc.),	*dāgh(a)*,	*dāghā*,	*dāgh(i)pa*.
danning,[1]	take away,	*da, dar*,	*darē*,	*dappa*.
daṛing,	descend,	*daṛ(a)*,	*daṛā*,	*daṛ(i)pa*.
daṛinging,	descend,	*daṛing*,	*daṛingā*,	*daṛingpa*.
dasing,	sow,	*dasa*,	*dasē, dasā*,	*dasipa*.
dassing,	give a fall,	*dassa*,	*dassā*,	*dassipa*.
dranjing,	hang,	*dranj(a)*,	*dranjā*,	*dranj(i)pa*.
drãzing,	throw up,	*drãz(a)*,	*drãzā*,	*drãz(i)pa*.
drikking,	jump,	*drik(ka)*,	*drikkā*,	*drik(ki)pa*.
dudēnging,	run,	*dudēng*,	*dudēngā*,	*dudēngpa*.
durring,	make an onslaught,	*durra*,	*durrā*,	*durripa*.
duzzing,	steal,	*duzza*,	*duzzā*,	*duzzipa*.
ḍakking,	hide,	*ḍakka*,	*ḍakkā*,	*ḍakkipa*.
ḍaling,	gnaw,	*ḍal(a)*,	*ḍalā*,	*ḍal(i)pa*.
ḍohing,	carry,	*ḍoha*,	*ḍohā*,	*ḍohipa*.
ḍūmbing,	cover up,	*ḍūmba*,	*ḍūmbā*,	*ḍūmbipa*.
fāming,	understand,	*fām*,	*fāmā*,	*fāmpa*.

[1] *Cf.* §259.

Infinitive.		Imperative. (2nd p. s.)	Past. (3rd p. s.)	Prohibitive. (2nd p. s.)
gagalling,	bleat (of goats),	*gagalla*,	*gagallā*,	*gagallipa*.
gārring,	bleat (of sheep),	*gārra*,	*gārrā*,	*gārripa*.
gārting,	belch,	*gārta*,	*gārtā*,	*gārtipa*.
gaṛing,	flatten,	*gaṛa*,	*gaṛā*,	*gaṛipa*.
gid(ā)rēng-ing,	pass over,	*gid(ā)rēng*,	*gid(ā)rēngā*,	*gid(ā)-rēngpa*.
giḍḍing,	nod with sleep,	*giḍḍa*,	*giḍḍā*,	*giḍḍipa*.
girring,	drag along,	*girra*,	*girrā*,	*girripa*.
going,	lose,	*goa*,	*goā*,	*goipa*.
goṭing,	pound,	*goṭa*,	*goṭā*,	*goṭipa*.
gūrring,	gurgle (of camels),	*gūrra*,	*gūrrā*,	*gūrripa*.
gūrting,	low,	*gūrta*,	*gūrtā*,	*gūrtipa*.
guṛēnging, }	be scared,	{ *guṛēng*,	*guṛēngā*,	*guṛēngpa*.
guṛing, }		{ *guṛa*,	*guṛā*,	*guṛipa*.
gwafing,	weave,	*gwaf(a)*,	*gwafē*, *gwafā*,	*gwaf(i)pa*.
ghakking,	bark,	*ghakka*,	*ghakkā*,	*ghakkipa*.
ghānḍing,	muddle,	*ghānḍa*,	*ghānḍā*,	*ghānḍipa*.
ghapping,	bark,	*ghappa*,	*ghappā*,	*ghappipa*
ghazhzhing,	swell (intr.)	*ghazhzha*,	*ghazhzhā*,	*ghazhzhipa*.
ghurring,	growl,	*ghurra*,	*ghurrā*,	*ghurripa*.
hakkaling,	drive,	*hakkal(a)*,	*hakkalā*,	*hakkal(i)pa*.
hāling,	cover (of animals),	*hāla*,	*hālā*,	*hālipa*.
halling,[1]	take,	*halh*,	*halk*,	*halpa*.

[1] Imp. plur. *halbo*, §197; pres. *halēr*, §203.

Infinitive.		Imperative. (2nd p. s.)	Past. (3rd p. s.)	Prohibitive. (2nd p. s.)
hamping,	load,	*hamp(a)*,	*hampē*,	*hamp(i)pa*.
haninging,	cohabit,	*haning*,	*haningā*,	*haningpa*.
harfing,	lift up,	*harf*,	*harfē*,	*harfpa*.
harrifing,	ask,	*harrif*,	*harrifē*,	*harrifpa*.
harring,	tear,	*harra*,	*harrā*,	*harripa*.
harsing,[1]	turn,	*hars(a)*,	*harsā*,	*hars(i)pa*.
hataring,[2]	bring,	*hatar*,	...	...
hating,		*hata*,	*hēs*,	*hatipa*.
hēfing,[3]	lift up,	*hēf*,	*hēfē*,	*hēfpa*.
hēling,	spread out,	*hēl(a)*,	*hēlā*,	*hēl(i)pa*.
hichchāning,	sneeze,	*hichchāna*,	*hichchānā*,	*hichchānipa*.
hījēnging,	be alarmed,	*hījēng*,	*hījēngā*,	*hījēngpa*.
hījing,		*hīja*,	*hījā*,	*hījipa*.
hikking,	hiccough,	*hikka*,	*hikkā*,	*hikkipa*.
hining,[4]	go,	*hin*,	*hinā*,	*himpa*.
hīning,	kid, lamb, etc.,	*hīn*,	*hīng*, *hīnā*,	*hīmpa*.
hīzhing,	whistle,	*hīzha*,	*hīzhā*,	*hīzhipa*.
hoghing,	weep,	*hogh*,[5]	*hoghā*,	*hoghpa*.[5]
hūlāi-ing,	howl,	*hūlāi*,	*hūlāi-ā*,	*hulāipa*.
hūling,		*hūl(a)*,	*hūlā*,	*hūl(i)pa*.
hunning,[6]	look,	*hur*,	*hurā*,	*huppa*.
huring,				
hūrēnging,	break out,	*hūrēng*,	*hūrēngā*,	*hūrēngpa*.
hushing,	burn,	*hush(a)*,	*hushā*,	*hush(i)pa*.

[1] Also *haṛsing*, §16; for derivatives *cf.* §274.
[2] Also *hatining*, *hatiring*, *cf.* §263.
[3] *Hēfing* is of course intimately related to *harfing*.
[4] Pres. *kāv*, *cf.* §264.
[5] Occasionally also *ho*, *hopa*, *cf.* §§ 190, 230.
[6] *Cf.* §262.

Infinitive.		Imperative. (2nd p. s.)	Past. (3rd p. s.)	Prohibitive. (2nd p. s.)
illing,[1]	leave,	*illa, ille,*	*illā*,	*illipa.*
		illē,	...	*illēpa.*
jakking,	cough,	*jakka*,	*jakkā*,	*jakkipa.*
jalling,	herd (trs.),	*jalla*,	*jallā*,	*jallipa.*
jupping,	jump over,	*juppa*,	*juppā*,	*juppipa.*
kahing,[2]	die,	*kah*,	*kask*,	*kaspa.*
kanning,[3]	do,	*ka, kar*,	*karē*,	*kappa.*
karghing,	shear,	*kargh(a)*,	*karghā*,	*kargh(i)pa.*
karring,	scrape out,	*karra*,	*karrā*,	*karripa.*
kashshing,	eject,	*kashsha*,	*kashshā*,	*kashshipa.*
kaṭṭing,	win,	*kaṭṭa*,	*kaṭṭā*,	*kaṭṭipa.*
kāvāring,	poison,	*kāvāra*,	*kāvārā*,	*kāvāripa.*
kishking,[4]	pluck off,	*kishk(a)*,	*kishkā*,	*kishk(i)pa.*
kitting,	groan,	*kitta*,	*kittā*,	*kittipa.*
konḍing,	bore out,	*konḍa*,	*konḍā*,	*konḍipa.*
koṭing,	cut in pieces,	*koṭa*,	*koṭā*,	*koṭipa.*
kuning,[5]	eat,	*kun*,	*kung*,	*kumpa.*
kūring,	roll up,	*kūr(a)*,	*kūrā*,	*kūr(i)pa.*
kurring,	keep back,	*kurra*,	*kurrā*,	*kurripa.*
kuṭṭing,	pound,	*kuṭṭa*,	*kuṭṭā*,	*kuṭṭipa.*
khāching,	sleep,	*khāch(a)*,	*khāchā*,	*khāch(i)pa.*
khalling,[6]	strike,	*khalh*,	*khalk*,	*khalpa.*

1 Pres. *illiv, illēv*, §202.

2 Pres. *kahēv*, §203; for *kas-* *cf.* §217; *kasning* is occasionally used in some hill dialects, *e. g.*, the Kidrani.

3 *Cf.* §258.

4 The included *-k-* is sometimes omitted, espec. in the pres. neg.: *kishpar*.

5 Pres. *kunēv*, §203.

6 Imp. plur. *khalbo*, §197; pres. *khalēv*, §203.

Infinitive.		Imperative. (2nd p. s.)	Past. (3rd p. s.)	Prohibitive. (2nd p. s.)
khaning,	see,	*khan*,	*khanā*,	*khampa*.
kharring,	sprout,	*kharra*,	*kharris*, *kharrā*,	*kharripa*.
kharring,	proceed,	*kharre*,	*kharrā*,	*kharripa*.
khasāling,	chew,	*khasāl(a)*,	*khasālā*,	*khasāl(i)pa*.
khassing,	throw,	*khassa*,	*khassā*,	*khassipa*.
khoshking,[1]	rub,	*khoshk(a)*,	*khoshkā*,	*khoshk(i)pa*.
khuling,	fear,	*khul(a)*,	*khulā*,	*khul(i)pa*.
khulīng,		*khulī*,	*khulīs*,	*khulīpa*.
khulling,	pierce,	*khulla*,	*khullā*,	*khullipa*.
khutting,	dig,	*khutta*,	*khuttā*,	*khuttipa*.
khwāhing,	graze (trs.),	*khwāha*,	*khwāhā*,	*khwāhipa*.
khwāhing,	desire,	*khwāha*,	*khwāhis*, *khwāhā*,	*khwāhipa*.
khwāning,	read,	*khwān(a)*,	*khwānā*,	*khwāmpa*, *khwānipa*.
lagging,	climb,	*lagga*,	*laggā*,	*laggipa*.
lakking,	lap up,	*lakka*,	*lakkā*,	*lakkipa*.
lānching,	gird up,	*lānch(a)*,	*lānchā*,	*lānch(i)pa*.
larzing,[2]	tremble,	*larza*,	*larzā*,	*larzipa*.
lēṭing,	lie down,	*lēṭ(a)*,	*lēṭā*,	*lēṭ(i)pa*.
lichching,	stick,	*lichcha*,	*lichchā*,	*lichchipa*.
lojing,	smear,	*loja*,	*lojā*,	*lojipa*.
loṛing,	root up,	*loṛa*,	*loṛā*,	*loṛipa*.
makhing,	laugh,	*makh(a)*,	*makhā*,	*makh(i)pa*.
maling,	open,	*mal(a)*,	*malā*,	*mal(i)pa*.

[1] Occasionally also *khoshing*, *khosha*, etc.

[2] Also *laṛzing*, §16.

Infinitive.		Imperative. (2nd p. s.)	Past. (3rd p. s.)	Prohibitive. (2nd p. s.)
manning,[1]	become,	*ma, mar*,	*mass*,	*mafa*.
manning,	obey,	*manna*,	*mannā*,	*mannipa*.
marring,	obey,	*marra*,	*marrā*,	*marripa*.
mashing,	wash (the head),	*mash(a)*,	*mashā*,	*mash(i)pa*.
miṛing,	drive out,	*miṛ(a)*,	*miṛā*,	*miṛ(i)pa*.
mūg͟hing,	sew,	*mūg͟h(a)*,	*mūg͟hā*,	*mūg͟h(i)pa*.
mukking,	stammer,	*mukka*,	*mukkā*,	*mukkipa*.
murīfing,	stretch out,	*murīf*,	*murīfē*,	*murīfpa*.
mūshkking,	rub,	*mūshk(a)*,	*mūshkā*,	*mūshk(i)pa*.
nāling,	groan,	*nāl(a)*,	*nālā*,	*nāl(i)pa*.
narring,	flee,	*narra*,	*narrā*,	*narripa*.
nusing,	grind (corn),	*nus(a)*,	*nusā*,	*nus(i)pa*.
pāching,	peel,	*pāch(a)*,	*pāchā*,	*pāch(i)pa*.
pākāling,	strain (through cloth),	*pākāl(a)*,	*pākālā*,	*pākāl(i)pa*.
palēfing,	boil,	*palēf*,	*palēfē*,	*palēfpa*.
pāling,	become wet,	*pāla, pāle*,[2]	*pālis*,	*pālipa*.
pāning,[3]	say,	*pā, pār*,	*pārē*,	*pāpa*.
paṭṭing,	seek,	*paṭṭa*,	*paṭṭā*,	*paṭṭipa*.
pēhing,	enter,	*pēha*,	*pēhā*,	*pēhipa*.
pēṛing,	roll up,	*pēṛa*,	*pēṛā*,	*pēṛipa*.
pil͟hing,	squeeze,	*pil͟h(a)*,	*pil͟hā*,	*pil͟h(i)pa*.
pinḍing,	beg,	*pinḍa*,	*pinḍā*,	*pinḍipa*.
pinning,	be broken,	*pinna*,	*pinnā*,	*pinnipa*.
pirāi-ing,	run dry,	*pirāi*,	*pirāi-is*,	*pirāipa*.
pirāi-inging	run dry,	*pirāi-ing*,	*pirāi-ingā*,	*pirāi-ingpa*.

[1] *Cf.* §256. [2] Also *pālē*, *cf.* §194. [3] Pres. *pāv*, §204; prob. fut. *pāroṭ*, §207.

Infinitive.		Imperative. (2nd p. s.)	Past. (3rd p. s.)	Prohibitive. (2nd p. s.)
pirghing,	break,	*pirgh(a)*,	*pirghā*,	*pirgh(i)pa.*
piring,	swell (intr.),	*pira*,	*piris*,	*piripa.*
pirring,	blink,	*pirra*,	*pirrā*,	*pirripa.*
piṭṭing,	curse,	*piṭṭa*,	*piṭṭā*,	*piṭṭipa.*
porring,	hatch,	*porra*,	*porrā*,	*porripa.*
poshing,	suck,	*posh(a)*,	*poshā*,	*posh(i)pa.*
prinching,	squeeze,	*princh(a)*,	*princhā*,	*princh(i)pa.*
puling,	rob,	*pul(a)*,	*pulā*,	*pul(i)pa.*
putrēnging,	enter,	*putrēng*,	*putrēngā*,	*putrēngpa.*
rabaṛing,	be delirious,	*rabaṛa*,	*rabaṛā*,	*rabaṛipa.*
raghāming,	instruct,	*raghām(a)*,	*raghāmā*,	*raghām(i) pa.*
rapaṭing,	talk in one's sleep,	*rapaṭa*,	*rapaṭā*,	*rapaṭipa.*
rasēnging, }	arrive,	{ *rasēng*,	*rasēngā*,	*rasēngpa.*
rasing, }		{ *rasa*,	*rasā*,	*rasipa.*
raṭing,	grumble,	*raṭ(a)*,	*raṭā*,	*raṭ(i)pa.*
rēfing,	cheat,	*rēf(a)*,	*rēfē*, *rēfā*,	*rēf(i)pa.*
rēsing,	spin,	*rēs(a)*,	*rēsā*,	*rēs(i)pa.*
rofing,	sweep up,	*rof(a)*,	*rofē*, *rofā*,	*rof(i)pa.*
rūsing,	pluck,	*rūs(a)*,	*rūsā*,	*rūs(i)pa.*
rūting,	reap,	*rūt(a)*,	*rūtā*,	*rūt(i)pa.*
saghing,	pound,	*sagh(a)*,	*saghā*,	*sagh(i)pa.*
saling, }	stand,	{ *sal(a)*,	...	*sal(i)pa.*
salīng, }		{ *salī*,	*salīs*,	*salīpa.*
sambarēnging, }	get ready,	{ *sambarēng*,	*sambarēngā*,	*sambarēngpa.*
sambaring, }		{ *sambara*,	*sambarā*,	*sambaripa.*
sangarēnging,	filtrate,	*sangarēng*,	*sangarēngā*,	*sangarēngpa.*

Infinitive.		Imperative. (2nd p. s.)	Past. (3rd p. s.)	Prohibitive. (2nd p. s.)
sarring,	grow up,	*sarra*,	*sarris*, *sarrā*,	*sarripa*.
saṛēnging, *saṛing*,	rot,	*saṛēng*, *saṛ(a)*,	*saṛēngā*, *saṛā*, *saṛis*,	*saṛēngpa*. *saṛ(i)pa*.
silling,	wash,	*sil(la)*,[1]	*sillā*,	*sil(li)pa*.
sīrring,	recoil,	*sīrra*,	*sīrrā*,	*sīrripa*.
sīṛing,	wait for,	*sīṛ(a)*,	*sīṛā*,	*sīṛ(i)pa*.
siṭṭing,	hop,	*siṭṭa*,	*siṭṭā*,	*siṭṭipa*.
soṭēfing,	provoke,	*soṭēf*,	*soṭēfē*,	*soṭēfpa*.
suring,	move,	*sur(a)*,	*surā*,	*sur(i)pa*.
shāg̲h̲ing,	pour,	*shā(g̲h̲)*,	*shāg̲h̲ā*,	*shā(g̲h̲)pa*.
shalāping,	wash (clothes),	*shalāp(a)*,	*shalāpā*,	*shalāp(i)pa*.
shĩṛshĩṛing,	neigh,	*shĩṛshĩṛ(a)*,	*shĩṛshĩṛā*,	*shĩṛshĩṛ(i)pa*.
shīring,	smooth out,	*shīra*,	*shīrā*,	*shīripa*.
sholing,	throw,	*shol(a)*,	*sholā*,	*shol(i)pa*.
shūling,	hem,	*shūl(a)*,	*shūlā*,	*shūl(i)pa*.
shurring,	scratch,	*shurra*,	*shurrā*,	*shurripa*.
tafing,	bind,	*taf*,	*tafē*,	*tafpa*.
takking,	covet,	*takka*,	*takkā*,	*takkipa*.
tamming,	fall,	*tam(ma)*,	*tammā*,	*tam(mi)pa*.
taring,	spin,	*tar(a)*,	*tarā*,	*tar(i)pa*.
taṛing,	cut,	*taṛ*,	*taṛē*,	*taṛpa*.
tassing,	pant,	*tassa*,	*tassā*,	*tassipa*.
tik̲h̲ing,	place,	*tik̲h̲*,	*tik̲h̲ā*,	*tik̲h̲pa*.
tining,[2]	give,	*ēte*,	*tiss*,	*tifa*.
toning,[3] *toring*,	hold,	*to*, *tor*,	*torē*,	*topa*.

[1] Also *sillē*, *cf.* §194. [2] *Cf.* §260.
[3] Pres. *toriv*, §204; prob. fut. *torot*, §207.

Infinitive.		Imperative. (2nd p. s.)	Past. (3rd p. s.)	Prohibitive. (2nd p. s.)
trakhkhing,	burst (intr.),	*trakh(kha)*,	*trakhkhā*,	*trakh(khi)pa*.
traḍḍing,	prance,	*traḍḍa*,	*traḍḍā*,	*traḍḍipa*.
trāshing,	plane,	*trāsh(a)*,	*trāshā*,	*trāsh(i)pa*.
trikking,	sprout,	*trikka*,	*trikkā*,	*trikkipa*.
trujjing,	choke (intr.),	*trujja*,	*trujjā*,	*trujjipa*.
trukking,	pluck up,	*trukka*,	*trukkā*,	*trukkipa*.
tūling,[1]	sit,	*tūlh*,	*tūs*,	*tūlpa*.
tusēnging,	faint,	*tusēng*,	*tusēngā*,	*tusēngpa*.
tusing,	faint,	*tus(a)*,	*tusā*,	*tus(i)pa*.
tuṛēnging,	get unhemmed,	*tuṛēng*,	*tuṛēngā*,	*tuṛēngpa*.
ṭaghalēnging,	be displaced	*ṭaghalēng*,	*ṭaghalēngā*,	*ṭaghalēngpa*.
ṭaghaling,	be displaced	*ṭaghala*,	*ṭaghalā*,	*ṭaghalipa*.
ṭahing,	agree,	*ṭaha*,	*ṭahā*,	*ṭahipa*.
ṭanḍarēnging,	be numbed,	*ṭanḍarēng*,	*ṭanḍarēngā*,	*ṭanḍarēngpa*.
ṭanging,	hang (trs.),	*ṭanga*,	*ṭangā*,	*ṭangipa*.
ṭoking,	hammer,	*ṭoka*,	*ṭokā*,	*ṭokipa*.
vadding,	increase (intr.),	*vadda*,	*vaddā*,	*vaddipa*.
vahing,	flow,	*vaha*,	*vahā*,	*vahipa*.
vakking,	bark,	*vakka*,	*vakkā*,	*vakkipa*.
zumburēnging,	squat,	*zumburēng*,	*zumburēngā*,	*zumburēngpa*.
zumburing,	squat,	*zumbura*,	*zumburā*,	*zumburipa*.
zhūnging,	buzz,	*zhūnga*,	*zhūngā*,	*zhūngipa*.

[1] Imp. plur. *tūlbo*, §197: pres. *tūliv*. Dialectical variant *tūsing*, past *tūsī*, *tūsis*.

Verbal Derivatives.

§**266.** This list of verbs may be conveniently followed by a reference to nouns and adjectives which are either derived from, or intimately related to, verbal roots. These fall into two main classes, according as they are derived directly from a verbal base, or are formed by the addition of a formative ending.

§**267.** The former class is further subdivided. In many cases the noun coincides with the crude base: *drik*, jump; *hakkal*, shout; *hamp*, loading; *pul*, robbery; *shūl*, hem; *hichchān*, sneeze; *kaṭ*, winnings; *tak*, desire. In the last three instances the derivative seems to preserve the base in a purer form than the imperative singular. Like it, however, it sometimes takes on an apparently non-radical final *-a*: *chanḍa*, shock; *hikka*, hiccough; *jakka*, cough; *giḍḍa*, nodding with drowsiness. Again, in *halh* and *tūlh*, the use of which is confined to the compound phrases *halh o tiss*, taking and giving, *bash o tūlh*, uprising and down-sitting, it shows a peculiar phonetic modification of the crude base, only found otherwise in the imperative singular (§190). In a second group the derivative noun is identical with the past stem: *tiss*, generosity; *khulīs*, fear. In *pirēs*, swelling, there is a slight vowel change. *Murīs*, length, appears to be an analogous formation, but there is no simple verb to correspond to *murīfing*, to stretch out, to extend, which is a causal in form.

§**268.** *Khan*, eye, probably belongs to a different category, like the loan-words *bashkh* (Persian *bakhsh*), allotment, and *khwāst*, request, in which the nouns seem clearly prior to the verbs. Indeed, the form of the noun in the last instance is possibly responsible in part for the apparently abnormal appearance of a final sibilant in the past stem of the derived verb *khwāhing*, to request.

§**269.** Conspicuous among the formative endings is *-āra*, which is employed to form a large group of nouns denoting sound: *gārrāra*, bleating; *ghurrāra*, growling; *hīzhāra*, whistling; *shīṛshīṛāra*, neighing; *vakkāra*, barking; *zhūngāra*, buzzing. There are one or two miscellaneous formations: *trakhkhas*, crack; *buruṭ*, crumb. In *kharrisī*, green (grass), a formative *-ī* has apparently been attached to the past stem. A final *-ī* serves as an adjectival formative in *marrī*, tame. But the chief adjectival formative is *-un* (*cf.* §77), which is probably not unconnected with the perfect formative *-un* (§223): *kharrun*, green; *bārun*, dry; *pālun*, wet; *bāsun*, hot; *bissun*, ripe. The doubling of the final consonant of the base in the last example is worth noting.

§**270.** A few illustrations of the use of these derivative nouns may be of interest: *ballo drikkas khalk*, he made a big jump; *asi chanḍato drakht tammā*, the tree fell with one shock; *o tēnā māranā kulle kaṭṭe tēnaṭ-a kunēk*, he enjoys all his son's earnings himself; *ī nē pātanuṭ ki kanto halh o tiss karak*, I haven't invited you to have dealings with me; *tissān bandagh dam-a dēk, khudā dam-a dappak*, though man wearies of giving, God never wearies; *kanā khulīsān onā jānaṭī laṛza tammā*, through fear of me, trembling seized his body.

The Passive.

§**271.** Although there are in a few isolated cases separate verbs for the active and passive, *e.g.*, *pirghing*, to break, *pinning*, to be broken, the passive is regularly formed from the transitive verb by suffixing the formative *-ing* to the base, and attaching the ordinary conjugational terminations :—

tikhing,	to place;	*tikhing-ing*,	to be placed.
ḍakking,	to hide;	*ḍakking-ing*,	to be hidden.
khaning,	to see;	*khaning-ing*,	to be seen.

§**272.** In cases like *illing*, to leave, *khuling*, *khulīng*, to fear, in which the base is really two-fold (*cf.* §194), there may be two forms of the passive: *illinging*, *illēnging*, to be left; *khulinging*, *khulīnging*, to be feared. The case is of course different with variants like *sholinging*, *sholanging*, to be poured, in which *-ang* is merely a variant of the passive formative. It obtains chiefly in cases like *malanging* (*mąlinging*), to be opened, in which the attraction of the vowel of the base appears to have made itself felt.

§**273.** Verbs in *-n* generally, though irregularly, retain the nasal in the passive: *kanning*, to do, *kanninging*, to be done; *danning*, to take away, *danninging*, to be taken away; *pāning*, to say, *pāninging*, to be said; *toning*, to hold, *toninging*, to be held. But except in the case of *kanning*, there are also secondary forms founded regularly on the base in *-r*: *daringing*, *pāringing*, *toringing*. The passive of *tining*, to give, is similarly *tininging*, less commonly *tiringing*.

§**274.** A passive is formed from the causal of an intransitive verb (§285): *kahing*, to die, *kasfing*, to kill, *kasfinging*, to be killed; *tūling*, to sit, *tūlifing*, to seat, *tūlifinging*, to be seated. Somewhat analogous is the complicated case of *harsēfinging* (*hąrsēfinging*), to be made to turn oneself; it is the passive of *harsēfing*, to make a man turn himself; *harsēfing* is the causal of *harsēnging*, to turn oneself; and *harsēnging* is the middle or neuter (§277) of the transitive verb *harsing* (*hąrsing*), to turn. The passive of the simple verb is *harsinging* (*hąrsinging*), to be turned.

§**275.** Except as regards the adjectival participle and the noun of obligation, the conjugation of the passive verb, both affirmative and negative, is perfectly normal, the ordinary conjugational terminations being suffixed to the passive base in the usual manner. It has already been pointed out that the *-g* of the passive formative may be dropped at pleasure before the imperative plural termination *-bo* (§197) and the present-negative sign *-pa* (§230), the *n* changing in consequence to *m*; that the past stem in the affirmative ends in *-ā* (§215); that the adjectival participle and the noun of obligation in the affirmative coincide with the forms in the active verb (§§212, 213); and that the same remark applies in the negative to the latter (§242), the passive like the ordinary verb being devoid of a negative participle as well as of a negative infinitive (§225). It will thus suffice to give a skeleton conjugation of a typical passive verb, *harsinging* (*haṛsinging*), to be turned.

	Affirmative.	Negative.
Infinitive:	*harsinging.*	...
Pres. adv. part.:	*harsingisa.*	...
Pres. adj. part.:	*harsok.*	...
Noun of obligation:	*harsoī.*	*harsparoī.* *harsiparoī.*
Imperative:	*harsing.*	*harsingpa.* *harsimpa.*
Present indefinite:	*harsingiv.*	*harsingpar.* *harsimpar.*
Present-future:	*harsingiva.*	*harsingpara.* *harsimpara.*
Probable future:	*harsingoṭ.*	*harsingparoṭ.* *harsimparoṭ.*
Past conditional:	*harsingosuṭ.*	*harsingparosuṭ.* *harsimparosuṭ.*
Past:	*harsingāṭ.*	*harsingtavaṭ.*
Imperfect:	*harsingāṭa.*	*harsingtavaṭa.*
Pluperfect:	*harsingāsuṭ.*	*harsingtavēsuṭ.*
Perfect	*harsingānuṭ.*	*harsingtanuṭ.*

The Neuter Verb.

§**276.** There is a class of verbs which, while on the whole resembling passives rather than actives in form, differ in certain respects from both, and lie in meaning midway between the two. The formative of such verbs is *-ēng*, which is suffixed to the base in the same way as the passive formative *-ing*: *harsēnging* (*haṛsēnging*), to return; *rasēnging*, to arrive; *dudēnging*, to run; *putrēnging*, to enter; *saṛēnging*, to rot, to be well cooked; *chirrēnging*, to roam; *tusēnging*, to faint. Such verbs have frequently a secondary simple form with the same meaning: *rasing*, *saṛing*, *tusing*.

§**277.** In the somewhat rare cases in which there is also a simple transitive verb in existence the derivative verb has a distinctly middle force: *harsing* (*haṛsing*), to turn, *harsēnging* (*haṛsēnging*), to turn oneself, to return, as opposed to the passive *harsinging* (*haṛsinging*), to be turned (§274). Again, *halēnging* in the compound *kī halēnging*, to set (of the sun), is a middle from *halling*, to take, and the compound literally means 'to take oneself below' (§295). The passive on the other hand is of course *hallinging*, to be taken, in which the consonant of the root is doubled as in the infinitive of the simple verb (§185). Similarly the relationship of *danning*, to take away, to *darēnging* in the compounds *dam danning*, *dam darēnging*, to be tired, to tire oneself, is clearly that of a transitive to a middle verb, though a distinction is hardly ever marked.

§**278.** The conjugation of the neuter verb differs in some respects from the conjugation of the passive. The infinitive termination is frequently dropped: *harsēng*, *rasēng*, *dudēng*. This is more especially the case in the so-called tenses of actuality: *ī harsēngaṭī uṭ*, I am returning; *ī rasēngaṭī assuṭ*, I was arriving; *ī dudēngaṭī affaṭ*, I am not running. In the adjectival participle and the noun of obligation the formative is not dropped as in the passive, which the conjugation, both affirmative and negative, otherwise resembles :—

	Affirmative.	Negative.
Infinitive:	*harsēng(ing).*	...
Pres. adv. part.:	*harsēngisa.*	...
Pres. adj. part.:	*harsēngok.*	...
Noun of obligation:	*harsēngoī.*	*harsēngparoī.* *harsēmparoī.*
Imperative:	*harsēng.*	*harsēngpa.* *harsēmpa.*
Present indefinite:	*harsēngiv.*	*harsēngpar.* *harsēmpar.*
Present-future:	*harsēngiva.*	*harsēngpara.* *harsēmpara.*
Probable future:	*harsēngoṭ.*	*harsēngparoṭ.* *harsēmparoṭ.*
Past conditional:	*harsēngosuṭ.*	*harsēngparosuṭ.* *harsēmparosuṭ.*
Past:	*harsēngāṭ.*	*harsēngtavaṭ.*
Imperfect:	*harsēngāṭa.*	*harsēngtavaṭa.*
Pluperfect:	*harsēngāsuṭ.*	*harsēngtavēsuṭ.*
Perfect:	*harsēngānuṭ.*	*harsēngtanuṭ.*

Of course if there is also a simple form besides the neuter form, both persist side by side throughout the conjugation: *rasēng(ing)*, *rasing*, to arrive; *rasēngisa*, *rasisa*; *rasēngok*, *rasok*; *rasēngoī*, *rasoī*; *rasēngparoī*, *rasēmparoī*, *rasiparoī*, etc. Both forms moreover are represented in the causal (§284).

§279. The verb *baṭinging*, to summon, which also appears as *baṭanging* (*cf.* §272 *fin.*), partakes somewhat of the nature of a deponent: it is similar in form to a passive, though purely active in meaning. It is, however, conjugated on the lines of the neuter verb: *ī baṭingaṭī* (*baṭangaṭī*) *uṭ*, *baṭingisa*, *baṭingok*, *baṭingoī*, etc. In the causal *baṭingifing* it displays a marked divergence from the neuter (§284). Somewhat similar is the case of *daṛinging*, to descend: *daṛingok*, *daṛingoī*, etc. But the simple forms *daṛing*, *daṛok*, *daṛoī*, etc., are at least equally common, while the causal *daṛifing* is regular. There are a few other instances of the same kind.

The Causal.

§280. A causal may be formed from practically every verb in the language by suffixing the causal formative *-if* to the base and adding the ordinary conjugational terminations:—

bining, to hear;	*binifing*, to make to hear.
bārring, to become dry;	*bārifing*, to make dry.
shāghing, to pour;	*shāghifing*, to cause to be poured.
tikhing, to place;	*tikhifing*, to cause to be placed.

§281. If the base ends in a long vowel, it is of course retained in the causal, and there may thus be alternative forms of the causal corresponding to alternative forms of the imperative and other parts of the simple verb: *illēfing*, *illifing*, to cause to be left; *khulīfing*, *khulifing*, to frighten; *salīfing*, *salifing*, to make to stand.

§282. The verbs in *-n* form their causal from the strengthened base in *-r*:—

manning, to become;	*marifing*, to make to become.
banning, to come;	*barifing*, to make to come.
kanning, to do;	*karifing*, to cause to be done.
danning, to take away;	*darifing*, to cause to be taken away.
pāning, to say;	*pārifing*, to cause to be said.
toning, to hold;	*torifing*, to cause to be held.

In the causal *tining*, to give, again follows the model of these verbs: *tirifing*, to cause to be given. *Bēning*, to wear, forms its causal in two ways: *bēnifing*, *bērifing*, to clothe.

§283. There are one or two irregular formations. The causal of *kahing*, to die, is formed from the same base as the past and the negative: *kasfing* (*kasifing*), to kill, the included vowel of the formative being usually dropped. The vowel is similarly dropped in *k͟hwāfing*, to graze (trs.), the causal of *k͟hwāhing*, to graze (intr.), the superfluous aspirate being dropped at the same time. On the other hand the causal of *k͟hwāhing*, to ask for, is formed regularly: *k͟hwāhifing*, to cause to be asked for.

§284. Neuter verbs in forming their causal retain the vowel only of the neuter formative: *harsēnging*, to return, *harsēfing*, to make to return; *dudēnging*, to run, *dudēfing*, to make to run. If there is a secondary simple form of the neuter verb, the causal is similarly two-fold: *rasēnging*, *rasing*, to arrive, *rasēfing*, *rasifing*, to make to arrive. The verb *baṭinging* (*baṭanging*), to summon, has been already shown (§279) to be on a different footing; its causal is *baṭingifing*. The causal of *daṛinging*, to descend, on the other hand is regular: *daṛifing*.

§285. It will have been observed that the causals fall naturally into two groups, according to the nature of the simple verb from which they are derived. Causals derived from intransitives are active causals and frequently take the place of the corresponding transitive verb: *kahing*, to die, *kasfing*, to kill; *tūling*, to sit, *tūlifing*, to seat; *k͟hulīng*, to be afraid, *k͟hulīfing*, to frighten. On the other hand causals derived from transitives are passive causals: *ḍakking*, to hide, *ḍakkifing*, to cause to be hidden; *k͟halling*, to strike, *k͟halifing*, to cause to be struck; *gwafing*, to weave, *gwafifing*, to cause to be woven; *kanning*, to do, *karifing*, to cause to be done.

§**286.** It follows that if the verb is at once transitive and intransitive, its causal may be either active or passive: *pāning*, to speak, to say, *pārifing*, to make to speak, to cause to be said; *khaning*, to see, *khanifing*, to make to see, to cause to be seen; *bining*, to hear, *binifing*, to make to hear, to cause to be heard; *kuning*, to eat, *kunifing*, to feed, to cause to be eaten.

§**287.** There may be a double causal, *i.e.*, a passive causal of the causal of an intransitive verb: *kahing*, to die, *kasfing*, to kill, *kasfifing*, to cause to be killed; *khulīng*, to be afraid, *khulīfing*, to frighten, *khulīfifing*, to cause to be frightened.

§**288.** A few verbs, such as *harrifing*, to ask, *harfing*, to lift up, *soṭēfing* (*soṭifing*), to provoke, are causals in appearance, but if they are really causals, the simple verbs have dropped out of the language. Similarly *murīfing*, to stretch out, has the appearance of being a causal derived from a base *murī-*, which seems to be contained in the noun *murīs*, length (§267 *fin.*), but the place of the simple verb is taken by the compound *murr manning*, to be far.

§**289.** The conjugation of the causal verb is perfectly regular both in the affirmative and negative; the past stem in the affirmative ends in *-ē* (§216).

	Affirmative.	Negative.
Infinitive:	*tikhifing.*	...
Pres. adv. part.:	*tikhifisa.*	...
Pres. adj. part.:	*tikhifok.*	...
Noun of obligation:	*tikhifoī.*	*tikhifparoī.*
Imperative:	*tikhif.*	*tikhifpa.*
Present indefinite:	*tikhifiv.*	*tikhifpar.*
Present-future:	*tikhifiva.*	*tikhifpara.*
Probable future:	*tikhifoṭ.*	*tikhifparoṭ.*
Past conditional:	*tikhifosuṭ.*	*tikhifparosuṭ.*
Past:	*tikhifēṭ.*	*tikhiftavaṭ.*
Imperfect:	*tikhifēṭa.*	*tikhiftavaṭa.*
Pluperfect:	*tikhifēsuṭ.*	*tikhiftavēsuṭ.*
Perfect:	*tikhifēnuṭ.*	*tikhiftanuṭ.*

Compound Verbs.

§290. Though the term 'compound verbs' is for the most part a misnomer, it serves as a convenient heading to bring together certain important classes of circumlocutory phrases.

Nominal Compounds.

§291. For lack of a better term we may designate as nominal compounds such phrases as are compounded of a predicative noun (substantive or adjective) and a verb. These of course are not real compounds, and belong rather to the dictionary than to grammar. But they bulk largely in the language, somewhat scantily provided as it is with simple verbs. A small selection will therefore be made from the profusion which offers itself, and these characteristic examples will sufficiently indicate the nature of this important class of phrase.

§292. Several useful couplets are formed with *kanning*, to do, and *manning*, to become :—

bash kanning, to raise up ;	*bash manning*, to arise.
chaṭ kanning, to destroy ;	*chaṭ manning*, to be destroyed.
gaṭ kanning, to engage ;	*gaṭ manning*, to be engaged.
lāb kanning, to harvest ;	*lāb manning*, to be harvested.
much kanning, to collect (trs.) ;	*much manning*, to collect (intr.).
rāhī kanning, to despatch ;	*rāhī manning*, to set out.
tud kanning, to send with ;	*tud manning*, to go in company with.
ṭung kanning, to bore a hole in ;	*ṭung manning*, to be breached.
yala kanning, to release ;	*yala manning*, to be released.

§**293.** *Kanning* indeed is particularly often employed: *aḍ kanning*, to wait, to halt; *barām kanning*, to marry; *kēb kanning*, to approach; *hīt kanning*, to chat; *langār kanning*, to plough; *khar kanning*, to get annoyed; *marrām kanning*, to call out for; *pāṭ kanning*, to pick up sticks. So is *tining*, to give: *aḍ tining*, to restrain; *barām tining*, to give in marriage; *bash tining*, to throw up (in the air); *chaṭ tining*, to sprinkle; *kirēng tining*, to abuse; *mon tining*, to send; *musiṭ tining*, lit. to give three stones, to divorce; *nishān tining*, to show; *ṭik tining*, lit. to give a ray, to rise (of the sun). A few miscellaneous examples may be given: *chak khalling*, to look back (in running); *tūfak khalling*, to fire (at, with abl.); *aḍ halling*, to take shelter; *khaf toning*, to give ear to; *taḍ toning*, to resist; *dīr shāghing*, to bathe; *dū shāghing*, to put one's hand in, to meddle; *pēsh tamming*, to come forth; *drogh taṛing*, to lie; *chūcha khaning*, to give birth to a child; *gīrām hining*, to escape the memory; *gīrām illing*, to forget; *dam kashshing*, to take a rest; *dam danning* (*darēnging*), to be tired; *dam darifing*, to tire out.

§**294.** Somewhat analogous are the compounds which contain a noun in some oblique case: *monaṭī tamming*, to go in front; *monaṭī kanning*, to put in front; *monaṭī shāghing*, to drive ahead, to admit into one's presence; *monaṭī harsēnging*, to face, to oppose; *dūṭī banning*, *dūṭī tamming*, to fall to one's hand, to be secured. The last two examples usually appear abbreviated: *dū banning*, *du tamming.* It seems possible that the first element of the compound phrase *tungān hining*, to go off into a sound sleep, is an ablative of an otherwise obsolete noun, *tung*, sleep (*cf. tugh*).

§**295.** There remain three groups of especial interest: (1) *kī halēnging*, to set (of the sun); *kē danning*, to swallow; *kē harsing*, to usurp; *ki banning*, to knock against; *ki tamming*, to descend; (2) *bē sholing*, to bathe (intr.);

bē khalling, to cross through (water); *bē harsing*, to turn over; *bē harsēnging*, to return back; *bē harsēfing*, to turn over; *bē bāling*, to cross over; (3) *ī-kashshing*, to thrust in; *ī-khalling*, to insert bit by bit.

Of these, *ki tamming*, *ki banning* are practically confined to the particular form of the Jhalawan dialect spoken by the Mengals of Saruna, but the phrases are linguistically of some importance. With the exception of *bāling*, which is otherwise obsolete, the last element in each case is a verb in common use. It seems clear that *ki* (*kē, kī*) is a stunted form of the full-word *kēragh*, bottom (§356), or at any rate a derivative from the same root. Thus *kī halēnging* means literally to take oneself below (§277), *kē danning*, to take away down, and so on. Similarly *bē* seems to be intimately related to *bāṭagh*, top (§355); a link between the two exists in the adjective *bēṭ*, on: *kho khākharāi bēṭ e*, the pot's on the fire; *hamē tūfakas ki nī khalkus, rad mass yā bēṭ?* did the shot you fired miss or hit? Thus *bē sholing* means literally to pour (water) on oneself; *bē khalling*, to strike over or across, and so on. The derivation of the first element in the third group is probably of a similar nature, but it is not easy to trace.

§296. The curious dialectical *kiballing* (past *kibalkuṭ*), to stumble, does not belong to the first group. The peculiar form of the past shows clearly that it is compounded with *halling*, to seize, and it seems no less clear that the other element in the compound is the word *kēb*, near, (§367). Nor has the first element *bāi* in the compound *bāi tining*, to lose (in a race or in gambling), any connection with *bē* in the second group. It is found also in the Pashtu *bailēdal*, and the Dehwari *bai dādan*; from it is formed a causal *bāifing*, to make to lose, as well as the somewhat rare passive *bāinging*, to be lost.

Potential Compounds.

§**297.** Ability to perform an action is expressed by coupling the infinitive with the finite parts of *kanning*, to do: *hining kēv*, I may be able to go; *halling-a kēva*, I can seize; *kanning kattavaṭ*, I could not do; *pāning kapparoṭ*, I shall probably not be able to speak, and so on.

§**298.** Similarly the possibility of an action being performed may be expressed by coupling the infinitive with *manning*, to become: *ī halling-a marēva*, I can be caught; *kanning matau*, it could not be done. But this periphrasis is also employed instead of the ordinary passive without suggesting any question of possibility: I will be caught; it was not done.

Inceptive Compounds.

§**299.** Inception is expressed by a phrase composed of *tamming*, to fall, and the infinitive of the verb in the locative in *-aṭī*: *hoghingaṭī tammipa*, don't fall a-weeping; *ī narringaṭī tammiva*, I'll set off running.

Frequentative and Continuative Compounds.

§**300.** The ideas of frequent and continuous action are expressed in one and the same way by coupling the adverbial participle of the verb with *hining*, to go, or *banning*, to come. The rest of the sentence or the context alone indicates whether the force of the phrase is frequentative or continuative: *narrisa kāik*, (i) he is always running away; (ii) he persists in his flight; *ī pārisa bassunuṭ*, (i) I have said times without number; (ii) I have never ceased saying.

Intensive or Completive Compounds.

§**301.** An intensive or completive force may be given in a few stereotyped cases by coupling the verb with *hining*, to go, both in the same tense: *o kunēk kāik*, he will devour up; *kask hinā*, he died outright; *num khalkure hināre*, you thrashed soundly.

The Syntax of the Verb.

§302. The following notes on the use of the various parts of the verb will ordinarily be of general application, a few remarks being added separately on the negative, the passive and the causal, with illustrations of the use of the so-called compound verbs. The neuter verb does not call for special comment.

The Infinitive.

§303. The infinitive is a verbal noun, declinable throughout the singular: *dushmannā khalling jwān e*, 'tis pleasant to strike the foe; *nanā tūlingnā jāga dād e*, this is our sitting place; *tēnā drogh taṛinge machchi ka*, cut your lying short; *narringān jang karosun*, oh that we had fought instead of running away; *duzzī kanningaṭ o tēne kharāb karē*, he ruined himself by thieving; *kane numā hīt kanningto chikār aff*, I've nothing to do with your talking; *bash manningki illēpēs-ta*, please don't let him get up; *nane khudā kahingiskā jitā kapp*, may God not part us till death. The two ordinary locatives are particularly important: *kanā īlum rāhī manningaṭī ass*, my brother was in the act of starting (§306); *tūfak khallingaṭī tammā*, he began to fire (§349); *ī ode dudēngāi khanāṭ*, I saw him on the point of running.

§304. In past narration the nominative of the infinitive is sometimes used for vividness in the place of a finite verb: *oftā tavār kanning, nanā urānā pēhing*, the moment they cried out, we entered the house.

§305. It will be observed that the infinitive, being a substantive, is ordinarily qualified by the object in the genitive. In this respect, however, it may also be treated as a verb: *dushmane khalling jwān e; oftā tavār kanning, nanā urāṭī pēhing*.

The Tenses of Actuality.

§**306.** The idiomatic use of the locative of the infinitive coupled with the auxiliary to form *quasi*-tenses of actuality deserves separate illustration. The regular expression for the true present, as distinguished from the present of habit, is of the form *ī tikhingaṭī uṭ*, I am in the act of placing, I am placing, and other tenses of the kind are formed on this analogy: *ballā apok tēnā arighe tēnā chunā apokāi soṭēfingaṭī e*, the elder wife is engaged in stirring up her husband against her young rival; *nan tēnaṭ numā pāraghāi banningaṭī assun, num tēne nāhak halāk karēre*, as a matter of fact we were on our way to you of our own accord, so you put yourselves out for nothing; *nēmrochāi ki sardār barē, ī lāb kanningaṭī maroṭ*, should the chief come at noon, I shall be in the middle of harvesting; *bāz vakht ī gobaṭ kanningaṭī massunuṭ ki od bassune*, many a time has he found me busy threshing on his arrival.

§**307.** The present of actuality is sometimes used with vivid effect in past narration: *kasaraṭ hināra, ant khanir? huchchīā banningaṭī e*, they were going on their way and what do you think they see?—the camelman is coming; *nāgumān murrān kuchakas khanān ki dudēngisa banningaṭī e*, all of a sudden we saw a dog from afar—it's coming at a run.

§**308.** No doubt the fact that the ordinary present is at the same time a future gave rise to this convenient mode of expression, as in the analogous case of Baluchi. There is an instructive parallel in the history of the English language. In Old English the present served also as a future, and recourse had to be had to some device to express distinctions of tense. Thus 'I am doing' came gradually to represent the type of the true present. The expressions 'I was doing,' 'I have been doing,' etc., are formed naturally on the present, but belong to later stages of development, and by these and similar devices the nicest shades of tense-distinction have been rendered possible. In Brahui there are traces of a like development: the present of actuality is firmly established, the use of the past is not uncommon, but the need for the other tenses has not yet made itself widely enough felt to give them a significant place in the language.

The Imperative and the Present Indefinite.

§309. The present indefinite, which might perhaps be appropriately termed the present subjunctive, supplements the imperative in two ways: it furnishes secondary forms in the second persons, and it supplies the missing forms in the other two.

Whereas the imperative expresses a direct and definite command, the present indefinite used as such in the second persons is less direct, and generally therefore more polite: *dā kārēme karak*, do this work; *dā kārēme kēs*, you will please do this work. The tense is moreover appropriate when the request or command is to be carried out at some later date: *dā ḍaghāre ēnakho das, ē ḍaghāre losāl dasis*, sow this land this year, and that land next year.

§310. As the imperative is confined to the second persons, recourse is had in the case of the other two to the present indefinite: *barēv*, let me come; *khudā khair kē*, God speed it; *jang kēn*, let us fight; *much marēr*, let them gather together. An appropriate imperative often introduces the present indefinite used in this manner: *ba ki kān*, come, let us go; *illē kāe*, let him go. The most important of such introductory words is *pānē*, which if an imperative at all—and in passing it may be noted that there are grounds for so regarding it—is not an imperative of any extant Brahui verb. It is more especially used in connection with the third persons of the present indefinite: *pānē* *tahṭī barē*, let him come in; *pānē tūlir*, let them sit down. But it is also used with the other persons: *pānē kāv*, let me go; *pānē asīka iragh kunēn*, let us eat for a while. It has at times a petulant or defiant force: *nā īlum pēshan salīsune—pānē sale*, your brother's standing outside—then let him stand. And this seems generally its force when used with the second persons of the present indefinite or of the imperative proper: *pānē kāre*, go, if you must go; *nī pānē duzzī ka, har vakhtas ki hallingās, nē tēnaṭ khabar tammoe*, go on with your thieving if you will, in the hour you're caught you'll learn the consequences without my help.

§**311.** The present indefinite is used potentially, more especially in interrogative sentences: *tūliv?* may I sit? *tūlis*, you may sit; *barē?* may he come? *barē*, he may come.

§**312.** It is used as an ordinary subjunctive in subordinate sentences: *jwān e ki ī dāsā kāv*, it's as well I should now take my departure; *jwān jwānangā hullīte bin o hata ki ī chēra kēv*, pick out the very best of the horses and bring them to me to examine. It is used as a subjunctive even in past narration: *o tēnā ustaṭī pārē ki ī duzziv-ta*, he inwardly made up his mind to steal it; *dastarkhānae malān ki iragh kunēn*, we opened out the table-cloth in order to eat a meal. In such cases the use of the imperfect, though not inadmissible, would be less idiomatic.

The Present-Future.

§**313.** The present-future, as its name implies, is used both as a present and a future. Treated as a present it is rather a present of habit than a true present, which is expressed by the so-called present of actuality (§306): *nan dā shahraṭī tūlina*, we live in this town, *i.e.*, we are resident here; *nan dā shahraṭī tūlingaṭī un*, we are at this moment actually living in this town, *i.e.*, we are resident elsewhere.

Although the context alone indicates whether the tense is used to denote a present of habit or a near future, its two-fold significance rarely presents any difficulty in practice: *Shālkoṭaṭī harvakht dā mosumāi pir-a kēk*, in Quetta it always rains at this time of the year; *pir dāsā dasik*, it'll rain presently. With the last example may be contrasted: *pir dāsā dasingaṭī e*, it's actually raining now.

The Probable Future.

§**314.** While the present-future in its future significance implies on the whole nearness of time and certainty of the event in the future, the probable future, at any rate in the standard language, contains almost always an element of uncertainty: *pagga nok khaningoe*, to-morrow (we hope) the new moon will be visible; *aino nok khaningtau, pagga khaningik*, the new moon wasn't visible to-day, it's sure to be visible to-morrow; *zinda massuṭ, losāle hajjāi hinoṭ*, if I'm alive, I propose to make the pilgrimage next year. In the Jhalawan dialect the tense is regularly used as a future proper: *ī hinoṭ*, I will go. This use is of course not unknown in the standard language, and is indeed quite common in the case of the first person singular affirmative of causals and verbs whose base ends in *-f*, in which the ordinary future would present an awkward sequence of labials: *e.g.*, *ī khulīfoṭ*, I will frighten, comes more naturally to the tongue than *ī khulīfiva*.

§**315.** The probable future is often employed idiomatically to express indefiniteness without any futuric meaning at all: *numā shahraṭī aṭ urā o? dah dwāzda-as maror*, how many houses are there in your village? some ten or twelve or so; *nā īlum tēnā urāṭī e, aff? hin hur-ta, urāṭī maroe, aga oṛē matau, shahraṭī maroe*, is your brother in his house or not? go and look for him, he's probably at home, and if he's not there, he'll be in the village; *nā mār aṭ sāla maroe?*

shash sāla maroe, how old's your boy? he'll be about six years old. The Brahui in fact makes use of a colloquialism not unfamiliar in English.

The Past Conditional.

§316. The past conditional is chiefly affected in the Jhalawan dialects; in the standard language it is generally displaced by the imperfect. It is used in past conditional sentences (§413), more particularly in the antecedent clause: *nī aga narrosus, nā padaṭ bafarosuṭ*, had you taken to your heels, I wouldn't have come after you; *ī aga numā pāraghāi barosuṭ, dāṛān must barosuṭ*, had I been coming to you, I'd have come before this; *khālī chirrēngān kārēm karosus, nā guzrān marosas*, had you worked instead of simply loafing, you'd have got a living; *faujanā banningān must pēsh tammosure, numā māl hintavaka*, had you set forth before the army arrived, your property would never have been lost.

§317. Closely allied to this conditional use is its use as a past optative: *tēnā hullīe daunangā lāgharīāi khamparosuṭ*, oh that I had never seen my horse in so skinny a condition; *narringān kahosas*, would that he had died sooner than run away; *iragh kuningān must dūte sillosus, dīraṭī pēhingān must puchchāte kashshosus*, you ought to have washed your hands before eating, and doffed your clothes before entering the water. As a past optative also the imperfect is generally preferred in the standard language (§330).

The Present Adverbial Participle.

§318. The adverbial participle despite its name does not participate in the nature of an adjective, and always requires a verb to complete its sense. Its three forms are sometimes used indifferently: *o kasaraṭ chinjik binisa* (*binisau, binisa-aṭ*) *hināka*, he went along the road picking up twigs. But as the form in *-isau* seems unmistakably a combination of the simple termination with the conjunction *o*, 'and' (§211), it is most commonly used when two participles are coupled together: *o hoghisau piṭṭisa tēnā khalkanā pāraghāi dudēngāka*, she was running towards her encampment weeping and beating her breast. Similarly the form in *-isa-aṭ*, which can hardly be anything but an instrumental, is obviously appropriate, if at all, when the participle is used absolutely: *kasarāi nane shikār karisa-aṭ nan tammā*, shooting on the road, night fell upon us.

§319. A repetition of the participle to express gradual process is not uncommon: *khado karraīāi dākā rāhī massun, hinisa hinisa irā tūān guḍ Kēche rasēngān*, last year in the early spring we set out from here, and travelling bit by bit we arrived two months later in Kech.

The special use of this participle to form frequentatives and continuatives (§300) will be illustrated later (§350).

The Present Adjectival Participle.

§320. The adjectival participle, whether active or passive in significance, is an ordinary adjective. It is only in the predicate that it appears in its simple form: *duzzāk khāchok assur ki nan kāṭumāi-tā tammān*, the thieves were asleep when we fell upon them; *ī ode bassuṭ, kahok khanāṭ*, when I reached him I found him dead; *oftā kuchak sakht kunok e*, their dog's a terrible biter; *o ḍaulān narrok khaningāka*, he appeared to be a deserter from his manner; *kanā puchchāk aga sillok o, zū hata-tā*, if my clothes are washed bring them without delay; *nā hullī aga daun-a kāik, ainonā maizile khalok chās*, if your horse covers the ground like this, you may regard to-day's march as over (lit. understand to-day's march as traversed).

§321. Used attributively the participle takes on the definite and indefinite endings in the ordinary manner: *dā ṭūloko masiṛas e, yā bash massune?* is she a maid or married?

(lit. a sitting girl, or has she risen up?—the usual idiom); *tēnā <u>kh</u>alokā <u>kh</u>arāse aga guḍḍis, nēki jwān e,* it would be good for you to slaughter your tossing bull. The definite form is as usual employed with a plural noun and in proverbs (§82): *<u>kh</u>āchokā aristā mēhī nar-a kēk,* the she-buffalo of sluggards will bring forth a male, *i.e.*, the early bird catches the worm; *salokā dīr bandag<u>h</u>e buḍḍējik,* standing water drowns the man, *i.e.*, still waters run deep. The definite form when used as a substantive is of course declinable: *kahokātā randaṭ dēr hināne?* who has ever followed after the dead? (a rebuke of excessive mourning).

§**322.** It is not always easy or even possible to render the adjectival participle by a participle or an adjective in English. A relative sentence is often the nearest equivalent: *<u>kh</u>alokā <u>kh</u>arās,* the bull which is always tossing people; *<u>kh</u>āchokā arisk,* the persons who lie a-bed; *<u>kh</u>udānā karokā kārēm,* the work that is done by God. This adjectival or relative participle, as it might be termed, helps in fact to supply the place of the missing relative pronouns.

The Noun of Obligation.

§**323.** The use of this form of the verb in the case of intransitives is complicated by the fact that it may be used either personally or impersonally. Thus 'I must go' may be rendered in one of two ways: either personally *ī hinoī uṭ,* or impersonally, and this is perhaps the more common idiom, *kane hinoī e,* (*mihi eundum est*).

§**324.** But the case of the transitive verb is much more complicated. In the first place the active and passive forms are identical. Thus 'I must do this work' may be rendered either actively *ī dā kārēme karoī uṭ,* or passively *dā kārēm kane karoī e.* If the logical object of the sentence is inanimate, as in this example, the case is comparatively simple. But if agent and object are on an equal footing, this mode of expression is ambiguous in the extreme, not only on account of the identity of the active and passive forms, but also on account of the identity of the dative and accusative case-suffixes. To take a concrete example, *ī nē illoī uṭ* may mean, as far as grammar goes, either 'I must leave you' or 'I must be left by you'; in the former *nē* is the object in the accusative governed by the active verb, in the latter *nē* is the dative of the agent with the verb in the passive. From a grammatical point of view the confusion is the worse confounded by the fact that *nī kane illoī us* is open to exactly the same two-fold interpretation as *ī nē illoī uṭ*, and for the same reasons. In practice of course the ambiguity is usually resolved by the context and the intonation of the voice, and unless there is some indication to the contrary, the idiom in such cases is generally limited to the active significance of the verbal noun.

§325. Yet one more construction has to be noted. In cases of marked emphasis and especially in interrogations of surprise or defiance the ordinary idiom is to employ the passive form with the agent in the genitive: *dā kārēm kanā karoī e, pēn kasas kanning kappak-ta*, this work is for *me* to do, no one else can do it; *dā kārēm kanā karoī e?* is this work *mine* to do? *ī nā khaloī uṭ ki nī daun-a pāsa?* am *I* to be struck by you, that you speak in this tone of voice?

§326. The negative form of the verbal noun is too cumbrous for common use: *nē nanā urāghāi baroī e, hum pā, bafaroī e, hum pā*, if you're to come to our house, say so, if you're not to come, say so no less; *ī dā kārēme kapparoī uṭ* (*kane dā kārēm kapparoī e*), I haven't to do this work. In such cases the negative noun of obligation is generally avoided by expressing negation in the auxiliary: *nī baroī affēs; dā kārēm kane karoī aff.* No change in the meaning of the sentence is involved.

§327. The force of this form of the verb is not always that of obligation or necessity. It often dwindles down through the idea of fitness or propriety to mere intention or wish: *o daun nājoṛ e ki onā mon huroī aff*, he's so ill that his face isn't fit to be seen; *kane aga pēnanā iragh kunoī-a massaka, ī har dē nā jahāi bassuṭa*, had it been decent for me to eat another man's food, I'd have come every day to your place; *kane aga Noshkē illoī massaka, guṛā ī tēnā tumane hattavaṭa*, had I contemplated leaving Nushki, I would never have brought my family; *nē naukarī karoī aff ki nī kārēm-a kappēsa?* so you've no taste for service that you refuse to work? *kane Shāl illoī aff, ī antei bandaghāteto jang kēv?* I've no desire to leave Quetta, so why should I brawl?

§328. Used attributively the noun of obligation takes on the usual definite and indefinite endings: *tēnā musāfirīāi daroīāte giṛāte jitā ka*, put aside the things you've to take for the journey; *dā giṛā-as ki nī-a pāsa, kanā karoīo kārēmas aff*, this thing you mention does not lie within my sphere of action. The use of a negative attributive adjective is hardly admissible.

The Tenses of Past Time.

§329. **The past** is the ordinary tense of past narration and as such requires no illustration. It is used idiomatically in the protasis of a future conditional sentence (§411): *ī aga nē narringāi khanāṭ, nā mone haloṭ*, if I see you attempt to run, I'll block your way. It may have an analogous contingent-futuric force in a relative sentence (§426): *harkas ki tēnā hullīe rasēngā, swār marē*, every man who can overtake his horse may mount. It may be similarly used in a temporal sentence (§418).

§330. **The imperfect** has four main uses. It expresses imperfect or continuous action in the past: *harchi ki nan* *must-a bassuna, ofk-a narrāra*, the more we were pressing forward, the faster they continued to run. It expresses habitual action in the past: *nan dā mulke har sāl-a dasēna*, we used to cultivate this land every year. It is the regular tense used to express an unfulfilled condition (§412 : *ī aga nē narringāi khanāṭa, nā mone halkuṭa*, had I seen you attempt to run, I'd have blocked your way. And finally it is used as a past optative, an offshoot of its use as a past conditional: *armān ki onā badalān ī kaskuṭa*, ah, would I had died in his stead. In the last two uses its place is regularly taken by the past conditional in the Jhalawan dialect (§§316, 317).

§**331.** **The perfect and pluperfect** have ordinarily the same force as in English, and examples would be superfluous. In temporal sentences introduced by the conjunction *tā ki* in the sense of 'until,' the perfect and pluperfect of the negative verb are used idiomatically with reference to future and past time respectively (§422).

§**332.** In the case of a few verbs, like *tūling*, to sit, *saling*, to stand, *khāching*, to sleep (to lie down), the tenses of past time present some little difficulty. Thus the pluperfect is used when the imperfect might at first sight seem more natural: *mēmānk tūsusur, iraghāte kunisa hināra*, the guests were seated and went on eating their food; *oftā narringān must nan hamoṛē salīsasun*, before they ran off, we were standing there; *num ki hināre, ofk tūsusur yā khāchāsur?* when you went, were they sitting up or lying down? The use of the imperfect, which from the English might seem to be the natural tense to employ, would entail a marked difference in the meaning: *tūsura*, they were about to sit; *salīsuna*, we were about to stand; *tūsura yā khāchāra?* were they going to sit up or lie down? The perfect is similarly used with what may seem present force: *tā ki nī kās barēs, ī hanaārē salīsunuṭ*, until you return, I stand here; *ofk* *khāchāno yā dāiskā tūsuno?* are they asleep or still sitting up? As a matter of fact the meaning of the verb in such cases is not so much to sit, to stand, to sleep (to lie down), as to seat oneself, to adopt a standing position, to go to sleep (to lay oneself down).

The final -*a* of the Present-Future and Imperfect.

§333. It has been shown that the present-future and the imperfect, both affirmative and negative, are formed from the present indefinite and the past respectively by the addition of a final -*a*, except in the second person plural, which is left unchanged, while the formation of the third person singular, though containing a final -*a* in the past, is in many ways peculiar. The structure of the sentence in which one of these tenses appears is of considerable interest. As a rule a final -*a* is added—apparently by attraction—to the word immediately preceding the verb. This applies in particular to the case of the so-called nominal compounds (§291): *ī ḍaghāre namb-a kēva*, I moisten the ground; *ofk jang-a karēra*, they were fighting; *tēnā māle līlām-a kappēsa?* won't you sell your goods by auction? The omission of -*a* in such cases would be a mark of *suruṭ* or broken Brahui. If the word immediately preceding the verb is a pronoun or ends in a case-sign or other suffix, the addition of -*a*, though not imperative, is regarded as more elegant: *ī-a kāva, num handāṛē tūlbo*, I'll go, but you remain here; *aino kanā bandaghāk-a hināra, pir torē-tā*, my men were going to-day, but the rain stopped them; *ī tēnaṭ-a bassuṭa, nī antei kane baṭingās?* I was coming of my own accord, so why did you summon me? *ofk Noshkēāi-a kāra*, they're going to Nushki; *ī nē-a dēva, ēlofte-a dappara*, I'll take you, but I won't take the others. If the word preceding the verb is a conjunction, it is better to omit -*a*: *nan ki hināna, nanā īlum bass*, when we were starting, our brother came.

§334. These rules apply to the third person singular even in the present-future, affirmative and negative, though it ends in *-k*, not *-a*: *kasase ki kur-a marēk, o shwān-a torik,* whoever has a flock, keeps a shepherd; *kanā bandagh-a himpak,* my man won't go; *ode toris ki kane-a khalēk,* please stop him or he'll beat me; *hushik-ta kharvālh, huff-a kēk panēre,* the hot milk scalds him, and he blows on the cream cheese (*kharvālh,* milk given three days after calving), a proverbial expression implying that the man is avenging himself on the wrong person.

§335. In the second person plural the present indefinite coincides with the present-future, and the past with the imperfect, and it is thus clear that the addition or omission of final *-a* to the word immediately preceding the verb in this person will make a material difference in the meaning of the sentence. The tense of the verb is in fact defined by the ending of the word it follows: *dā ḍaghāre namb kēre,* you will please moisten this ground (*kēre,* pres. indef.); *dā ḍaghāre namb-a kēre?* will you moisten this ground? (*kēre,* pres.-fut.); *antas ki num pārēre, kane manzūr e,* whatever you said (or: whatever you may say, *cf.* §329), I accept (*pārēre,* past); *antas ki num-a pārēre, kane manzūr e,* whatever you were saying, I accept (*pārēre,* imperf.).

The Negative Verb.

§336. The negative verb is so integral a part of the language and has been illustrated so frequently in these pages, that a multiplication of examples would be superfluous. Practically the only idiomatic use which merits separate comment will be found in the temporal sentence (§§420, 422).

§337. It is rather the avoidance of the negative verb which calls for illustration. The use of a separate word of negation, as distinct from the negative verb, is in fact alien to the genius of the language. It is almost unknown among the wilder Brahuis, with whom even the negative interjection becomes a mere click (§443) which hardly belongs to the sphere of articulate speech, while the less unsophisticated Brahui contents himself with an occasional use of some particle of negation, picked up from one of the neighbouring languages.

§**338**. Chief among such negative particles are *navā*, lest, and *nei* ... *nei*, neither ... nor, both obvious loan-words: *navā dākā barēs*, mind you don't come by here; *mulkāi ki hināṭ, jahas jola allau, oṟē nei bazghak assur nei kharāsk*, when I went to the field, there wasn't a soul (lit. a spider's web) anywhere, there were neither labourer, nor bullocks. But the Brahui has found even in these simple particles of negation occasions for stumbling, for he sometimes uses *navā* as a noun, and inserts a pleonastic conjunction between *nei* ... *nei* : *navā kēs, kās narris*, take care you don't go and run away; *nī nei kaneāi tēnaṭ bassus o nei tēnā āvāle mon tissus*, you neither came to see me yourself, nor sent me your news. In passing it may be noted that he even robs *navā* of its negative force: *navā khudā e, aino pir-a kēk*, pray God it rain to-day; but in a case like this the idea of the negative seems to be contemplated though euphemistically suppressed.

The Passive Verb.

§**339**. The passive hardly calls for detailed comment. It is indeed not infrequently avoided, chiefly by the inversion of the sentence, and to some small degree by coupling the infinitive of the active verb with the auxiliary *manning*, to become (§298 *fin.*).

§**340**. The imperative is rare, though it finds a place in uncomplimentary expressions: *kasfingbo ki numeān* *chuṭṭēngin*, be killed that we may be rid of you. The adverbial participle is hardly more common: *Mēngalnā lashkar ki pinnā, tā Vadiskā khallingisa hināka*, when the Mengal army was broken, it continued to be harassed as far as Wad. On the other hand the adjectival participle and the noun of obligation—it will be remembered that these are identical with the forms in the active—are used freely: *lashkarnā khalok ābād-a marēk, urānā khalok ābād-a mafak*, plundered by an army a man will yet prosper, plundered at home—never; *kanā ēnakhonā kholum kane makhlūkān ḍakkoī e*, I must hide my wheat crop this year from the people. Of the tenses the presents and the perfect are probably the ones most commonly used, especially in the third persons: *dā giṛāk handāṛē tikhingir, jwān e*, if these things are placed here, well; *Murdār dākān khaningik, Chiltan dākān khaningpak*, Murdar is visible from here, but not Chiltan; *nanā silāk kul ballā urāṭī tikhingāno*, all our arms have been stored in the large house.

The Causal Verb.

§341. The use of the causal verb varies with the nature of the simple verb from which it is derived (§285). If the causal simply supplies the place of a missing transitive verb, the fact that it happens to be a causal in form makes no difference to the structure of the sentence: *tēnā īlume antei kaṣfē?* why did he kill his brother? *shwān mēlhte khwāfik*, the shepherd will graze the sheep.

§342. The difference in use between the active and passive causal is best illustrated by those verbs, at once transitive and intransitive, from which both classes of causal may be derived (§286). The active causal is generally treated like an ordinary transitive, the agent which is the object of the causation being put in the accusative: *o gung e, maga ī ode pārifoṭ*, he's dumb, but I'll make him speak;

o karr e, maga ī ode binifēṭ, deaf though he is, I made him hear; *nī bīngum affēs, maga ī nē kunifiva*, you're not hungry, but I'll make you eat. But if the object on which the agent is made to act has to be specified, it also is put into the accusative, and the causal may therefore govern two accusatives as in the ordinary Indo-European idiom: *ī nē dā iraghe kunifiva*, I'll make you eat this food; *o kane dā khalate bēnifē*, he made me put on this robe of honour.

§**343.** In the case of a passive causal, *i.e.*, a causal derived from a transitive verb, the object is placed in the accusative; the agent by whom the object is acted upon is often omitted, but if it is specified, it is placed in the instrumental: *nī dā āvāle antei binifēs?* why did you get this news noised abroad? *ī dā āvāle tēnā īlumaṭ makhlūkaṭī pārifoṭ*, I'll get this news spoken of among the people through my brother; *o nē tēnā kuchakaṭ kunifik*, he'll get you bitten by his dog.

§**344.** The double passive causal (§287) is used in exactly the same way as the ordinary passive causal: *ī ode nēaṭ kasfifēṭ*, I got him killed by you; *kanā mēlhte tēnā shwānaṭ khwāfif*, have my sheep grazed by your shepherd; *ī nē sarkāraṭ khulīfifoṭ*, I'll get you frightened by Government. But the double causal is a mouthful, and the simple causal is often used loosely in its stead: *ī ode nēaṭ kasfēṭ; kanā mēlhte tēnā shwānaṭ khwāf; ī nē sarkāraṭ khulīfoṭ.*

§**345.** Several causals are used in a peculiar sense; *e.g.*, *khāchifing*, lit. to make to sleep: *ī ode asi tūfakto khāchifēṭ.* I gave him his quietus with one shot; *rasēfing*, lit. to make to arrive: *ī nē dāsā rasēfiva*, I'll overtake you presently; *hampifing*, lit. to cause to be loaded: *huchchāte hampif*, help to load the camels; *laggifing*, lit. to make to climb: *ī chirāghe laggifēnuṭ*, I've lit the lamp; *daṛifing*, lit. to make to descend: *o kanā dīvāle daṛifēne*, he's razed my wall to the ground; *bārifing*, lit. to make dry: *ī nē hītaṭī bārifiva*, I'll out-talk you in conversation.

Compound Verbs.

§**346. Nominal compounds:** *nī handāṛē asīka aḍ ka, ī dāsā barēva*, wait here for a moment, I'll come presently; *tēnā illanā malhe zara-as aḍ ēte ki iraghe tayār kēv*, detain your cousin for a minute while I get the food ready; *ī dam darēngāsuṭ, hullīān daṛingāṭ*, I had tired myself out and got down from my horse; *har-vakhtas ki nī kanto kārēmāi salīsus, ī nē dam-a darifiva*, every time you pit yourself against me in work, I'll tire you out; *o dāsā gaṭṭ e, marrām kappa-ta*, he's now engaged, don't call him; *shikārāi pēsh tammāṭ, hich dū tammitau kane*, I went out shooting, but nothing fell to my gun; *aga o padāi chakk-a khaltavaka, ala goe bāi titavaka*, had he not cast a look back, why he wouldn't have lost the race; *dāsā ki o chūcha khanāne, ode musiṭ tining nēki mayār e*, for you to divorce her now that she has borne a child, would be scandalous; *o tungān hināne, sār kappa-ta*, he's fallen into a sound sleep, don't wake him up; *ī dīrān chavaṭṭāteto bē khalkuṭ*, I passed through the water, sandals on feet; *aino Sariāvāi kāv, dahimīko dē khalkanā pāraghāi bē harsēngiva*, if I start for Sariab to-day, I'll return to the village in ten days' time; *ē vakhtas ki dē kī halēngā, ode hilh karē, vakhtas ki dē ṭik tiss, hilh illā-ta*, when the sun set, the fever seized him, when the sun rose, the fever left him; *hullīāi swār, dū-ka drakhtasēto ki bass, ṭap mass*, as I was riding my horse, my hand struck against a tree and got hurt; *kasaraṭ-a bassuṭa, nāgumān khalasēṭī kibalkuṭ tammāṭ*, as I was walking along the road, I suddenly stumbled against a stone and fell; *daske sīla-aṭī ī-kashshā, sīlanā duk pinnā*, she thrust the thread into the needle, and the eye of the needle broke.

§347. Potentials: *nī ode khalling-a kēsa?* can you thrash him? *ī nēto drogh pāning-a kappara,* I can't tell lies with you; *dā hullī Mastungiskā hining kapparoç,* this horse won't be able to get as far as Mastung, I think; *nī kane dākān danning kattavēs,* you weren't able to remove me from here.

§348. The passive compounds are analogous: *o kaneaṭ khalling-a marēk,* he can be beaten by me; *dā kharās dēraṭ tafing-a marēk?* by whom can this bull be tied? Such phrases, however, are often devoid of any idea of possibility, and are used as ordinary passives: he will be beaten by me; by whom will this bull be tied?

§349. Inceptives: *kanā khaningto o dudēngaṭī tammā,* as soon as he saw me, he took to his heels; *har-vakht ki nē khanik, hoghingaṭī-a tammik,* every time she sees you, she bursts into tears; *kharmānā rasēngto mēlhk trah karēr, narringaṭī tammār, harchi ki ī jallāṭa-tā, jalling-a matavasa, narrisa hināra,* at the appearance of the wolf the sheep were panic-stricken and took to flight, in spite of my efforts they wouldn't be folded and continued to scatter.

§350. Frequentatives and continuatives are distinguishable only from the context; the difference between them is indeed often fluid: *o dushmanān har-vakht narrisa kāik,* he's for ever running away from the enemy; *nī arīza tirisa hināsa, o nā hīte bintavaka,* you never used to lose an opportunity to present a petition, but he declined to listen to what you had to say; *ī nē pārisa bassunuṭ ki dākā bafa,* I've told you time after time not to come this way; *ī tīvaghā dē ode pārisa bassunuṭ ki daun kappa,* from morning till night I haven't ceased telling him not to behave like this; *isto khāching-vakhtān ki sangaraṭī tūsuno, tā dāiskā tūfak khalisa kāra,* from bed-time last night when they entered the sangar up to now they've been keeping up a continuous fire;

tā ki nan batanun, nī ḍaghāre dasisa kās, don't leave off sowing the field till we come; *nanā sardār bāva o pīraghān iragh tirisa barēk, onā mār umēd e ki handun iragh tirisa hinoe*, our chief keeps up the family tradition of never-failing hospitality, and we may hope that his son will follow in his steps; *dēanā ṭikkato taho ziāt marisa hinā*, at dawn the wind continued to increase. Significantly enough, if the object governed by the compound phrase is an enclitic pronoun, it is attached to the latter element, notwithstanding the fact that this is an intransitive verb: *dushmane monaṭī shāghāsas, ḍak tirisa hināka-ta*, he had driven the foe ahead and kept goading him on.

§351. **Intensives and completives**: *tēnā kharāse taf, kanā beite kulle kunēk kāik*, tie up your bullock or it'll devour up all my grass; *ī aga rasēngtavaṭa, huchchāk nā kulle kadīmāte kungura hināra*, had I not arrived, the camels would have finished off all your grain; *daunangā droghātēki ki nī pāsa, ī nēkonā chandīte khalkunuṭ hinānuṭ*, I've thrashed many a man like you within an inch of his life for such lies as you tell; *hināṭ ki tēnā hullīe halēv, kanā rasēngān must kaskas hināsas*, I went to fetch my horse, but before I got to the spot he was stone dead. If the object of the sentence is an enclitic pronoun, it is attached to the last verb of the compound, intransitive though it is: *harkas ki kanā monaṭī harsēngāne, ī khalkunuṭ hinānuṭ-ta*, I've thrashed soundly every man who has stood in my way.

POSTPOSITIONAL NOUNS, POSTPOSITIONS AND PREPOSITIONS.

§352. Postpositional nouns are postpositions in the making. They are in fact ordinary nouns employed in some oblique case to perform the functions of a postposition, and govern of course the genitive. In the absence of any real dividing line between the ordinary noun and the noun used in this postpositional manner, a selection will be made of such nouns in which the literal nominal meaning is apt to become most clearly subordinated, but in each case the opportunity will be taken to illustrate the use of the full-word. In the postposition evolution has reached a further stage; it is no longer in an oblique case, and the governed noun is in the ablative. A still further stage is represented of course by the case-suffixes. The prepositions, which, like the postpositions, govern the ablative, are comparatively recent refinements borrowed from other languages. There remains one word, also a loan-word, which is rather an interposition (if the term may be allowed) than a postposition or a preposition; the noun which precedes it is the same as the noun by which it is followed, and both are undeclined.[1]

Postpositional Nouns.

§353. ***Pāragh* (*pāra*),** side:— *dā mashanā rāstīko pāragh āvār e*, the right side of this hill is smooth. This word sometimes helps to form a compound noun: *ī aino dēṭik-pāraghāi shikārāi-a kāva*, to-day I'll go eastwards to shoot.

Postpositional: *kanā pāraghāi ki bass, nā pāraghāi um barēk*, if he comes to me, he'll come to you also; *onā kharābī khudānā pāraghān ass*, his ruin came from God; *o ē mashanā pāraghān rāhī massune*, he has set out from the direction of that hill.

[1] Except in one special case, *cf.* §385, *fin.*

§354. ***Nēma,*** **side,** is used in exactly the same way and with the same meaning as *pāra: kanā nēmaghāi,* to me; *nā nēmaghāi,* to you; *khudānā nēmaghān,* from God; *ē mashanā nēmaghān,* from the direction of that hill.

§355. ***Bāṭagh,*** **upper side, top:**—*dā sundūkhnā bāṭaghe dēr joṛ karēne?* who has made the top of this box? *zorākā dīr bāṭaghān kasar-a kēk,* the flood forces its way from the top, *i.e.*, might is right; *bāṭaghko kasaraṭ kās,* please go by the upper road.

Postpositional: *kanā bāṭaghāi tūlpa, ēṛē tūlh,* don't sit on me, sit over there; *o dīte nanā bāṭaghāi chaṭ tiss,* he sprinkled the water over us.

§356. ***Kēragh,*** **lower side, bottom:**—*dā shahranā kēragh kul dīr e,* the lower side of this village is water-logged; *kēraghko mashān kārēzas pēsh tammāne,* a karez has been made from the lower hill.

Postpositional: *sardār drakhtanā kēraghān kachārī e,* the chief is in court beneath the tree; *o tēne karodnā kēraghān ḍakkāsas,* he had hidden himself under the river-bank; *dā ḍrakhtanā kēraghaṭī ballo koḍas e,* there's a big cave underneath this tree.

§357. ***Zī,*** **top:**—*dā mashanā zī kul bei e,* the top of this hill is all grass.

Postpositional: *Murdārnā zīāi bil-a-sum karē,* there was a rainbow over Murdar; *dīvālnā zīāi laggāṭ,* I climbed on to the top of the wall; *sangarnā zīān tūfakāk-a gidārēngāra,* bullets were flying over the sangar.

§358. ***Mās,*** **bottom:**—*dā dīvālnā zīe barf daṛifēne, mās-ta annā salāmat e,* the snow has knocked down the top of this wall, but the bottom of it is still intact. In combination with *mash,* hill, *mās* generally forms a compound noun: *nanā khalk mash-māsāiṭ e,* our village is at the foot of the hill; *mashanā mās,* however, is also used.

Postpositional: *ē drakhtanā māsāi mungītā kutām e*, the wasps' nest is at the foot of that tree; *duzz tēne kumbanā māsāi rasēfē, mishanā chankas kashshā*, the thief plunged to the bottom of the pool, and brought up two handfuls of earth (referring to an ordeal by water); *dā machchīe dīranā māsān kashshānuṭ*, I've drawn up this fish from the bottom of the water.

§359. ***Mon***, front, face:— *kanā monāi pīuno ṭikkas e*, there's a white spot on my face; *nanā urānā mon dēṭikkāiṭ e*, the front of our village is towards the east.

Postpositional: *nī aga kanto jang-a kēsa, ī nē hākimnā monāi-a dēva*, if you fight with me, I'll hale you before the ruler; *aino shikāraṭī chār murū kanā monān pēsh tammār*, in to-day's hunt four hares got up in front of me; *o chaṭṭo bandaghas e, tēnā monaṭ-a chirrēngik*, he's a worthless fellow and follows his own nose; *kasarīas kanā monaṭī bass, nā banningnā āvāle tiss*, a wayfarer came across me, and gave me news of your coming.

§360. ***Muh***, front:—*muhe kilbaghāi ka, rāst pā*, turn your face towards Mecca, and speak the truth.

Postpositional: *nā mār nā muhato dākā rāhī mass*, your son left here just before you; *numeān kasas nanā muhāi batau*, not one of you came out to receive us; *nī kulle kārēme tēnā muhaṭ-a kēsa, kasān harrifpēsa*, you do all your work after your own bent and consult no one.

§361. ***Pad***, back:—*nanā urānā pad jahndumāiṭ e*, the back of our house is towards the south.

Postpositional: *nā padaṭ bandaghas bassune, nē tavār-a kēk*, a man has come after you and is giving you a shout; *dushmank nā padaṭ tammāno, khudā chāe nēto ant kēr*, the enemies are in pursuit of you, God knows what they may do with you; *o kanā padān bass*, he came from behind me; *o nā padato naneān narrā*, he fled from us just behind you.

§362. ***Baj,*** **back**:—*kanā baj khalh-a kēk*, my back aches; *onā baj nā mon barēbar affas*, there's no comparison between his back and your face, *i.e.*, his influence even in his absence is greater than yours even though you are present.

Postpositional: *dīr dā shahranā bajaṭ-a kāik*, the water flows behind this town; *nā bajāi ī drogh tarṭanuṭ*, I haven't lied against you.

§363. ***Tah,*** **interior, inside**:—*dā tūfaknā tah khāzgī e*, the inside of this gun is dirty.

Postpositional: *masītnā tahṭī pēhāṭ*, I entered inside the mosque; *o nanā kishārnā tahaṭ hiningaṭī e*, he's walking within our crops; *vatākhnā tahān tūfake khākhar tissuṭ*, I fired the gun from inside the encamping-ground; *kane khanā, urānā tahāi mon karē*, when he saw me, he made for the inside of the house.

§364. ***Niām,*** **(Jhalawan, *yām*), middle**:—*sēlhanā niāmaṭī nanā mulk hinoī aff*, in the middle of winter our country is no place to go to; *kasarnā yāmāi nan-a-o asiṭ ēloe khanān*, we saw each other midway.

Postpositional: *tēn-pa-tēn jang kabo, nan numā niāmaṭī tammipana*, go on fighting among yourselves, we won't come between you; *kanā o kanā bāvanā niāmaṭī jitāī aff, murū nanā niāmān sham-a kappak*, there's such perfect union between me and my father, a hare couldn't run between us.

§365. ***Rah, rahī,*** **bank, side**:—*dā jalanā rahk burz o*, the banks of this torrent are steep; *joanā rahīaṭ hiningaṭī ass ki musi hanj monān-ta bāl karēr*, he was going by the side of the stream when three ducks got up in front of him.

Postpositional: *lashkar sobato nanā urānā rahān gidārēngā*, the army passed by our house early in the morning; *o daun nājoṛ e ki kasas rahīāi-ta himpak*, he's so ill that no one goes near him; *dā bāghanā rahato kasar-a kāik*, the road goes by the side of this garden; *nanā shahranā rahāi kirrīnā ladas e,* there's a tamarisk grove by our village.

§366. ***Rand,*** track:—*duzzātā rande gum karēnun,* we've lost the thieves' tracks.

Postpositional: *har-vakht ki darbār mass, ī nā randaṭ-a barēva,* as soon as the meeting takes place, I'll come for you; *nā randaṭ-a chār bandagh-a chirrēngāra, nē khanār, khantavas?* four men were roaming about after you, did they find you or not?

§367. ***Kēb,*** (*khēb*), near, nearness:—*ī khazmāte kēb karēṭ,* I got near to the deer.

Postpositional: *kanā kēbāi bafēs,* please don't come near me; *bīshe margh-a massaka, kase tēnā kēbaṭ illētavaka,* if the ass had had horns, he would never have allowed any one near him.

§368. ***Khuṛk,*** near, nearness:—*Kānak khuṛk e, murr e?* is Kanak near or far? *ī ode bēkhī khuṛk khanāṭ,* I saw him quite close.

Postpositional: *dā shahranā khuṛkāi ballo talāfas e,* there's a large tank near this village; *onā khuṛkāi ki hināṭ, zaghme kashshā, kaneāi rāst mass,* as soon as I got near him, he drew his sword and made straight for me; *dā arē Bēlaunā khuṛkān-a barēk,* this man comes from near Las Bela.

Postpositions.

§369. Of the postpositions two are in a transitional stage and may be treated as postpositional nouns governing the genitive, while the rest with the exception of *-bā(r)*, like, are also used independently as nouns, adjectives or adverbs, from which they are indeed at times hardly distinguishable.

§370. ***Dā rah*** (*rahī*), this side; ***ē rah*** (*rahī*), that side:—*jalān dā rahī massuṭ, tēnā huchche khanāṭ,* when I got this side of the torrent, I saw my camel; *dā shahrān ē ra'h sardārnā urā e*, the chief's house is that side of this village. These phrases may also govern the genitive like the ordinary postpositional noun: *Mastungnā dā rah bei bāz e, ē rah-ta bārun e*, on this side of Mastung there's plenty of grass, that side it's dry.

§371. ***Dā mon***, this side; ***hē mon*** (***ēmon***), that side:—*Noshkēnā kanḍān dā mon massun, asi khazmas bash mass*, when we reached this side of the Nushki pass, a deer got up; *dā parraghān ki hē mon massus, khalkanā molhe khanisa*, when you get the other side of this hillock you'll see the smoke of the village. These phrases may also be used as postpositional nouns: *Murdārnā dā mon pir kattane*, it hasn't rained this side of Murdar.

§372. ***Must***, before:—*kaneān must tūlpa*, don't sit in front of me (or: don't sit before I do); *ainoān must ī nē khantanuṭ*, I haven't set eyes on you before to-day; *kasaraṭ ballāṛān must tammipa*, don't go in front of your elders on the road; *dā mār bāvaghān must vadī e*, this lad (to judge by his impudence) was born before his father.

§373. ***Guḍ***, after:—*zara-aseān guḍ barak*, come after a while; *ēkān guḍ gap o shap mass*, after that the gossip began; *dah dēān guḍḍ-a barēva*, I'll come after ten days; *paltannā rāhī manningān guḍ pir karē*, it began to rain after the regiment started.

§374. ***Pad***, after:—*ī dah dēān paḍ-a barēva*, I'll come after ten days; *o nēān pad hinā*, he went after you did.

§375. ***Pizzēr***, after, behind:—*o kasaraṭ naneān pizzēr āhīs*, he was left behind us on the road; *sālaseān pizzēr nā līte gīrām karēṭ*, I forgot your words after a year; *nanā rāhī manningān pizzēr oftā khalk khākhar halk*, their village caught fire after we started.

§376. ***Khuṛk,*** near:—*ī ode shahrān khuṛk khanāṭ*, I saw him near the village; *sardārkhēlaṭī sardārān khuṛk dēr e?* in the chief's family who comes nearest the chief?

§377. ***Murr,*** far from:—*kaneān murr tūlh*, sit far from me; *dākān murr ka-ta ki nan tūlin*, take it right away from here that we may sit down.

§378. ***Pēshan,*** outside:—*urāghān pēshan salīsune*, he's standing outside the house; *nanā shahrān pēshan ballo muchchīas e*, there's a large gathering outside our village.

§379. ***Shēf,*** below:—*mashān shēf dīranā chakkulas e*, there's a spring of water below the hill; *nanā shahrān shēf pēn ābādī aff*, there's no habitation below our village.

§380. ***Bā, bār,*** like:—Unlike other postpositions *bā, bār* has no existence except as a postposition. It is indeed so closely connected with the noun it governs that the ablative case-suffix *-ān* changes before the labial to *-ām*: *o tēnā kārēme dāṛām-bā karē*, he did his work like this; *ē huch hullīām-bā dudēngik*, that camel gets over the ground like a horse; *māranā shaunk buṭaunā jalhām-bār e*, the desire of a youth is like a bush-fire. It will be noticed that the final consonant is ordinarily omitted unless the postposition immediately precedes the copula. So closely incorporated is this combination of noun and postposition, that it is freely employed as an attributive adjective (§83 *fin.*): *dāṛāmbāro pēn hullīas khanānus?* have you seen such another horse as this?

Prepositions.

§381. ***Baghair (baghaire),*** except, without:—*kunoīo giṛā-as pēn allau baghair hamo musi kaṭangarān*, there was nothing else to eat save those three sandgrouse; *baghair kanā hukmān dākān himpēs*, don't go from here without my orders; *baghaire oṛān pēn kane kasas aff*, I've no one but him; *baghaire nēān ī shikārāi himpara*, I won't go shooting without you.

§**382.** ***Bē, bēd (bēde),*** **without, except:**—*bē nēān kane ārām-a bafak*, I'm restless without you; *bē pāningān kane dā khalat rasēngā*, I got this robe of honour without saying a word; *bēd nā hukmān ī dāṛē bafara*, I won't come here without your orders; *bēde nēān ī tēnā āvāle kasasė pātanuṭ*, with the exception of yourself I've told my news to no one.

§**383.** ***Savā (savāe),*** **except, without:**—*savā dah hēṭān pēn kulle kure garr halkune*, with the exception of ten she-goats the whole flock has got the mange; *savāe khudāghān pēn dēr kanā arze binoe?* who else save God is likely to listen to my prayer?

§**384.** The three prepositions may also be used postpositionally, but only in the forms *baghair*, *bēd*, *savā*, which seems to indicate that the incremental *-e* is a reminiscence of the *izāfat* (*cf.* §156): *nēān nā māteān baghair ī pēn kasato siālī kappara*, I won't have relations with any one save with you and your sons; *pīr pakhīrāteān bēd ī dā shahre hushiva*, with the exception of the saints and the holy men I'll fire this town; *nēān savā pēn kasas dā duzze halling-a kappak*, no one but you can catch this robber.

§**385.** ***Pa,*** **to, etc.:**—*nī ama mon pa mon drogh-a pāsa?* how can you lie face to face? *dū pa dū hināra*, they were going along hand in hand; *tēn pa tēn hīt-a karēra*, they were talking one to another; *hullīk goaṭī khaf pa khaf dudēngaṭī o*, the horses are racing neck to neck (lit. ear to ear). Though *pa*, which is of course a loan-word, is never used except between two identical words, it appears to approximate to a preposition proper in such examples as the following: *dū pa dū halkusa hināra*, they went along holding hand in hand; *huchchāk likh pa likh tissuno jang-a* *kēra,* the camels have put neck to neck and are engaged in fight. On the other hand *tēn-pa-tēn* (§119), self by self, is frequently treated as a compound noun pure and simple: *tēn-pa-tēnān vām halpabo,* don't borrow from one another. So completely is the phrase regarded as a compound, that its declension, instead of following the lines of the reflexive pronoun, is perfectly regular.

THE ADVERB.

§386. The majority of the adverbs are palpably cases of nouns or pronouns. The latter fall into a group by themselves which will be conveniently exhibited later (§388). The former are exceedingly numerous: *e.g.*, ***monaṭī***, ahead; ***padāi***, back; ***hurēāi***, ***vaḍērāi***, late; ***bēgato***, in the evening; ***sobato***, in the early morning; ***dīgarto***, in the latter part of the afternoon; ***pēshīmāi***, in the afternoon; ***vakht-i-nanaseāi***, at the dead of night; ***jwānīaṭ***, ***jwānīkā***, ***sharrīaṭ***, ***sharrīkā*** (from ***jwānī***, ***sharrī***, goodness), well. Such adverbs might be multiplied indefinitely, and illustrations of their use seem hardly necessary: ***monaṭī tammipa***, ***padāi ma***, don't forge ahead, fall back; ***o isto vaḍērāi bass***, he came late last night; ***ī bēgato hurēāi rasēngāṭ***, I arrived late in the evening; ***tēnā ḍaghāre jwānīkā das***, sow your land properly; ***kanā hītāte ode sharrīaṭ binifis***, repeat my words to him accurately. One couple will repay special note: though 'by day' is expressed by the ordinary ablative ***dēān***, 'by night' is not ***nanān*** as might have been expected, but ***nanikān***, which appears to be an example of the fusion of two case-suffixes.

§387. The foregoing adverbs are formed from nouns still in common use. In a few similar formations the derivation is less obvious, the noun being otherwise obsolete: *e.g.*, ***bisaṭ***, straight, outright; ***kala-aṭ***, with difficulty; ***hastīn***, everywhere, ***pēntīn***, elsewhere, ***hichtīn*** (with negative), nowhere.[1] These adverbs are important enough to deserve passing illustration: ***tūfaknā sum bisaṭ nishānanā tahṭī laggā***, the rifle-bullet hit straight on the centre of the target; ***taho drakhtāte bisaṭ bēkhān loṛā***, the wind plucked the trees up bodily from

---

[1] These three compounds are occasionally declined: *e.g.*, ***nī ode hastīnaṭī khaning-a kēsa***, you can see him everywhere.

the roots; *hastīn kās, khudānā āsmān e*, wherever you go, God's heaven is above you, *i.e.*, you can't escape from the cares of this world; *dāṛē nā guzrān mafak, pēntīn hin*, if you can't get a living here, go elsewhere; *Makurānnā huch pēn hichtīn vadī-a mafak*, the Mekran camel is procurable nowhere else.

§388. A very important group is comprised of adverbs formed from pronominal bases :—

	Demonstrative.			Interrogative.
	Proximate.	Mediate.	Remote.	
	dā.	*o*.	*ē*.	*arā? a-?*
Time.				
1. at:	*dāsā*, now.	...	...	...
2. up to:	*dāskā(n)*, up to now.	*oskā(n)*.	*ēskā(n)*.	...
Place.				
1. at, to:	*dāṛē(k)*, here.	*oṛē(k)*.	*ēṛē(k)*.	*arāṛē(k)?*
	**dāṛēsk*.	**oṛēsk*.	**ēṛēsk*.	**arāṛēsk?*
2. from:	*dākā(n)*, hence.	*okā(n)*.	*ēkā(n)*.	*arākā(n)?*
3. up to:	*dāṛēskā(n)*, up to here.	*oṛēskā(n)*.	*ēṛēskā(n)*.	*arāṛēskā(n)?*
	**dāṛēkā(n)*.	**oṛēkā(n)*.	**ēṛēkā(n)*.	**arāṛēkā(n)?*
Direction.				
1. in:	*dāng(ī)*, in this direction.	*ong(ī)*.	*ēng(ī)*.	*arāng(ī)?*
2. towards:	*dāngāi*, towards this direction.	*ongāi*.	*ēngāi*.	*arāngāi?*
3. from:	*dāngān*, from this direction.	*ongān*.	*ēngān*.	*arāngān?*
Manner.	**dahun*, thus.	*ohun*.	*ēhun*.	*ama(r)?*
	daun.			
	**duhun*.			

It will be observed that the series *dāṛēk*, etc., bears the same relation to the series *dāṛēkān*, etc., as the series *dāṛēsk*, etc., bears to the series *dāṛēskān*, etc. The forms marked with an asterisk are comparatively rare. There are a few other variants; thus *ēng*(*ī*), *ēngāi*, *ēngān* are not infrequently aspirated, *hēng*(*ī*), *hēngāi*, *hēngān*, while *dāskā*(*n*) is often displaced by *dāiskā*(*n*), both forms moreover varying with *tāskā*(*n*), *tāiskā*(*n*). The full forms *dāṛēk*, *dāṛēskān*, etc., are imperative if immediately followed by the copula (*cf.* §42), and are occasionally used in other connections. The demonstratives are frequently employed in the intensive form: *handāskā*(*n*), *hamoskā*(*n*), *hamēskā*(*n*), etc. *Handun*, the ordinary form of the intensive adverb, is slightly irregular. Certain Jhalawans, notably the Haruni Muhammad Hasnis, who corrupt the intensive proximate demonstrative pronoun to *ḥannā* (§129), corrupt the corresponding adverbs in a similar manner: *hannāskā*(*n*), *hannāṛē*(*k*), etc. The conversion of the adverbs of manner into attributive adjectives has already been discussed (§182). To this pronominal group belongs *antei?* why? which is apparently an accusative from *ant?* what? and may possibly contain an older form of the accusative case-suffix (§139).

§**389.** Examples: *nī antei dāsā bassunus? ē handāsā rāhī massune*, why have you come now? he has just started; *ēskā ki nī batanus, ī handāṛēk uṭ*, until you come, I remain here; *ī daun nājoṛ massuṭ ki kaneān dākha matau ki ī ēkān handāṛēskā barēv*, I became so ill that I hadn't it in me to get as far as from there to here; *mēlhk dāngāiṭ o, hēng paṭṭipa tā*, the sheep are towards this direction don't search for them over there; *arāngān-a barēsa? arāngī kāsa?* whence do you come and whither do you go? *ama bassus, piāda yā swār?* how did you come, afoot or riding? *mon arāngāi pēsh tammānus?* facing in what direction have you set out?

§390. Except in the case of the interrogatives the force of the various series is somewhat fluid. Thus *dākān, okān, ēkān*, which properly denote motion from, and *dāngī, ongī, ēngī*, which denote direction in, may be used of time, like 'hereafter.' 'henceforth,' and similar adverbs in English: *dākān guḍ drakhtāk pann-a sholira*, after this the trees will shed their leaves; *ē dēaseān ki ī nē khanānuṭ, okān dāngī ī joṛ matanuṭ*, from the day I saw you, yes, from that time to this I haven't been well; *ainoān ēngī kane nēto kārēm aff*, from this day henceforth I wash my hands of you. Again, the series *dākā(n), okā(n), ēkā(n)*, though primarily denoting motion from, is sometimes used with reference to motion along or rest in the vicinity of a place: *Sarāvānnā lashkar sobato okān gidārēngā*, the Sarawan army passed by thereabouts at dawn; *ē būchāteāi tūlpa ki nā puchchātēṭī lichchor, dākā tūlh*, don't sit on that rubbish or it'll stick to your clothes, sit somewhere over here.

§391. The missing adverbs of time are supplied by combinations of the noun *vakht*, time, with *arā?* which? or with the corresponding loan-word *chi?*: *arā vakht? chivakht?* (commonly corrupted to *chiva?*) when? *arā vakhtān? chi vakhtān? chivaghān?* from what time? *arā vakhtiskā? chi vakhtiskā? chiva-iskā?* up to what time?

§392. The interrogative adverb of manner also appears as an abstract noun, *amarī?* (lit. 'howness'?) whether undeclined or in the construct state, *amarīaṭ? amarīāi? amarīkā?*: *hamo rupaīte ki nī darēs, amarī gum karēs-tā?* how did you lose those rupees you took away? *nī amarīaṭ bassunus, jangaṭ yā khairaṭ?* how have you come, for war or in peace? *nī amarīkā kanā siāl us?* in what way are you relation of mine?

§393. Another important group of adverbs has reference to days, nights and years:—

aino, dāvadī, to-day.

daro,	yesterday.	*pagga,*	to-morrow.
mulkhudo,	the day before yesterday.	*palmē,*	the day after to-morrow.
kūmulkhudo,	three days ago.	*kūdē,*	three days hence.
		kūmādē,	four days hence.

bēgāi, to-night.

isto,	last night.	*panā bēgāi,*	to-morrow night.
dare nan,	the night before last.	*palmē bēgāi,*	two nights hence.
mulkho nan,	three nights ago.	*kūdē bēgāi,*	three nights hence.

ēnakho, this year.

khado,	last year.	*lo-sāl,*	next year.
mustirkhado,	the year before last.	*musiṭimīko sāl,*	the year after next.

A discussion of the derivation of these adverbs, which presents in some cases considerable difficulty, lies outside the scope of the present volume. The fact that the Brahui reckons the 24 hours as beginning with the evening, accounts for the meaning of *dare nan.* Though *kūmulkho nan* and *kūmādē bēgāi* are occasionally heard, the series is rarely carried so far back. Indeed, one or two adverbs included in the series hardly belong to the workaday vocabulary. There are a few local variants: *pagga na, ēlodē,* not to-morrow, the next day, and even *ēlodē* by itself are sometimes used for the ordinary *palmē; ainakho,* this year, occasionally displaces *ēnakho:* the Zahris corrupt *isto* to *ishto*, while the Nicharis employ *musi<u>kh</u>ado* for *mustir<u>kh</u>ado*.

§394. These words are used in the first instance as adverbs: *kanā īlum aino rāhī mass, kūdē yā kūmādē dāṛē rasēngik*, my brother started to-day and will arrive here three or four days from now. But they are for the most part susceptible of being used as declinable substantives: *<u>kh</u>ado ainonā dē kanā bāva Kēchāi hinā, dāskā batane*, this very day last year my father went to Kech and has not come back yet; *ī dāṛē dāvadī-iskā āsūda matanuṭ*, up to this present day I haven't been happy here. *Bēgāi* is of course already in an oblique case.

§395. The concluding portion of this section has been reserved for a few miscellaneous adverbs which do not range themselves readily in any of the groups already discussed, and which seem to merit detailed illustration by reason either of the obscurity of their derivation or the idiomatic part they play in the language.

§396. ***Annā***, still; (with negative) yet:— *ī nē pārēṭ hinak, nī annā tūsunus?* I told you to go and are you still seated? *ēna<u>kh</u>o annā Kachchīāi hintanun*, we haven't gone to Kachhi yet this year; *annā tūfak tavār karē kattau, gaḍ tammā*, the crack of the rifle had hardly yet been heard, when the hill-sheep fell; *ḍorvāge annā much kattanus ki kanā kuchak murūe halēk*, as soon as you gather up the leash, my hound will seize the hare. Very occasionally the case-suffix *-iskā* is added: *annāskā batane*, he's not come yet.

§397. ***Vā***, again, back:— *ī nē pārēṭ bafa, nī vā bassunus?* I told you not to come, and have you come again? *chukkāte harchi ki miṛāna, o vā dīrāi-a bassura*, in spite of our efforts to drive the birds, they kept coming back to the water; *ēna<u>kh</u>o ki hināṭ, vā losāl-a barēva*, if I go this year, I'll come back next.

§398. ***Guṛā,*** then, later:—*asīka kanā pāraghāi ba, guṛā ēngī hin,* first come to me and then go over there; *dāsā gaṭṭ uṭ, guṛā ba,* I'm busy now, come later.

§399. ***Āskār,*** wantonly:—*kanā onā laṭṭas ṭappas allau, o āskār bass kane khalk,* he and I had no feud between us, he came and struck me wantonly; *ī ama ode tēnā ḍaghārnā fasle bashkhiv? o āskār kure hēs, kanā ḍaghāre khwāfē,* why should I make him a present of my crops? it wasn't by accident that he brought his flock along and grazed them on my land; *nī chāsa ki ī naukar uṭ, nī āskār-a barēsa, saibe kaneāi soṭēfisa,* you know I'm an inferior, so you come without rhyme or reason and stir up the Sahib against me. *Āskār* also appears in the construct state, *āskāraṭ, āskārān,* with the same meaning.

§400. ***Rūmalās,*** openly:—*nī rūmalās ama drogh-a pāsa?* how can you lie openly? *nā īlum kane rūmalās ḍaghārān javāb karē,* your brother declined in public to give me the land; *duzz rūmalās kanā monān khēr karē,* the thief ran barefacedly away from me.

§401. ***Nēṭ,*** at last:—*nī aga duzzī-a kēsa, nēṭ asi dēas hallingos,* if you go on thieving, you stand to be caught one fine day; *kanā pāningaṭ kārēm kattau nēṭ tā ki tēne kharāb karifē,* he declined to act according to my advice until in the end he brought himself to ruin.

§402. ***Nillā,*** simply, purely, altogether:—*drogh pāpa, nillā rāst pā,* don't lie, speak nothing but the truth; *ī nillā nā khātirān dā mulke illēva,* it's purely on your account that I leave this country; *dā hullīki sad rupaī nillā zar tissunuṭ,* I've given a hundred rupees, hard cash, for this horse.

§403. ***Bīra,*** simply, etc.:—*bēdīte bīra dīr karēnus,* you've made the broth nothing but water; *ēnakho darbāraṭī bīra Jhalāvānīk bassuno, Sarāvānīk kul narrāno mash karēno,* this year only the Jhalawans have come to the durbar, the

Sarawans have all fled and taken to the hills; *o bīra shāmato bass*, he came quite after sunset. The definite attributive adjective or what appears to be such, *bīraghā*, is used in a similar manner: *bīraghā droghaṭ khalās-a mafēsa, giṛā rāst hum pā*, you won't get off by simply lying, tell a modicum of truth also. Compare the use of *tīva, tīvaghā* (§161), and of the two words below.

§**404.** ***Shana,*** **simply, etc.**:—*ī nē pārēṭ pālh hata, n. shana dīr hēsunus*, I told you to bring milk, and you've brought simply water; *dā drakht shana pann e*, this tree is all leaf; *nā ḍaghār shana pāṭ e, kharrisīnā pin aff tahṭī-ta*. your land's nothing but wood, there isn't the name of grass in it. *Shanaghā* is also used: *dā māshte ki nā īlum kaneāi bahā karēne, shanaghā būch o*, this pulse your brother sold me is pure refuse.

§**405.** ***Chaṛa,*** **simply, etc.**:—*o kanā pāraghāi chaṛa asīka bassune*, he has come to me once only; *kane chaṛa bei bakār e, pēn giṛā-as khwāhipara*, I need grass only, I want nothing else. *Chaṛaghā* is also in use.

§**406.** ***Chā,*** **please understand**[1]:—*kane chā nā kāṭum bakār e*, I'd have you know it's simply your welfare (lit. head) that I desire. Emphasis and intonation, however, furnish the best equivalent for this highly idiomatic word: *tēnā rāhī manningān must nī chā kane sahī-a karēsa ki ī nā monāi-a bassuṭa*, you ought to have *told* me before you started, that I might have come out to receive you; *nī chā rāst-a pārēsa, ki nā hīte khaf-a torēra*, you should have spoken the *truth*, so that they might have given ear to what you said; *o chā duzzī kapp, ant kē?* suppose he *doesn't* thieve, what *is* he to do? *ī chā drogh-a pāva, rāst pārokā nī us*, ho, ho, so *I* am the one who tells lies, and *you* are Mr. Truthful.

---

[1] Though now used as a true adverb, *chā* is in origin simply the imperative singular of *chā-ing*. Hence the dialectical variants *tā, tiā* (§261).

THE CONJUNCTION.

§**407.** It is natural that the conjunction should play a minor part in the language, for the working of the Brahui mind is simple and finds expression in the simplest terms. Sentence follows sentence, knit together as a rule, not by conjunctions, but by the sequence of ideas. Of the conjunctions which are found in the language, the large majority have been borrowed from outside, and not one has yet succeeded in making itself indispensable. They are as it were still on their trial, though with the Brahui's ever-widening intercourse with the outside world their survival in the struggle for existence is for the most part a foregone conclusion. The best illustration of these remarks will be found in the conditional sentence.

The Conditional Sentence.

§**408.** In most highly developed languages supposition and conclusion are usually fused together into one complex whole. But even in such languages, notably, for instance, in German, the more primitive method of splitting up the hypothetical idea into its component parts has maintained its place, especially in proverbs and poetry, in which archaic expressions are preserved by a kind of atavism.

§**409.** In Brahui the idiom varies not only with the tribe, but with the individual. The more the tribe and the more the individual have come into contact with alien languages, the greater the tendency to affect the use of conjunctions. In the language of the unsophisticated Brahui the use of the conjunction is the exception and not the rule. Supposition and conclusion are presented side by side as independent statements, or rather the supposition is put in the form of a query, which is answered by the conclusion in the form of a rejoinder.

§410. To take the simple conditional: ***nī kāsa, ī nēto barēva***, you're going, you say, I'll come with you; or: are you going? I'll come with you; if you're going, I'll come with you; ***paisa affak ītonā, ī nē ētiva***, if you've no money with you, I'll give you some. The conclusion may of course be contained in an imperative or an interrogation: ***gaṭ affēs, dīr ēte-ka***, if you're not busy, give me water; ***nī kanto salīpēs, ī arāng kāv?*** if you won't stand by me, whither shall I go?

§411. If the condition refers to a remoter or improbable future, the idiom is somewhat peculiar. The supposition is presented vividly to the mind as a *fait accompli;* the conclusion follows pat, like the conclusion of a syllogism. The verb of the protasis is in the past, while the verb of the apodosis is in the present-future, etc., as the case may be: ***sardār bing, nanā bēkhe kashshik***, (suppose) the chief heard—he'll pluck up our root, *i.e.*, if the chief hears, he'll cast us out root and branch; ***mass īānka, baroṭ***, if I can, I'll probably come; ***kanā banningnā bingus, kasase pāpēs***, if you hear of my arrival, please tell no one; ***nī narrās, ī dā mulkaṭī tūlparoṭ***, if you run away, I don't intend to stay in this country.

§412. To express a past unfulfilled condition the verb is placed in the imperfect in both sentences: ***ī narrāṭa, lashkar muchchāi-a narrāka***, had I run, the army would have run in a body; ***jwāno īlumas-a massusa, aino kanā dūe halkusa***, had you been a true brother, you would have grasped my hand (in friendship) to-day. In the case of the substantive verb the past is commonly used for the imperfect, especially for vividness: ***pinḍingān nī kaskusa, jwān ass***, it were well you had died sooner than beg.

§413. In the Jhalawan dialect the place of the imperfect is preferably taken by the past conditional (§316): ***nī***

kanā hēṭe duzzosus, ī nā māre khalosuṭ, had you stolen my she-goat, I would have beaten your son; *nī mahālau rāhī marosus, dāṛē iraghān must rasēngosus*, had you started betimes, you would have arrived here before dinner. If, as sometimes happens, both tenses are used side by side, the past conditional is generally found in the protasis, the imperfect in the apodosis: *ī nā urāghāi barosuṭ, nī zarūr-a narrāsa*, had I come to your house, you would certainly have run away.

§**414. The conditional conjunctions** ***aga (agar), ki,*** **if.** In view of the possible ambiguity in these disjunct sentences, it is not surprising that the Brahui makes an ever-increasing use of the conditional conjunctions, which not only facilitate the expression of his ideas, but add to his mental machinery. The insertion of the conjunction simply binds the sentences together; the tense of the verbs is in no wise altered: *nī aga kāsa, ī nēto barēva*, if you're going, I'll come with you; *sardār aga bing, nanā bēkhe kashshik*, if the chief hears, he'll cast us out root and branch; *ī ki narrāṭa, lashkar muchchāi-a narrāka*, had I run, the army would have run in a body. It should be noted that *ki* never, *aga* rarely, stands first in the sentence; their proper place is immediately after the subject. *Ki* has often a temporal rather than a conditional force (§419).

§**415. The conclusive conjunctions** ***guṛā, ala, to.*** The conclusion is itself not infrequently introduced by one of the conjunctions *guṛā, ala, to*, which may be rendered by 'then,' 'well,' 'why,' or some such word: *o aga aino batau, guṛā chās ki dāvae bāi tiss*, if he doesn't turn up to-day, then you may take it that he lost his case; *kanā hītāk aga rāst affas, ala drogh hum mafaror*, if my words don't come true, well they won't prove lies at any rate; *aino aga bassus, to kullān jwān e*, if you come to-day, why that's the best of all. In such sentences also the conditional conjunction is frequently omitted: *narritavana, ala ant-a karēna?* if we hadn't fled, what on earth were we to do? *kanā arighe kasfēr. gurā ī nē barām-a kēva,* if they kill my husband, then I'll marry you; *bohar asi sāl rasēmpak-ta, to mulke sunn-a kēk,* if one fine year he doesn't receive the revenue, well he'll lay the country waste.

§416. **The conditional conjunction *aga na,* if not.** The ordinary way of expressing the idea conveyed by 'otherwise' is to repeat the verb of the first clause in the negative: *nī (aga) bassus, jwān, (aga) batavēs, nā mulk sarkārī-a marēk,* if you come in, well and good, otherwise your land will become confiscated to Government. The negative verb may, however, be omitted and its place taken by *aga na*: *nī aga bassus, jwān, aga na, nā mulk sarkārī-a marēk; o khākhar, lagga, aga na, apokas īkinā hatarēna,* burn, oh fire, or we'll bring a rival for you (a regular child's saying to a fire that won't burn).

The Concessive Sentence.

§417. **The concessive conjunctions *aga, agaki,* although.** The concessive sentence is on all fours with the conditional. The use of the conjunction simply makes the concessive meaning the more explicit: *nī (aga, agaki) sadvār pās, ī nēāi bāvar-a kappara,* though you say it a hundred times, I won't trust you.

The Temporal Sentence.

§418. A temporal relation between two sentences can be expressed without employing a conjunction: *pir-a kēk, pudēn-a marēk,* when it rains, it turns cold; *harvakht ī onā jahāi hināṭa, ode khantavaṭa,* whenever I went to his place, I missed seeing him; *khalk tūlok ass, ḍung rasēfē,* the people were seated when the robber-band came down upon them. If there is some contingency implied in the temporal clause, the ordinary rule of the conditional applies to the tense of the verb (§411): *pāṭān harsēngā, kasaraṭ shikār karisa baroe,* when and if he returns from gathering wood, the chances are he'll shoot on the way home. The distinction between a temporal and a conditional sentence is of course often somewhat subtle.

§**419.** **The temporal conjunction** ***ki*****, when.** The insertion of a conjunction in such sentences merely makes the temporal relation explicit: *duzz ki narrik, kasase khabar-a tifak,* when the thief makes off, he doesn't advertise his movements; *handā ki khanāṭ-ta, tūfakaṭ khalēva-ta,* I'll shoot him on sight; *ī onā khalkāi ki hināṭa, o baj-a tissaka,* whenever I went to his encampment, he used to show me his heels; *beirake ki pulār, Jhalāvānnā lashkar pinnā,* when they seized the banner, the army of the Jhalawans was broken.

§**420.** The negative plays an important part in temporal sentences of past narration. Its use in the first clause implies an abrupt interruption in the action by the second, which is usually, but not necessarily, introduced by the conjunction: *o narritavēsas ki nan rasēfēn-ta,* he had scarcely begun to run away when we overtook him; *o shahre kēb kattavēsas, pulūs halk-ta,* no sooner had he approached the town than he was arrested by the police. This idea is idiomatically expressed by coupling affirmative and negative together: *o iraghe kungas kuntavēsas ki mēmānk bassur,* he had barely tackled his meal when the guests arrived; *nan urāghān pēsh tammān pēsh tammitavan, pir malingā,* we no sooner put our face out of doors than the rain began.

§**421.** **The temporal conjunction** ***tā ki*****.** Used with the affirmative verb, *tā ki* means as long as, whilst, since: *tā ki zinda uṭ, nē yāt-a kēva,* as long as I live, I'll remember you; *tā ki ī kārēm karēnuṭ, nī khāchok massunus*, whilst I've been toiling, you've been asleep; *tā ki ī dāṛē bassunuṭ, ī nē shahraṭī khantanuṭ*, since I've come here, I haven't set eyes on you in the village.

§**422.** Used with the negative verb the conjunction denotes until. If reference is made to future time, the ordinary tense is the perfect, though the present indefinite is also used; in past narration similarly the verb is generally in the pluperfect: *tā ki ī batanuṭ, dākā bash mafēs*, mind you don't rise from here until I come; *tā ki nī bafēs, ī handāṛēk uṭ*, until you come, I remain here; *tā ki onā tūfaknā tavāre bintavēsun, jang kattavan*, until we heard the sound of his rifle, we didn't show fight.

§**423.** The compound *hamēskā ki*, lit. up to that time, that, is used in the same manner and with the same meanings. In some parts *dāng ki*, lit. in this direction, that, may be heard, and also *tān-ki*, which may be a corrupted form of either *tā ki* or *dāng ki*.

The Final Sentence.

§**424. The final conjunctions *ki, (han)dārki ki* (lit. for the sake of this, that), that, in order that; *navā, ki navā*, lest.** The present indefinite, or subjunctive as it might be called, is generally used in the subordinate clause even in past narration (§312): *hullīe zēn ka ki ī swār marēv*, saddle the horse that I may ride; *ī onā pāraghāi handāṛki hināṭ ki o kanā arze bine*, I went to him that he might listen to my petition; *ī khulīva navā o nē khane*, I'm afraid he may see you; *khākhare kasfif ki navā nanā urāe hushe*, put out the fire or it'll burn down our house. In past narration the subordinate verb is occasionally in the imperfect, and imperfect and present indefinite are sometimes even used loosely side by side: *ī handāṛki khulīsusuṭ ki navā o nē khanāka, giṛā-as pārēka*, I had feared he might see you and say something; *ī handāṛki bassusuṭ ki o kanā hīte khaf-a torēka, dāṛki batavēsuṭ ki kane ghurrānk ēte*, I had come that he might lend an ear to what I had to say, not that he might rebuke me.

The Relative Sentence.

§425. The language is devoid of a relative pronoun, and the place of one is partially supplied by the adjectival participle (§322). The most primitive way of expressing the idea conveyed by a relative pronoun in other languages is to state two apparently independent sentences side by side. In the forefront is placed the element common to both. If this is a noun, it is usually qualified by one or other of the demonstrative pronouns especially in the intensive form (*cf.* §131). Its case depends of course on its function in the sentence to which it primarily belongs. If it happens to be the subject of the second sentence, it is generally omitted altogether in it; otherwise it is represented as a rule by a pronoun: *hamē kaizī narrāne, kanā khalkanā aff*, that prisoner who has escaped, doesn't belong to my encampment; *hamo shahrān ī pēsh tammāṭ, dēṭik-pāraghāiṭ e*, the village I came from, lies to the east; *hamo māhrīāi ī swār assuṭ, pīr assaka*, the riding camel I rode on, was old; *hamo hullīe ī khado halkusuṭ, ēnakho padāi sad rupaīāi tissuṭ-ta*, that horse I had bought last year, I gave back this year for a hundred rupees.

§426. If the relation between the two sentences is hypothetical, the tense is governed by the rules in the conditional sentence: *harkas kanā hukme mannitau, ī dā shahrān kashshiva-ta*, every man who dares to disobey my order, I'll turn out of this village; *harkas kanā hukme mannitavaka, ī dā shahrān kashshāṭa-ta*, I would have turned out of this village any man who dared to disobey my order.

§**427.** The antecedent, as it may conveniently be called, frequently receives the addition of the enclitic indefinite article, unless it is in the plural, or is qualified by an attributive adjective in the definite form, or happens to be a personal pronoun (*cf.* §74). The force of the enclitic so used is of course in no way indefinite; on the contrary it has the effect of particularising more directly the person or object referred to: ***hamē huchchas ī nē nishān tissuṭ, nataṭī-ta pitas hināne,*** that particular camel I pointed out to you has had a thorn run into its foot; ***hamo bandaghaseān ī dā hullīe halkuṭ, dāsā Kachchīāi hināne,*** that very man from whom I bought this horse, has just gone to Kachhi.

§**428. The relative conjunction *ki*.** Except in the simpler cases there is a growing tendency to knit the sentences together by means of the relative conjunction ***ki***. Its insertion does not necessarily make any formal difference in the structure of the sentences; the enclitic ***-as*** is generally attached to the antecedent except in the cases noted in the preceding paragraph: ***ē bandaghas ki nē khanāne, nā sifate-a kēk,*** every man who has ever seen you, sings your praises; ***hamo nī assus ki khado dāṛē bassusus,*** you were the man who had come here last year; ***antas ki nī pāroī us, dāsā pā,*** say what you have to say, now; ***giṛā-as ki kanā īlumnā mēlhk assur, ēnakho kul hīnguno,*** whatever sheep my brother had, have lambed this year; ***dākān guḍ antas ki kanā Khudā karē, kane kabūl e,*** henceforth whatever my God may do, I accept; ***hamo sajjīe ki nī bisēnus, jalh hushānc-ta,*** the flame has singed the meat you've roasted; ***ē asiṭ ki drogh-a pāik, mon-ta maun e,*** the face of the liar is blackened; ***bandaghase ki dauno bakhtas marē, khudānā shukre kē,*** let the man to whom such a lot may fall, give God the thanks; ***hamo mārato ki nī daro hīt-a karēsa, aino padāi bassune,*** the lad with whom you were talking yesterday, has come back to-day.

§**429.** The antecedent may stand structurally outside the dependent clause, and be represented in it instead by a pronoun as in Persian: *hamē māras ki nī daro ītota hīt-a karēsa, aino padāi bassune*, that lad with whom you were talking yesterday, has come back to-day; *hamēas zaghm-a khalēk ki muskok-ta khalkuno*, that man will wield the sword whose forefathers have wielded the sword; *hamo sardāras ki dūṭī-ta bil ass, Shā Bāz Khān ass*, the chief who had the bow in his hand, was Shah Baz Khan.

§**430.** Even in such sentences the conjunction is not infrequently omitted, though its omission is often awkward enough. There is indeed considerable looseness in the structure of these relative sentences. The antecedent may be a nominative *pendens*, standing without structural relation to either clause: *hamo hullīas ki dū-ta huson ass, pēn aib hum ass-ta*, that horse whose forefoot was injured—there was also some other unsoundness in it; *hamo bandaghas ki bāva-ta duzz mass, jind-ta zarūr duzz-a marēk*, the man whose father turned thief, he is sure to turn thief himself. And finally sentences like the following are not uncommon, in which the meaning is clear, but a logical analysis impossible: *bandaghasēnā ki bāva-ta duzz mass, mār-ta zarūr duzz-a marēk.*

The Causal Sentence.

§**431.** **The causal conjunction *ki*, because.** Though *ki* is used by itself as a causal conjunction it is generally preceded by a pronominal phrase, *e.g.*, *antei ki*, lit. why? that, *antasēki ki*, lit. for the sake of what? that, *handāṛki ki*, for the sake of this, that: *khalpa-ta ki kāik*, don't beat him or he'll go; *ī nē sizā ētiva antei ki nī duzzī karēnus*, I'll punish you because you have committed theft; *onā khank khaṛīnkān purr assur antasēki ki onā mār kaskas*, his eyes were full of tears at the death of his son; *ī handāṛki khwash uṭ ki o batau*, I'm glad he didn't come.

Miscellaneous Conjunctions.

§432. *Ki*, that. In addition to the other uses noted above *ki* is used to introduce the *oratio recta* after verbs of saying, thinking, etc.: *o pārē ki ī pagga barēva,* he said he would come to-morrow. The *oratio obliqua* is rarely employed: *o pārē ki o pagga baroe.* The verb of saying, etc., may be idiomatically omitted: *sardār tēnā bandag͟hāte much karē ki tēnā tūfakāte palīta kabo,* the chief collected his men and told them to put the match to their guns.

§433. *O*, and. This conjunction is frequently omitted, especially between nouns and verbs in the same grammatical relation: *kanā urā hog͟hā* (*o*) *pārē,* my wife wept and said. It is sounded in close connection with the preceding word; thus if this ends in *-ā*, the long vowel may coalesce with the conjunction to form the diphthong *-au: hog͟hau pārē,* she wept and said; while a final short *-a* followed by the conjunction is as a rule hardly sounded at all: *dā lumm' o mār drog͟h-a pāpasa,* this mother and son don't lie.

§434. *A*, and. This form of the conjunction is regularly used in certain pronominal combinations: *ī-a-nī rāst pān, naneāi kas bāvar-a kappak,* though you and I may speak the truth, not a soul will credit us; *dā hamē lashkar e ki nan-a-num dāṛē k͟hanān-ta,* this is that army we and you saw here. It is seemingly preserved in the compound word *bil-a-sum,* bow and arrow, rainbow, and it is possibly the original form of the conjunction.

§435. *Um, hum,* also:—*nī aga jwān us, ī hum duzzī kattanuṭ,* righteous though you are, I too have committed no theft; *ī hum k͟halkuṭ-ta, kanā mār um k͟halk-ta,* not only did I myself beat him, but my son beat him into the bargain. The Persian form *ham* is sometimes used, but it is generally regarded as *suruṭ,* and the same applies in a greater degree to *bī*, which has been introduced from Sindhi: *nī bī daun-a pāsa*, you too will say so.

§436. ***Yā***, or; ***yā . . . yā***, either . . . or:— *dā hullīteān dāde harf yā ēde*, of these horses take this one or that; *har-vakht ki ī nē pēndwār baṭingāṭ, yā tēnaṭ barēs, yā tēnā īlume mon ētis*, the next time I summon you, please either come yourself or send your brother.

§437. ***Nei . . . (o) nei***, neither . . . nor (§336):— *ī nei khudāghān khulīva nei bandaghān*, I fear neither God nor man; *ī nei oṛān narrānuṭ o nei nēān narroṭ*, I have neither fled from him nor am I likely to flee from you.

§438. ***Maga (magar)***, but:— *ī bassuṭa, maga kane kasarāi pēn khabaras rasēngā*, I would have come, but I received other tidings on the road; *o pārē asiṭ, maga karē pēn kārēmas*, he said one thing, but did another. The form *magar* may be regarded as *suruṭ*.

THE INTERJECTION.

§439. It will be useful to note a few of the commoner sounds and exclamations used to express emotion. These include not only 'vocal gestures,' but also words which have been, and in some cases still are, full parts of speech.

§440. ***Hau,*** **yes**:—*kurato kāsa? hau,* will you go with the flock? yes. The verb used in the interrogation is generally repeated in the answer: *dā hullī nā e? hau, kanā e,* is this horse yours? yes, it's mine.

§441. ***H-m,*** **yes**:—*nī kanā hīte jwānīaṭ bingus? h-m,* did you catch my remarks properly? oh yes; *tūfaknā tavār nā khafāi tammā? h-m, tammā,* did the sound of the gun reach your ear? yes, it did.

§442. ***Jī,*** **yes (to superiors)**:—*hullīteki ispust rūtānus? jī,* have you cut lucerne for the horses? yes, sir; *huchche pākuṛo karēnus? jī khwāja, karēnuṭ?* have you saddled the camel? yes, master, I have. It is often coupled with *hau*: *jī hau.*

§443. ***'Chik,'*** **no.** The most primitive mode of expressing dissent is to emit a clicking noise called, but not sounded, *chik*: *iragh kungunus?* (*chik*), have you had your food? no. The sound, which resembles the click of the cab-driver, is accompanied by a side-toss of the head.

§444. ***Āhah,*** **no**:—*dā bandaghe must khanānus? āhah,* have you seen this person before? no; *guzhghe kashshāno? āhah, aino kashshitano,* have they pulled up the lucerne roots? no, not to-day. The final syllable of *āhah* is clipped exceedingly short.

§445. ***Nah*** **(*na*), no**:—*dam darēnus? nah,* are you tired? no; *kharāste bei karēnus? nah dāiskā kattanuṭ-tā,* have you given the bullocks grass? no, I haven't yet.

§**446.** ***Jwān,*** very well:—*ī aino Sēbīāi kāva, jwān, hin,* I'm off to Sibi to-day, very well, go.

§**447.** ***Shukr,*** thank goodness:—*shukr khanāṭ-ne,* thank goodness I saw you.

§**448.** ***Mār,*** oh:—*mār dā chūcha amaro jwānoas e,* oh my, what a fine baby he is.

§**449.** ***Jī khudā,*** my God:—*jī khudā dā amaro sādāras e,* my God, what a curious creature. The Garr Sasolis[1] make use of an extraordinary expletive: *o kanā kharrunā khudā, dā khalkanā kullanā kāṭum sholok e,* oh my green God, all the men in this village have their head shaven.

§**450.** ***Vah vā,*** hullo:—*vah vā, jwānangā aristā kārēm handād e ki nī karēnus?* hullo, is this work you've done the work of honest men? *vah vā, aino jwāno kūsas bēnānus,* bless us, you've put on a mighty fine shirt to-day.

§**451.** ***Shābās,*** bravo:—*shābās, hullīe sharr khar-kharra karēnus,* bravo, you've currycombed the horse splendidly. It may be used ironically, especially when preceded by *vā*: *vā shābās, kanā mēlhte gum karēnus, bassunus?* capital, have you come back after letting my sheep go astray?

§**452.** ***Puhū,*** by Jove:—*puhū, ballo vallaras e,* by Jove it's a big flock of birds.

§**453.** ***Puh,*** pshaw:—*puh, nī arākā ballo arēas massus?* pshaw, what made you such a fine fellow? The same contemptuous meaning is expressed vulgarly by *ṭurt* and *purt.*

---

[1] The Garr Sasolis are the Brahui men of Gotham or Abdera: *bīshe harrifēr: nē dunyāṭī siāl arē? pārē: Sasolī jakkas-a khalēk,* they asked the ass whether he had any relations in the world; 'well,' quoth he, 'the Sasoli is always *boasting* of the connection.'

§454. ***Ala, alavā, alavā chā,*** ho ho:—*nī chaṛa drogh-a pāsa—alavā rāst pārokā nī us*, you tell nothing but a pack of lies—ho ho, so you're the only man who speaks the truth.

§455. ***Shāla (shalla),*** pray God:—*shāla, zū barē*, pray God he come quickly. Its obvious derivation from *in shā 'llāh* is not always felt: *shāla, khudā kanā duāe āmīn kē*, pray heaven, God fulfil my prayer.

§456. ***Khabardār,*** take care:—*khabardār, hullī khaloe-ne*, take care, the horse'll kick you.

§457. ***Vāe nā jānāi, (jānaki),*** woe betide you:—*vāe nā jānāi aga kanā huchche sār kattavēs*, woe betide you if you don't look after my camel; *sobato hāzir matavēre, vāe numā jānaki*, if you're not present to-morrow early, on your head be it. The expression is an adaptation from Persian.

§458. ***Armān,*** alas:—*armān, kanā tūfak dāsā radd-a matavaka, ala aino sūān sēr-a karēna*, alas, had my shot not missed just now, we would to-day have had our fill of meat.

§459. ***Aboe,*** woe:—*aboe kanā arigh tāiska jangān harsēngtane*, woe, my husband has not yet returned from the battle.

§460. ***Toba,*** fie:—*toba, balā-asēṭī aṛēngānun*, fie, we are caught in a calamity.

§461. To this category belong the various sounds addressed to animals. The following are some of the calls: ***kich***, to a kid, *ḍ-r-r-r-r,.....*, to a sheep, ***chuh***, to a dog. *Chakh, chih, chī* are used to drive on a dog, a goat and cattle respectively; from the last sound is derived the child's word for cattle, *chīā*. Commands to halt are ***hash-sh-sh*** ......, to a donkey, *pasht*, to a horse. *Hush-sh-sh......* is used to make a camel kneel down. *P-r-r-r-o* is the general command to drink.

BIBLIOGRAPHY

BIBLIOGRAPHY.

LEECH, R.,—*Epitome of the Grammar of the Brahuiky, the Balochky and the Panjabi languages, with Vocabularies of the Baraky, the Pashi, the Laghmani, the Cashgari, the Teerhai, and the Deer Dialects.* Journal of the Asiatic Society of Bengal, Vol. vii, 1838.

LASSEN, CHR.,—*Untersuchungen über die ethnographische Stellung der Völker im Westen Indiens.* (4) *Die Brahui und ihre Sprache.* Zeitschrift für die Kunde des Morgenlandes, Vol. v, 1844.

CALDWELL, REV. ROBERT,—*A Comparative Grammar of the Dravidian or South-Indian Family of Languages.* London, 1856. (Second edition, 1875.)

FINZI, FELICE,—*Il Brahui. Studio di etnologia linguistica.* Bolletino della societá geographica Italiana, Fasc. v, 1870.

BELLEW, DR.,—*From the Indus to the Tigris.* (Appendix.) London, 1874.

ALLA BUX,—*Handbook of the Birouhi Language.* Karachi, 1877.

NICOLSON, CAPT. M.,—*Meanee, &c., a Compilation of extracts from Napier's Conquest of Scinde, Grant Duff's Mahratta History, &c., &c., translated into the Biroohi Language.* Karachi, 1877.

TRUMPP, DR. ERNEST,—*Grammatische Untersuchungen über die Sprache der Brāhūīs.* Sitzungsberichte der k. b. Akademie der Wissenschaften, München, 1880.

DUKA, DR. THEODORE,—*An Essay on the Brāhūī Grammar, after the German of the late Dr. Trumpp, of Munich University.* Journal of the Royal Asiatic Society, New Series, Vol. xix, 1887.

BIGG-WITHER, F.,—*A Guide to the Study of Brahui.* Allahabad, 1902.

(KONOW, DR. STEN,)—*Linguistic Survey of India, Vol. iv. Muṇḍā and Dravidian Languages.* Calcutta, 1906. General editor, Dr. G. A. Grierson.

MAYER, REV. T. J. L.,—*A Brahui Reading Book, Part I.* Ludhiana, 1906.

JAMIAT RAI, R. S. DIWAN,—*Notes on the Study of the Brahui Language.* Quetta, 1907.

END OF PART I.